104622

**HOW TO SURVIVE
THE BUSINESS RAT RACE**

OTHER BOOKS BY ROBERT C. SAMPSON

The Staff Role in Management: Its Creative Uses

Managing the Managers: A Realistic Approach to Applying the Behavioral Sciences

How to Survive
the Business Rat Race

ROBERT C. SAMPSON

President, Sampson Associates, Inc.
Management Counselors

MCGRAW-HILL BOOK COMPANY

New York   St. Louis   San Francisco   Düsseldorf
London   Mexico   Panama   Sydney   Toronto

Sponsoring Editors   M. Joseph Dooher/Dale L. Dutton
Director of Production   Stephen J. Boldish
Editing Supervisors   Barbara Church/Carolyn Nagy
Designer   Naomi Auerbach
Editing and Production Staff Gretlyn Blau, Teresa F. Leaden, George E.
  Oechsner

HOW TO SURVIVE THE BUSINESS RAT RACE

07-054510-3

1234567890 VBVB 7543210

*To Lucille, who has helped me practice
what I preach*

Preface

THE BUSINESS RAT RACE is the major epidemic of our high-speed, competitive, industrial life, and it is the exceptional businessman who does not suffer from it to some degree. Essential causes of the stress are in-company politics, the growth of bureaucracy, power plays, underutilization of talent, and the growing communication barriers between generalists and an ever-increasing variety of specialists. For many men the business rat race is a harried and hurried existence, with its hectic pace, long hours, and "briefcase-itis." The most prevalent symptoms are "frustration fatigue," tenseness, anxiety, and in many cases, physical discomfort. At the other extreme some men suffer personal uneasiness from underwork, boredom, apathy, and pretended busyness. But be it overwork or underwork, the business rat race adversely affects a man as well as his personal and family life.

This book—solidly based on the findings of the behavioral sciences—offers a total program for the total man. It is a guide to living a full, well-rounded business, personal, and family life. It tells how not to be a victim of the business rat race. You discover here (1) how to survive *in* the rat race, (2) how to *reduce* it where possible, and (3) how to survive *beyond* it. To survive *in* the rat race includes building a career within the various kinds of success and learning about the variety of work needs, as well as making sense out of the management mess and developing a professional stance. To *reduce* the rat race includes developing greater self-awareness and learning how to help others who will in turn help you. To survive *beyond* the rat race is to get more satisfaction out of personal and family life.

Both the research and my suggestions built on these findings have been tested for usefulness and effectiveness by our firm in consulting with clients, installing behavioral sciences management systems in companies, personal counseling with businessmen, evaluating management people, doing executive search, and conducting management development programs, as well as applying the research to every facet of a business.

The knowledge and how-to in this book have met the test of business reaction in the hundreds of management conferences our firm has run. The criticisms and suggestions have been most useful in reworking the material for this book to make it meaningful and helpful to the businessman. For example, in the interest of easy reading I have followed the recommendation of readers of my earlier books to eliminate quotations and keep footnotes to a minimum.

My books are evidence of my own increasing reliance on the basic findings about men. In my first book I urged staff people to stop trying to grab line authority or using personal pressure to get their way. I suggested instead a helping approach, essentially counseling. This approach is presented in *The Staff Role in Management: Its Creative Uses,* Harper & Row, Publishers, Incorporated, New York, 1955. Then I discovered research had found that the power struggles between managers made grabs for power among staff people relatively insignificant. Hence my second book, *Managing the Managers: A Realistic Approach to Applying the Behavioral Sciences,* McGraw-Hill Book Company, New York, 1965, tells of the power struggle within management and what should be done about it.

I am indebted to the key authors listed in the Bibliography for their research, observations, and findings. They have made this book possible. There are also many other researchers whose contributions, while not as great, have aided substantially in making this a comprehensive, factual guide. To add their names to the Bibliography would have made it much too long. In the interest of economy of sources, I have not always used the original source on finding that another author had combined some of the original research efforts. This is, after all, not a treatise for academicians, who might want more "purity" in a textbook than a businessman would like in a guide for himself.

Finally, I am in great debt to my wife, Lucille Jolliffe Sampson, a former social worker. She continues to be not only my best critic, editor, and typist, but also an achieving companion.

Robert C. Sampson

Contents

xi

Contents

List of Exhibits

1

A Total Program
for the Total Man

> There is no meaning to life except the meaning man
> gives his life by the unfolding of his powers, by liv-
> ing productively; and that only constant vigilance,
> activity, and effort can keep us from failing in the
> one task that matters—the full development of our
> powers within the limitations set by the laws of our
> existence. —ERICH FROMM, M.D., *Man for Himself* [1]

IF YOU ARE GOING TO SURVIVE in and beyond the business rat race,
you need a total program for you as a total man—something which
I have not been able to find in the inspirational books, how-to
books, or the many books based on experience, personal opinion, or
even research.

In this book, you have the common findings about man. First,
common in that they are interrelated. They provide a total approach that is internally consistent. Second, common in that the
findings are a consensus drawn from many fields. Divergent findings
are excluded. Third, common in that the findings are within the
understanding of the businessman. Extensive and complex backup
theories are omitted. Fourth, common in that the findings are trans-

[1] Holt, Rinehart and Winston, Inc., New York, 1947, pp. 44–45.

lated into the language of the businessman. This book is in plain English. Professional and academic jargon have been eliminated wherever possible. Where it is necessary to use the jargon, including management jargon, it is defined.

Business Rat Race

Rat race. No other term is so universally accepted as describing business life today. It is tragic. You were brought up to value work. Without it you are nothing. Yet, the odds are that you seldom have a feeling of exhilaration, accomplishment, and personal growth. You feel frustrated, uncertain, and pressured.

Much of my time in the last several years has been spent consulting with businessmen and running management development conferences, large and small. I have worked with hundreds of management groups all over the country as well as beyond the United States. Let me ask you the questions I ask many of them. List your answers.

Do you feel that you are a success?

Do you feel that you operate somewhere near your optimum capabilities?

For those of you who went to college, do you feel that you are using more than 10 percent of what you learned?

Do you work, including what you take home and work-related reading, less than fifty hours a week?

Do you feel that your boss is interested in you, approves of what you are doing, and helps you?

Do you feel there is more helpful cooperation than competition among your associates?

Do you have any idea as to how far you are going to advance in your company?

If you were to have a nervous breakdown, would your company care for you indefinitely?

Well over nine out of ten men in my sessions have said no to each question. How did you do? If your answer was no to some of the questions, you are in the rat race. Even if you answer yes to almost all these questions, you may still be in the rat race—and not know it. You may have been "conditioned," as you will see later, to accept without question the business rat race. A surprising number of men do. It is an elementary fact that people in responding to surveys or questions about themselves often are incapable of giving an accurate answer. In one mail survey where men were asked if they were working too hard, over three-quarters of them said they did not feel so.[2] But I found in the report no reference, for example, to how many hours beyond the official hours for company employees these men worked. In my queries of businessmen in management groups, many say they are not working too hard. Yet I find that, in the main, management men at all levels work somewhere near sixty hours per week.

Rat Race Syndrome Look at these sad findings about business life today:

One, almost every man suffers "frustration fatigue" on a job which is neither physically nor mentally, but only emotionally exhausting. Yet, he is expected to show no feelings. Therefore, his insecurities, anxieties, frustrations, and even hostilities become imprisoned within him, eating away at his emotional structure.

Two, almost every businessman is actually underutilized at work. Man's primary fight in life is against boredom. Even when a man tries to delude himself that his work is fun, he cannot operate at uninteresting, boring routines without damage to himself.

Three, there is the speed up. Think what the telephone has done to business life. With it man moves at a much faster pace, for the telephone itself enables him to be involved in more things at one time. Worse, it means more stress. It can interrupt any conversation or time for quiet thinking.

Four, many a man regularly puts in very long hours. It is a popular but odd notion that no man can succeed without total personal commitment to his company. In many cases the long hours are contrary to stated company policy. But a man comes to feel he must put in long hours if he wants to get ahead. He must choose between his job and his family—to his own detriment.

Five, man finds himself overwhelmed with bureaucracy. A major modern nemesis is the rules and regulations, paper work, and red

[2] The Life Extension Foundation, *Report of a Survey on Executive Tension in Business*, Life Extension Institute, New York, about 1960.

tape—from both government agencies and most business organizations.

Six, man has a win-lose complex. For you to fail is as good as for me to succeed. Every man, except the Mr. Milquetoasts, is potentially the enemy of his fellow man. It causes much hostility, often well masked, and isolation from each other. Man's tenseness and anxieties are greatly increased.[3] Even the most conservative business journals accept the universality of the power struggle. Cooperation to you means giving in. "Committee" and "compromise" have become dirty words. Competition and rivalry are encouraged. It started when you were a child. Parents are found by sociologists to encourage rivalry between brothers and sisters while lecturing their children to love each other. Schools encourage competition in each class for grades and in promotion from grade to grade. Almost every extracurricular activity from sports to music is based on competing for the top spots. If you have ever had any help in how to cooperate or how to listen, you are a very rare bird. At least this is what I have found in my informal polls at my management conferences. Hell-bent on getting your own way, what you achieve is, as you see it, synonymous with corporate goals and company loyalty. Certain that your way is the best, when others do not go along, you pressure, manipulate, procrastinate, evade, ignore, or reinterpret to redound to your personal advantage. You increase the power struggle and your own rat race.

Seven, there is the increasing need to deal with several people to get anything done. More contacts. More negotiations. A wide range of problems and a multitude of diverse relationships. Most of these are external to the superior-subordinate relationship. More win-lose situations where a man unknowingly uses his specialty to secure more power. Many involve peers who operate under different standards of performance and with conflicting objectives. Dealing with hostility, feeling hostile, taking risks, resisting pressure, manipulation, gamesmanship, and uncertainty make negotiations a major factor in races that are never won. They are only run well in the rat race. These relationships tend to be uncomfortable, tense, and frustrating.

Eight, you are in a specialist explosion. You deal with people

[3] Rollo May, *Man's Search for Himself,* W. W. Norton & Company, Inc., New York, 1953, p. 48.

whose work you do not understand and who have their own jargon. New technologies and computers have spawned their own breeds. Even in the traditional business fields more specialists and new jargon are being spewed forth at an ever-increasing rate. Even you may be becoming more and more specialized. The communication barrier is rising higher and higher.

Nine, not only is almost everyone underutilized at work, man also underutilizes himself in his personal life and family life. After work, he tends to seek the easy life. He avoids thinking about what is really important to a well-balanced life. To get into management requires brains. Yet, many businessmen do not use their brains to see the bigger picture beyond work life.

Ten, the result? It is estimated by some experts that at least two-thirds of the businessmen have mild to severe emotional disturbances. One out of twelve persons in this country will spend part of his life in a mental hospital.

Rats in a Maze In this the most affluent society, there are several ways to become overly involved in the rat race. You are *caught* in the rat race if you are overworked but underutilized. You scramble along at a faster pace and work longer hours. At the other extreme, you are *lost* in the rat race if you have had to learn the boring art of loafing because there is just not enough for you to do. You are underworked and underutilized. Even worse, you are *trapped* in the rat race if you have a mild to severe emotional problem. And you have *succumbed* to the rat race if you have become emotionally incapable of doing an effective job even though you may be employed.

Like rats in an experimental maze, most of us rush or wander through a blind network of passages toward unknown ends. We wear a brave smile and a self-confident air. Emotionally we are too unsure of ourselves to see our life as it really is. We hide from tomorrow's rejections in our work life. Many of us will be passed over by younger men well before our retirement. Some of us will be "de-hired." Several of us will become obsolete. Almost all of us will be deeply disturbed when we realize that we face the rest of our work life with no more promotions. Most of us will receive the biggest shock of all, retirement. The high death rate shortly following retirement is sad testimony to the man who could not survive beyond the rat race. An empty, useless, and unhappy man dumped on the industrial ash heap.

A Life Plan

This total approach is your personal guide to survive in and beyond the business rat race. Your Goal? A life plan, carefully worked out, to achieve the greatest sense of mental, emotional, and physical well-being. You achieve a greater sense of well-being only when you make good use of your capabilities, feel comfortable with others, enjoy living, and are able to cope with stress. You decide for yourself who you are and what you want to become. There is no one else to fall back on.

There is much you can do in a lifetime to help yourself. However, you cannot easily free yourself from your own history in terms of the many hidden barriers within yourself. Unless you become aware of them, they block your further development as an adult, a businessman, and a family man. You can move from being an unthinking product of your past and your heritage to working out your own consciously planned life pattern. Goals for self-renewal, ideals, and dreams of personal excellence are excellent lures. Strive for them even though you may not be able to achieve them. They help you make better choices along the way.

Steps to Survival It is axiomatic that you need to be able to exercise competent judgment. To do this you need meaningful knowledge. You need awareness based on knowledge about yourself if you are going to help yourself. You also need awareness based on knowledge about others and the nature of the relationships in a business organization so that you can help yourself by helping others. Knowledge is paramount to awareness. Awareness is paramount to skills. Then and only then can skills or how-to be based on competent judgment.

Because this is a total approach for you as a total man, you are your greatest barrier. Strive to *unlearn* what you now believe about yourself and others when it does not square with the common findings outlined here. This is not easy. You impulsively pick and choose. Yet, you cannot learn how to survive in and beyond the business rat race if you accept only those things with which you agree and reject those with which you disagree. Nor can you rely on the two things you undoubtedly cherish most, your common sense and your experience.

Read this book with a mind that is as wide open as you can get it. Aids to your opening it even more are also provided. You learn about, understand, evaluate, and use your own powers to work for your own increased sense of well-being. I suggest that you pull in here, stretch yourself there, look at some things with a different slant, listen more openly, and start new positive habits to replace old negative ones.

Three Objectives   This book has three objectives: to enable you (1) to survive *in* the business rat race, (2) to *reduce* it where possible, and (3) to survive *beyond* the business rat race. For the first goal, to survive *in* the rat race, Part 1 of this book offers those things to help you have a more meaningful work life and a career. Part 2 includes the means to help yourself as a businessman in management. For the second objective, to *reduce* your rat race, you discover how to help yourself to greater awareness in Part 3. In Part 4 you find how to help yourself by helping others in your work life. For the third goal, survival *beyond* the business rat race (as well as in), Part 5 provides guides on how to live your personal life and family life to the fullest. Part 6 offers a longer and larger view on how to help yourself for the long pull.

There are three different sets of common findings. One consensus is designed to help you as an individual survive as an individual *in* the business rat race. Another consensus enables you to build your nonbusiness life so as to survive *in* the rat race as well as *beyond* it. A third consensus outlines a new comprehensive management system so that you can in your management practices actively *reduce* the business rat race.[4] You secure for both yourself and others greater productivity and work satisfaction with substantially less conflict.

Misuse and abuse of personal and organization power to the detriment of others is the major cause of the business rat race. His

---

[4] For this management system I draw from and in some instances expand on my recent book, *Managing the Managers: A Realistic Approach to Applying the Behavioral Sciences,* McGraw-Hill Book Company, New York, 1965.

pursuit of power is hard for a man to discover. Moreover, he unwittingly conceals it from others who are not schooled in the use of power. Finally, it is glossed over with many euphemisms so that most management men are unconscious of its unhealthy dimensions in business today. Yet, it is by becoming aware of personal and organization power that you reduce the rat race in management.

part **1**

Help Yourself at Work

*It is not difficult to understand why people who
think constantly about "doing better" are more apt
to do better at job-hunting, to set moderate,
achievable goals for themselves, . . . and to prefer
work situations where they can tell easily whether
they are improving or not.*
—DAVID C. MCCLELLAND, "That Urge to Achieve" [1]

WHAT DO YOU WANT out of your life? What are your
goals? Try these questions on yourself. You may be able to
say, "To be a successful businessman, a good husband, and
a good father." Rarely can anyone go beyond these in my
polls at management conferences. Many do not get to the
good husband part. You may be able to utter a few generalizations about your concept of success, your work needs,
and your career. But then you stop. If you cannot determine what it is you really want in and from your work life,
you are unable to set the best course for yourself. You have
your own blind rat race with its intricate maze toward unknown ends.

[1] *Think*, vol. 32, no. 6, published by IBM, November–December,
1966, pp. 19–23.

In your school life you could say with some conviction just how far in school you were going to go. You learned the fixed stages and the rules of the game. Schools in the main are dedicated to educate every young person to learn to his full potential. Yet they do not let students of every caliber graduate from high school, get into college, graduate from college, and go into graduate work. In spite of the democratic ideals of our culture, schools have been and still are hard-nosed about the record of a student and his performance. The college "gentlemanly C" of a few years ago is a thing of the past. It is harder to earn the "C" today.

Moreover, with the greater numbers of students wanting to get into college and graduate work, admission standards appear to be increasingly higher. Students also have to work harder and persist longer to get their degrees. As an example, undergraduate work in business administration is being eliminated in favor of graduate work. In high school, students are reported to be developing an alarming variety of psychosomatic disorders such as ulcers. As of now about half of the young people finish high school. Only a few will leave because of intellectual limitations. Most dropouts will be because of emotional problems.

There are no such stages in your work life. Yes, you can say to yourself that some day you want to be president of a company. Or you can say you want to retire early. These may be totally unrealistic. About all you can do if you face work life realistically is to have as successful a career as you can taking into account your capabilities, economic conditions, and the situation in your company and in your industry, to name a few of the many variables.

We toss around much too glibly such pat phrases as "integrating personal goals with organization goals," "success," "self-actualization," "achievement," and "management by objectives." In the next three chapters, you are going to have the opportunity to think about where you are now in terms of some basic guides. Then you can plan your own course of direction in light of the many uncertainties. First, you explore the matter of success—what it is and what it should be. Second, you find whether or not you are getting from your job what in general a businessman needs. Third, you have guides to work through what you should and can do about your career.

We start with the assumption, with good proof, that the average man in our country wants to work. But he needs work that is interesting, challenging, and changing. Then he will be more productive. In our society, man is taught as a small child that work is important. Many of the very rich appear to be hard workers though their wealth is increasing at a faster rate than that of anyone else.

Until the last few hundred years, there was no generally accepted notion of personal gain. Production and marketing systems are a recent innovation. Peasants, serfs, and slaves did the work of the lords under tradition or central rule. Striving to become a personal success as we know it today is still unknown to a large portion of the world's population.[2]

This country was peopled by have-nots from other countries who had enough gumption to leave their fellow have-nots who stayed in the old country and took it. No, people did not usually come to this country expecting the land of opportunity. They left misery. The same is true for the have-nots of the Eastern states who moved West. We dramatize them as pioneers who built the West. Admire them for their gumption, we should. Let us at the same time acknowledge that they were essentially have-nots who could not make it in the industrial East.

Today, the products of the have-nots with gumption are the haves who, in the main, keep trying. As the first part in the total program for the total man, help yourself at work. Determine your kind of success. Try for more for you from your work, not more work. Build your own career.

[2] Robert L. Heilbroner, *The Worldly Philosophers*, Simon & Schuster, Inc., New York, 1967, pp. 16–21.

2
Determine Your Kind of Success

Every manager must accept the cardinal fact that he lives and works in uncertainty and conflict, beginning with himself. He can become obsolescent at any age, or he can keep up with change by continuing to grow—by learning and by helping others. He should seek to use experimentally the latest ideas from the exploding behavioral sciences in practicing his art—and work not *against* but *for* himself and others—thereby reducing the rat race.

—ROBERT C. SAMPSON, *Managing the Managers* [1]

DO YOU FEEL that you are a success? You probably say no. Yet, odds are that you are already a business success. It is a matter of degree. You are successful if you have moved up from the clerical and blue-collar class. About nine out of ten people in this country never get much beyond their starting jobs in their entire work lives. If you are a college graduate, you are an even greater success for you are about one out of twenty-five. Surely, some men have done better than you, but most have not done nearly as well. Now you can see why I did not title this book *How to SUCCEED in the Business Rat Race.*

[1] McGraw-Hill Book Company, New York, 1965, p. 254.

Take your first step to survival. Start with the fact that you are a business success. Do not make success the impossible dream as so many do in my informal polls. (I too was unable to admit it at first when a psychiatrist asked me this question in a management conference.) Just to accept the simple fact of economic success can do much for your feeling of achievement, self-esteem, status, and well-being—an increase in your awareness. It does not mean that you slow down. On the contrary, you accomplish more with less strain. By becoming aware of your present success, you reduce some anxiety about yourself. To underevaluate your accomplishments often leads to indecisiveness, pessimism, and unwillingness to take risks. You work longer and harder with undue worry about and suspicion of others. You get more entrapped in the win-lose complex. You cannot distinguish between your push for personal status, increased personal leverage over others and organization authority, and your work for personal accomplishment.

Nor do you understand the stress and strain continuing conflict puts on your emotional structure and on those with whom you compete. If you win, you not only carry the additional emotional burden resulting from the stress of conflict. You also feel increased uncertainty stemming from the fact that you can seldom feel secure in your winning. You are said to fear failure. More accurately, you fear losing. For, if you lose, your emotional burden increases. You feel hostile toward the winner with the urge to get even. You also feel shamed in the eyes of others and personal disappointment. The organization suffers too, for it is less effective. Conflicts continue to spiral to the point where almost every man is in there fighting for what he personally can get out of it.

If you can *feel* that you are a business success, you can then examine with a greater sense of awareness what *concept* of success you have been following. There are four:

Salvation concept—new twists on the Puritan ethic

Organization concept—bureaucracy personified

Power concept—James's bitch goddess of success, now with a college degree

Maturation concept—trying to become as much of a person as you can become

Salvation Concept

"Serve God by working hard and making money." The salvation concept, first brought to America in the seventeenth century, started as the Protestant ethic. However, Jews and Catholics later brought with them what we should more properly call the Puritan ethic of piety, frugality, and industry. Making money is a relatively recent innovation. Do not confuse the salvation concept with the "divine right to be taken care of." People who have this feeling have a problem to be overcome. They feel gypped when their right is not honored.[2]

The early Protestants of our country were an earnest and godly people. Filled with puritanical exaltation, they were sure that strenuous toil was acceptable to Heaven. Cotton Mather preached that business was a calling and a vital part of religion. Success was the attainment of a respectable economic status in this world and eternal salvation in the next.

Religion and Success Today   Norman Vincent Peale with his power of positive thinking is a modern religion-and-success writer. A confidence man,[3] Peale offers a religious basis for the ideal of success without becoming involved in the conservative Protestant tradition. Through mental transformation, the road to success no longer requires hard work. Steps are outlined by Peale to acquire the higher power of positive thinking to a serene mental outlook. Then comes higher status and more money.

For those who want salvation without success, there is Billy Graham, the debunker of success.[4] In this new, modern version of Fundamentalism, you should be poised, gracious, and cultured. Laugh, yes, but through your own wholesomeness you rise above the low level of others—of other religions, other races.

The most recent twist of the salvation concept of success is not

[2] Rollo May, *Man's Search for Himself,* W. W. Norton & Company, Inc., New York, 1953, pp. 197–198.

[3] Donald B. Meyer, "The Confidence Man," *New Republic,* vol. 133, July 11, 1955, pp. 8–10.

[4] Donald B. Meyer, "Successful De-bunker of Success," *New Republic,* vol. 133, Aug. 22, 1955, pp. 8–10.

only how to serve God and mammon but also if and how to support the new revolution of the have-nots. A few religionists demand more than one's own salvation. They want the businessman to move out not so much to convert others as to help them economically and socially.

Organization Concept

"Be diligent in your work and the organization will take care of you." Such is the organization concept of success. Organization men are punctual, reliable, orderly, conscientious, underutilized, hard working, and unquestioning. Yet, they have the win-lose complex. They struggle to have their way. They have been erroneously labeled, I believe, the "passive conformist" or the "organization man." [5] More appropriate is the "local" who places himself in the arms of his company. The company becomes the source of many of his satisfactions. Here is a place where he can get ahead while not being committed to a particular career or specific skills.[6] His satisfactions come from his standing in the company, from company values, and from his fellow men. His attitude is typified by his belief that he will get ahead in his company by being devoted and working hard—although he may do neither.

The Road to Success   Many organization men are conscientious doers who work long hours without complaint. In the main they wear the mask of conformity. Yet, in their own way they strive for what they think is right. The pattern is clear. A young man starts to work. He is enthusiastic. He starts taking work home with him or staying late at the office to get something special done. Behind this is a normal, anxious need to make a good showing, the desire to get started off on the right foot by impressing the management. Soon he is spending the rest of his work life relying on his hard work and long

[5] David Riesman, Nathan Glazer, and Reuel Denny, *The Lonely Crowd*, Doubleday & Company, Inc., Garden City, N.Y., 1953; and William H. Whyte, Jr., *The Organization Man*, Simon & Schuster, Inc., New York, 1956. See also Chapter 9.

[6] A. W. Gouldner, "Cosmopolitans and Locals: Toward an Analysis of Latent Social Roles, I," *Administrative Science Quarterly*, vol. 2, December, 1957, pp. 281–306.

hours as the means to advancement. His primary need is to work with people he likes. Although he would deny it, he is neither trying to do better nor trying to learn more. In school he was found to get good grades in all subjects although he never developed an interest in learning. Nor is he usually creative.

A creative person may or may not have marked emotional problems. He is found to seek solutions to the ever more difficult problems that he continuously sets for himself. There is a difference between logical thinking and creative imagination. Intellection is the logical intellectual process. Creativity, on the other hand, is imagination that relies on irrational factors such as inspiration for the unusual, not the logical, weaving together of mental events. A creative person enjoys the risk and uncertainty of the unknown, with little fear of failure of his ideas. He tends to be less interested in future personal success than others. As a student he cares less about grades than does the conscientious student. Creative people are found to be more excited with a problem and to strive for multiple solutions. Creative problem-solvers tend to show physical symptoms of being excited and to ask less questions. Doers ask more questions without reaching solutions.

Power Concept

"I give ulcers. I don't get them." "Nice guys don't win." The drive for power in modern business was started by robber barons. Their game was rough and tough. There was no honesty and no regard for the finer points of the law. The players were interested not in producing goods or services useful to society, but only in their own wealth and power. They established empires which are now run by paid managements. Today, top managements exercise their own self-perpetuating, autonomous power without any significant ownership. Separation of control from ownership has nearly doubled in the last thirty years. About 85 percent of the 200 largest companies are now controlled by paid management, according to recent reports.

What kinds of men try to get to the top? Many kinds do. They include, among others, the authoritarian dictator and the neurotic competitor. Later we shall look into these varieties. Here we view those who follow William James's bitch goddess of success, now with a college degree. The highly competitive, success-oriented executive *makes* the business rat race.[7] He is not too concerned with improving his own work performance. His drive is to climb the pyramid of a large corporation to acquire power, status, wealth, and control of many others.

Machiavellian Manager A competitive business manager is deep in the dilemma of manipulation. Although he practices it, he must not get caught at it. In working for his own personal advantage, he searches out the corridors of comparative indifference and follows them. He avoids wherever possible complete, outspoken support or determined opposition. He capitalizes on opportunities and relationships so as to move his organization toward what he wants.[8]

A contrasting view of manipulators is that they are better fighters than thinkers. Those who get to the top still struggle for power. Analysis of meetings of boards of directors and top management proves that the level of trust is low. There are almost no instances in which an executive helps another to think through a new idea. No one builds upon another person's contribution. Often more than one person talks at the same time. Some pass written notes to each other. Most of the time is spent trying to show why another person is wrong and the speaker correct.[9]

Personal ethics give way to business ethics. Businessmen claim that while they are ethical, the average businessman is not. Most know of instances of supplying call girls to customers, price fixing, and bribery.[10]

Pathology of Power Religious or not, man cannot live with a sense of well-being unless his business ethics and his personal ethics have

---

[7] Research findings about followers of the power concept of success are so voluminous that only a few key points and a few authors are cited.

[8] Drawn from H. Edward Wrapp, "Good Managers Don't Make Policy Decisions," *Selected Papers*, no. 26, Graduate School of Business, University of Chicago, Chicago, Apr. 27, 1967.

[9] Chris Argyris, "How Tomorrow's Executives Will Make Decisions," *Think*, vol. 33, no. 6, published by IBM, November-December, 1967, pp. 18–24. Based on an analysis of 265 meetings.

[10] Raymond C. Baumhart, "How Ethical Are Businessmen?" *Harvard Business Review*, vol. 39, no. 4, July-August, 1961, pp. 6–7ff. Based on a survey of 1,700 businessmen.

the same basic ideals. In a single-minded pursuit of power, man comes to believe that all living is a power contest. Ends justify the means. He is emotionally incapable of developing his other resources. He can only pretend to have ethics, humility, a sense of humor, and concern for others. A power seeker does not trust others, for they are likely to let him down. He believes he must make his own way unaided. The extreme intensity with which he pursues his work leaves little time, energy, or interest for any other activities. A tense individual, he can never rest. He is impatient with others. His long hours and hard work isolate him from his family and friends.[11]

The emotional pathology of the power concept is hostility toward rivals and some anxiety and guilt because of that hostility. Even though he is not power mad, man's symbol of victory becomes the substance of victory. There can be no internal rewards in the feeling of having done a job well. The misuse and abuse of organization power at all management levels is the biggest factor in the rat race. Competition is the excuse for aggression and domination of others. Man plays to win regardless of the issue. Rivalry soon becomes compulsive. The differences between people are not about the immediate task but about beating each other.

Worse still, a man who has acquired organization power will one day lose it. Then what happens? The result may often be tragic. Although he may have made a rat race for others, he finally loses his power and with it he loses everything that is important to him.

Maturation Concept

"Try to become as much of a person as you can become." If you take the long and the large view, you find in this statement the essentials of the maturation concept of success. Maturation means that you consciously strive to become as mature as you can become— continuous intellectual, emotional, and physical self-development. It is more a course of direction than a destination. Maturation is a never-ending process of growth until death. Strive to live as long as you possibly can, as active in as many ways as you can. With what is known today, the mystique of both middle and old age, each with its cautionary measure of slowing down and its expected set of de-

[11] W. Lloyd Warner and James C. Abegglen, *Big Business Leaders in America*, Harper & Row, Publishers, Incorporated, New York, 1955, pp. 72–82.

bilitations, is the surest road to personal obsolescence and unhappiness as well as mental and physical ill health. The maturation motto might well be, "Fight to live to the fullest."

The Ancient Greek Way   The maturation concept of success is the ancient Greek invention with new depth and meaning as the result of modern knowledge. The Greeks strove for the full development of self through:

1. Pursuit of wisdom—known today by such terms as excellence, achievement, and effectiveness
2. A free mind, free of religion and state—today known as emotional maturity, autonomy, and well-being
3. Knowing yourself—now considered to be the knowledge and awareness to face the reality of yourself
4. Learning through observing, study, and reasoning—known now as self-development, self-improvement, and self-renewal
5. Human progress in a democratic city-state [12]—today the democratic ideal, community service, helping others, and in this book, helping others to help yourself
6. Physical excellence—now physical fitness or physical well-being through vigorous exercise
7. Love of life—in today's terms, spontaneity, intimacy
8. Golden mean with everything in moderation—the *modern* golden mean of a balanced life to assure well-being, intellectual, emotional, and physical

In Athens, a little town on the western border of the civilized world 500 years before Christ, something very new and different happened. Athens rejected the ancient world of the despot who ruled a wretched people with a great priestly organization which governed the intellectual domain. The Greek way was worked out in a cold, mountainous, infertile land. In a democratic city-state, religion was split off into one compartment and everything else that mattered into another. Under the Greek way, happiness was exercising the vital powers for excellence in life. The first intellectuals with a passion for using their minds, these men of Athens were the first and probably the only free minds, free of state and religion.

[12] For themselves, not their slaves.

Mind, reason, observation, and the pursuit of wisdom became supreme through science, philosophy, and mathematics. They also played hard, the first people of the world to do so and on a scale not equaled since, in games and singing. Physical fitness was encouraged through athletic contests. They found the world delightful and tragic. Eating, drinking, and being with friends made their lives full and active.[13]

Since the ancient Greeks, many people have expressed concern over how man can develop himself toward maturity in an environment of human progress. Over the centuries the idealists of philosophy, literature, and politics provided the intellectual leadership. The other concepts of success had their supporters too. Religionists fought with power seekers, and followers of the organization concept of success were caught in between.

If we look at Europe, some time after the birth of Christ, we find again a closed world. Despots ruled over wretched illiterates with a priestly organization controlling the intellectual domain. Both scientific advances and the modern economics of money making, production, and marketing were blocked by the priestly organization. The priest stood between man and God until the revolt by Luther, who also opposed modern economics. It was Calvin who freed the businessman from the sin of usury by upholding the right to charge interest. The typical businessman today, however, is more like the ancient Roman than the ancient Greek. The Roman citizen was a commonsense man of affairs interested in building the Roman empire and exercising power.

Early American Self-made Man   In many ways the rebellion of the American Colonies to form a democratic nation resembles the early Greek discovery—more so than any other country. The self-made man who believed in self-improvement and in the opportunity for improvement for others is the early American version of the maturation concept. In the Declaration of Independence, Jefferson put into a government document for the first time the natural rights of man. These ideals, developed primarily by European thinkers in the seventeenth century, were common among the intellectuals of the Colonies. The American democratic nation is dedicated to the welfare of its people, who are created equal with inalienable rights

[13] As paraphrased from Edith Hamilton, *The Greek Way*, W. W. Norton & Company, New York, 1930, 1943. Copyright renewed in 1958 by Edith Hamilton.

to life, liberty, and the pursuit of happiness. Jefferson and Franklin were the chief public exponents of striving for individual potential. Jefferson was concerned about the kinds of democratic institutions that would ensure the development and selection of the best natural leaders, as opposed to the elite of power, wealth, or aristocracy. He believed that people enlightened by free education would, under our republican institutions, govern themselves more effectively than under any other system of government.

Franklin, whose talents were as remarkable as those of Washington and Jefferson, established himself as the folk hero of the self-made man in America. He enclosed his scientific genius, his literary and political skills, in simple middle-class garb; he was an ordinary-looking man with a dumpy figure. By his actions and in his "Memoirs," he became the American self-made man.

In the nineteenth century Ralph Waldo Emerson, poet and philosopher, became the outstanding exponent of self-improvement, success, and self-culture. Success comes with self-reliance, sensibility to beauty and truth. Abraham Lincoln is the epitome of the self-made man who believed in both personal development and human progress.[14]

Modern Maturation Concept of Success   Only since World War II have we become sufficiently sophisticated or knowledgeable, if not precisely scientific, to accept fully the ancient Greek way. The Greek way in modern dress means to strive for intellectual, emotional, and physical maturity. It is concerned with the material side and the human side of your life. I have found no one today who espouses all the tenets of the Greeks. Hence, I bring together a variety of specialties to form a consensus for the maturation concept of success. Its essential elements are enterprising achievement, self-actualization, autonomy, helpfulness, and physical fitness.

The first is enterprising achievement. If you are or can become an enterprising achiever, you have an intense urge to achieve, whereas the majority apparently do not care that much.

You continually strive to do better.
You are challenged by opportunity.
You are resourceful in adversity.

[14] Drawn from John G. Cawelti, *Apostles of the Self-made Man*, The University of Chicago Press, Chicago, 1965.

You prefer to work where you can see you are improving.
You seek a high degree of personal responsibility.
You search for areas where you can accomplish something.
You select moderately risky situations.
You set reasonable goals for yourself.
You choose experts rather than friends for help in problem-solving.
You work with others where you can see your personal contribution.[15]

The second element is self-actualization in and beyond work. This is at the top of five levels of man's needs. At the first level are the basic physiological needs: food, rest, shelter, and protection from the elements. When these are adequately satisfied, needs at the second level become important. These are safety needs: protection against deprivation, danger, and threat to life. Social needs constitute the third level: love, friendship, belonging, acceptance by one's fellows, and association. The fourth level of needs are egoistic needs of which there are two kinds: those that satisfy self-esteem (self-confidence, self-respect, achievement, knowledge, and competence); and those of reputation (recognition, status, appreciation, and respect).

Finally, at the fifth level are the needs for self-actualization: realization of one's potentialities and continuing self-development, creativity, and awareness. If you are a self-actualized person, you have a keen awareness of the reality of your own desires, impulses, opinions, and reactions. Moreover, with your awareness of external reality, you savor time after time life's simple, basic goods, however they might bore others.[16] The business rat race is such that the need for self-actualization, if it exists, is partially blocked. In

[15] Social psychologist David C. McClelland is the chief authority on this kind of an achiever. To differentiate this kind of an achiever from others, I have titled him "enterprising." McClelland uses no title. The qualities listed are given in his *The Achieving Society*, Litton Educational Publishing, Inc., New York, 1961, by permission of Van Nostrand Reinhold Co. and "That Urge to Achieve," *Think*, vol. 32, no. 6, published by IBM, November-December, 1966, pp. 19–23. In the latter he also describes the affiliate and the power achievers. The first is in my organization concept of success and the second is in the power concept where I have used some of his findings.

[16] Theoretical psychologist A. H. Maslow is the authority on these five levels of needs. See his *Motivation and Personality*, Harper & Row, Publishers, Incorporated, New York, 1954, especially pp. 210 and 214 for his description of awareness of the reality of the self and external reality.

the business rat race where people cannot satisfy their lower-level needs, they use their energies in attempting to satisfy those lower-level needs rather than self-actualization.

The third facet of maturation is autonomy, the overthrow of family, social, and cultural conditioning and tradition. The demands of society and friends must also be partly overthrown. You achieve autonomy through awareness, spontaneity, and intimacy.[17] Awareness is to see and accept the here and now of reality of both yourself and others, not as conditioned by parents. Spontaneity is to express your own feelings, not those you were taught to have. Intimacy is the spontaneous candidness of an aware person who is open and accepts the openness of others.

The fourth element is helpfulness. This is implied in all that you have read thus far about the maturation concept of success—in the democratic ideal of the Greek city-state and of this country, in the enterprising achiever, in self-actualization, and in the spontaneity and intimacy of autonomy. Helping others in your organization so that it can perform at its highest level is the keystone to organization development and economic effectiveness. When men are working against each other in an organization, it cannot achieve optimum performance. It is axiomatic that a man should compete only for promotions and should help others with their tasks. A boss ideally should help his subordinates develop for the long-term good of the organization.

To help another with no thought of personal gain is generally viewed by psychiatrists as the most personally rewarding act for man. This, then, is the mark of a mature person, whether he does it personally or works for those conditions which assure that others are helped for the total good of the entity of which he is a part— be it family, business, community, state, nation, or world. Put in purely selfish terms, it is vital that you at least help those who will help you in turn toward the maturation concept of success. And later on when you retire, once you have learned to help others, you will not suffer from a common problem of old people—the need to be needed.

The fifth facet is physical fitness. Through working to keep your

[17] Psychiatrist Eric Berne has become one of the most published exponents of autonomy. See his *Games People Play*, Grove Press, Inc., New York, 1964, pp. 178–182, and *A Layman's Guide to Psychiatry & Psychoanalysis*, Simon & Schuster, Inc., New York, 1947.

body in top physical condition, you achieve five benefits: a feeling of physical well-being, greater endurance, mental alertness, emotional stability, and longevity.[18] Side benefits include emotional therapy through release of aggressions and frustration as well as a sense of accomplishment.

In sum, you follow the modern maturation concept of success by (1) trying to do better as an enterprising achiever, (2) developing your full potential through self-actualization, (3) securing greater emotional and mental well-being through autonomy, (4) being helpful, and (5) striving for physical well-being through physical fitness.

Try for More Maturity

If you have some awareness of yourself, by your own actions you should be able to identify the route you have been using for your success. The first three concepts beyond business success cannot help you survive in and beyond the business rat race because they are essentially overly concerned with your personal salvation, with your dependency on an organization, or with power. If you can analyze your primary need for one of these and abandon it, you are likely to find the wish for maturation emerge and with it a move toward intellectual, emotional, and physical fitness.

Three Lives, in Three Activities, through Three Ways   The maturation concept of success offers you the only means I have found to survive the business rat race with a feeling of well-being. You try to live a full, well-rounded life, to become a more mature person. After assessing behavioral sciences and medical findings, I have found that the modern means to survival can be reduced to a deceptively simple formula. Survival is achieving by

Living fully three lives: Business, Personal, Family

In three activities: Work, Relaxation, Re-creation

Through three ways: Your mind, Your body, Other people

---

[18] Physician Kenneth H. Cooper, in his *Aerobics,* M. Evans and Company, Philadelphia, 1968, has developed a point system on the amount of exercise needed (discussed further in Chapter 15).

In following this "three by three by three" formula, you find a variety of suggestions on how to secure more maturity. Exhibit 1 summarizes the primary sources of the suggestions.

Exhibit 1   THREE BY THREE BY THREE
FORMULA FOR SURVIVAL

Achieving in three lives: Business, Personal, Family	Work	In Three Activities: Relaxation	Re-creation
Through: Your Mind	For self-esteem and accomplishment. See Chaps. 2–7, 10, 15, 16.	Play, escape, and rest. See Chaps. 7, 10, 15, 16.	Self-development in awareness, knowledge, and skills. See Chaps. 5–10, 14–16.
Your Body	For physiological or safety needs and achievement. See Chaps. 10, 15, 16.	Emotional and physiological needs for sleep and rest. See Chaps. 15, 16.	Physical fitness as well as physical and emotional therapy. See Chaps. 8, 15, 16.
Other People	Egoistic status needs and joint effort. See Chaps. 10, 11–17.	Social needs to accept and be accepted. See Chaps. 15–17.	Learning with and from others. See Chaps. 11, 12, 14–17.

You try to live as full a life as possible for as long as possible: through (1) your mind, (2) your body, and (3) other people, by (1) work, (2) relaxation, and (3) re-creation, in *each* of your three lives —business, personal, and family. Work means constructive activity. Relaxation covers diversion, refreshment, escape, play, and rest. Re-creation includes those activities which add to your personal growth as well as restore you emotionally, physically, and intellectually. Re-creation is continuously and constantly creating yourself again —rebuilding yourself. If you pick the right activities, much can be done in a little time. Re-creation, if successful, provides recognizable results:

Your reactivated curiosity makes learning not a chore but a joy.
Your reactivated vitality makes physical exercise something you

look forward to, not something to be avoided at every opportunity.
Your reactivated interest in learning from others enables you to
help others to help you.

You secure a greater sense of emotional well-being through your
mind, your body, and other people—and reduce your business rat
race.

As for your mind, the first of the three ways, common sense tells
you that your mind is an objective, thinking, learning, creative machine. A major breakthrough of the behavioral sciences is the primary finding that your mind is self-deceiving. It perceives what it
needs to perceive. It believes what it needs to believe. To become
aware is to see things for what they really are, not as you are conditioned to see them by parents or others. Your body, the second of
the three ways, not only suffers from the business rat race but can
enable you to survive the race provided you develop and use it as a
means for physical work, relaxation, and re-creation. As for other
people, the last of the three ways, the maxim is simple: help yourself by helping others. This is essentially selfish, not altruistic.

Achieving maturity is a state of becoming. Few people reach it
completely. The issue is life, not only as a biological and economic
fact, but as a process of growth. The trick is to try to live a full and
well-balanced life both within and beyond your career. To try for
more maturity is to be committed to and work at a worthwhile life
of broadening interests and accomplishments, of which your work is
only one facet. Power is desired, but not pursued to the sacrifice of
other goals. A multiplicity of resources and gratifications are developed so that you can turn to others when some fail.

You come to find that what you do off the job may be as important for you as what you do on the job, as vital as that is. To succeed by really trying means to strive for

Freedom of mind
An overview of life and the world
A greater sense of well-being
Better physical and emotional health
Avoidance of obsolescence
Greater longevity
Meaningful and interesting retirement

3

Try for More from Your Work

One wonders whether the sense of anomie, of the rootlessness and alienation which anthropologists, political scientists and psychiatrists have found so serious in our world, is not at least in part a consequence of overloading of interpersonal relationships due to the loss of the direct meaning of work.

—FREDERICK HERZBERG, BERNARD MAUSNER, and BARBARA SNYDERMAN, *The Motivation to Work* [1]

To REDUCE YOUR BUSINESS RAT RACE, you should try for more from your work. With almost no exceptions, businessmen in my informal polls say they are underutilized. But then when I ask them what they want from their work, they are able to utter only a few generalizations. Work for us is so basic, it is axiomatic that if a man is to find himself, he must do so in his work. Through work man is able to accomplish something and count for something. Not only does a job provide for life; it is a large part of life.

What do you want from your work? Try to make a list. Then see how well you have done in terms of what the research has found. In this chapter I consolidate the most prevalent findings on the work

[1] John Wiley & Sons, Inc., New York, 1959, p. 131.

needs of the normal management man, a consensus drawing from several researchers.[2] Exhibit 2 summarizes the normal work needs.

Exhibit 2 NORMAL WORK NEEDS

Intrinsic Work Needs

1. Intrinsic job satisfaction—the right type of work for you
2. Achievement—self-actualization, autonomy, accomplishment, variable pace, advancement
3. Decision making—the opportunity to make the decisions in your work and to participate in decisions affecting you and your work
4. Good boss—who has those key qualities of competence, effectiveness, and supportiveness
5. Good peers—compatibility with your fellow workers
6. Good subordinates—if you are a boss, subordinates who are competent and compatible

Extrinsic Work Needs

1. Compensation—by all odds the most important in this group
2. Status—the symbols that assure you your proper place in the pecking order
3. Fair organization—one that treats you and others fairly as judged by you
4. Effective organization—good administration
5. Good working conditions—right for your kind of occupation
6. Job security—so that you do not have to worry too much about retaining a job

Intrinsic Work Needs

Intrinsic work needs tend to increase work satisfaction and productivity. If they are not met satisfactorily, productivity tends to decrease.

Intrinsic Job Satisfaction   Even though you may be underutilized, it is imperative for your own well-being that you do the particular kind of work you like. This is intrinsic job satisfaction. You cannot do as well when you are doing work in which you are not interested. You usually react negatively. You may be unaware of the

[2] Many views of several specialists have been brought together here to form a consensus of the findings and a common language. I am particularly indebted to Frederick Herzberg and his associates, Chris Argyris, Rensis Likert, Douglas McGregor, Elton Mayo, F. J. Roethlisberger, William Foote Whyte, as well as others cited in the Bibliography. The split into two basic kinds of work needs is based on Herzberg's approach with the findings of the other behavioral sciences researchers brought in for a consensus.

source of your dissatisfaction and often "take it out" on yourself. Intrinsic job *dis*satisfaction is believed by some psychiatrists to be a significant source of emotional disturbances and psychosomatic illnesses.

Achievement Of the many items that might be put under achievement, almost all of them can be grouped under five key categories: self-actualization, autonomy, accomplishment, variable pace, and opportunity for advancement. Note that I use some of the terms of the maturation concept of success: self-actualization and autonomy covered in Chapter 2. Here, however, they describe a lower order for the normal man who is found to be underutilized at work. While he does not have the intense urge for doing better, the self-actualization and autonomy of the enterprising achiever, he does need a greater sense of self-actualization, autonomy, and accomplishment than his own work offers him.

Self-actualization in the work itself enables you to be more active than passive, more in control of your work, more expressive of your deep and complex abilities.[3] Ideally, you should also have the opportunity for personal growth on the job, re-creation to realize your potentials. For a continuing sense of self-development, you should have the opportunity to tackle and finish new and interesting tasks. Then you have job enlargement for a greater variety of work, and job enrichment for higher-level work. These are the primary means for re-creation on the job. In many organizations self-actualization in work poses a problem. Your need to fit your job to yourself is diametrically opposed to the organization's interest in fitting you to the job.

Autonomy enables you to be more independent than dependent in your work. In popular management theory, responsibility usually means being accountable for doing something a certain way within a certain time with certain results. If you, however, are going to have a sense of responsibility, you need the feeling of an autonomous adult. You should be able to do your own planning, generating courses of action and choosing among them, rather than being a servant for your superior. This means that you feel that you are being trusted and are not continuously on trial. You stand on your own two feet as a responsible, thinking adult. Important, too, is the

[3] Chris Argyris, *Personality and Organization,* Harper & Row, Publishers, Incorporated, New York, 1957, p. 53.

feeling that you can make mistakes as part of your "batting average."

Accomplishment means solving problems, completing tasks, and overcoming difficulties. Admittedly, there must necessarily be in every job a considerable amount of routine and trivia. Still, most of the time you should be able to feel that you are accomplishing something personally significant, being well utilized.

Variable pace permits you to work at a pace which is comfortable for you. You work faster sometimes and slower at other times, with opportunities for relaxation while at work. Artificial pressures to produce have been found to have a negative effect. Certainly you cannot do your best if you feel pressured. True, you like the feeling of internal tension when you are doing something you enjoy. You get excited about what you are doing and have a genuine feeling of happiness while working on some special, pleasing task. But no animals, and few humans, go at the continuous, rapid pace that the average businessman attempts. Animals rest often. When they are tired they sleep. Compared with the human animal, they are serene and unanxious. For relaxation you need opportunities to "goof off" without feeling guilty, a climate of acceptance so that you relax with your fellow workers, and an informality that enables you to be casual.

Advancement includes not only the likelihood of a promotion or transfer but also a situation in which you advance in your own work.

Decision Making   The core of organization authority is the power to make decisions. Unfortunately, decision making is thoroughly confused. As a management fad it has produced over 400 books and articles.[4] The situation is even more confounded with "democratic management" and "participation." We do managing no good by indulging in terms like "democratic management" when it can only be autocratic.

"Participation" got its start in the classic Hawthorne experiment in the late 1920s.[5] At the businessman's level participation should be

[4] Paul Wasserman and Fred S. Silander, *Decision-Making: An Annotated Bibliography*, Cornell University Press, Ithaca, N.Y., 1958.

[5] F. J. Roethlisberger and W. J. Dickson, *Management and the Worker*, Harvard University Press, Cambridge, Mass., 1947.

thought of in two senses: participation by one individual in decision making with his boss, and subordinate-group participation in decision making with its boss. You should be able to feel that your boss seeks to help you rather than to direct your work. You make the key decisions in your work. Also you should feel that you have something to say about decisions affecting your job and your career.

Good Boss The kinds of people you work with and their relations with you are vital. And yet *no one,* in the many management conferences I have held, has ever suggested that a good boss, good peers, and good subordinates are important to him in his work. It is my hunch that people are emotionally blocked on the subject, unable to recognize and voice their feelings.

Exhibit 3 QUALITIES OF A GOOD SUPERIOR

Competence	Effectiveness	Supportiveness	
Clear thinking	Active	Accepting	Patient
Unconventional	Aggressive	Democratic	Tolerant
Humorous	Ambitious	Fair	Responsible
Intuitive	Confident	Frank	Sensitive
Original	Not easily influenced	Informal	Tactful
Scientific	Enthusiastic	Good listener	Trusting
	Sophisticated	High integrity	Trustworthy
	Deep	Humble	Warm
		Kind	Helpful
		Likes teaching	Sincere

Charisma, rejected by many researchers as the basic quality of a good boss, now returns. Be he boss, parent, teacher, or anyone in an authority position, when he is good, he has been found to be very different from the poor "authority figure." Good bosses, parents, teachers, and counselors are viewed as having competence, effectiveness, and supportiveness.[6] Exhibit 3 lists the qualities of a good su-

[6] Edgar H. Schein and Douglas T. Hall, "The Student Image of the Teacher," *The Journal of Applied Behavioral Science,* vol. 3, no. 3, July-August-September, 1967, p. 325. "Effectiveness" is titled "potency" in the article. These authors have made a major breakthrough. After doing research on the student-teacher relationship, the authors found that much of the research on other "authority relationships" followed the same pattern. These include subordinate-boss, child-parent, student-teacher, and counselee-counselor.

perior. But for you it is also compatibility. A good boss must be someone you like personally or at a minimum feel indifferent to. If there is no compatibility to the point where there is active dislike or sparks fly, get another boss.

Good Peers   Good peers for the businessman are different than those for rank-and-file, blue- and white-collar workers. Historically, much has been made of the informal organization, the tightly knit, blue-collar work group opposed to the formal organization. These cliques come into existence primarily in defense against management. Management men do not form these kinds of cliques. While they keep their differences from the boss and try to "butter him up," they are highly competitive with each other.[7] Paradoxically, you want peers who will accept you and, with your win-lose complex, whom you can beat.

Good Subordinates   At a minimum you want subordinates who are technically competent, emotionally competent, and compatible and cooperative with others.

Extrinsic Work Needs

Although extrinsic factors must be adequate, so as not to have a negative impact, it has been found that increasing them does not tend to result in higher productivity or greater work satisfaction.[8] Much of the management literature has focused on the importance of the extrinsic factors while continuing to simplify jobs and reduce the intrinsic factors, both at the worker and management levels. In addition the number and variety of controls have increased, as well as stepped-up supervisory pressure on subordinates under the guise of leadership and motivation. Neither management nor union officials seem to have a clear impression of what is important to people.[9] Superiors, for example, consistently underestimate the impor-

[7] Chris Argyris, *Executive Leadership and Appraisal of a Manager in Action,* Harper & Row, Publishers, Incorporated, New York, 1953.

[8] Herzberg and his associates termed these "hygienic factors." In large measure our "extrinsic factors" are similar to his. See Herzberg et al., *op. cit.*

[9] R. L. Kahn, "The Prediction of Productivity," *Journal of Social Issues,* vol. 12, no. 2, Fall, 1956, pp. 41–49; T. Purcell, *The Worker Speaks His Mind on Company and Union,* Harvard University Press, Cambridge, Mass., 1953.

tance people attach to interpersonal relations and the opportunities to turn out good quality work. Superiors also seriously underestimate the extent to which their subordinates feel that their boss understands their problems.[10]

Compensation Although extremely important, compensation does not induce man to work hard. Almost everyone wants more salary and fringe benefits as well as bonuses and profit sharing. But salary is potentially more of a job dissatisfier than a job satisfier in affecting job attitudes.[11]

Status Status provides concrete indication that others hold a person in esteem.[12] Personal standing includes your egoistic needs for recognition and reputation, the status instinct in terms of the pecking order, vital to almost all animals including the human animal (see Chapter 8). Then there is the symbol of power and privilege, as mentioned, a part of the power concept of success. To be a status seeker is to try aggressively to secure additional leverage over others who are not one's subordinates through "the struggle for status." A man typically wants to move to those positions in the organization where he can make more initiations on others than others can make on him. He can put pressures on them and because they are of lower status they have little ability for rebuttal.[13]

Status symbols as indicators of the pecking order have been described so much that I shall not detail them here. A private office is the beginning, and from there on evidences of status within the private-office group stem from the size of the office to the quality of its furnishing and decor. Pay is another status symbol. Although salaries in most organizations are supposed to be secret, enough information leaks out so that individuals can tell their rank in the pecking order by the amount of money they receive. To gain greater personal status by having one's work considered a profession is a

[10] Rensis Likert, *New Patterns of Management,* McGraw-Hill Book Company, New York, 1961, pp. 49–51.

[11] Herzberg et al., *op. cit.,* p. 82; and William Foote Whyte, *Money and Motivation,* Harper & Row, Publishers, Incorporated, New York, 1955.

[12] Recall Maslow's fourth-level egoistic need of reputation which includes status.

[13] Leonard Sayles, *Managerial Behavior,* McGraw-Hill Book Company, New York, 1964, pp. 115–116.

popular American pastime. Almost every specialized occupation is striving to secure "professionalization." Think of the increasing number of times that management is being called a profession. Businessmen seem to be unaware of the differences between their formal preparation for their work, their ethics, and their standards and those of members of the true professions such as medicine and law.

Fair Organization Because of his dependence on his organization, be it a small company or a unit of a larger one, man is concerned about whether management and personnel policies are fair. In addition, he becomes concerned when there is no indication that his management or his company has concern for him as an individual.[14]

Effective Organization Poor administration is found by research to be an important factor in negative feelings about a job. In my own consulting with companies, I find how much men are concerned about company inefficiencies and ineffectiveness, duplication of effort, waste, and the like. How eager people at all levels are to suggest improvements. They want the opportunity to work more effectively and efficiently.

Good Working Conditions The physical working environment in terms of the particular industry, the community, and the status of the individual constitutes the working conditions for management people. Ventilation, air conditioning, lighting, space, decor, and housekeeping should not fall below the level of the industry or the community.

Job Security Included in job security are such things as tenure and company stability. Furthermore, if you have climbed up a good part of the management pyramid in your organization, you would normally be concerned about the loss of your job or important parts of it. This concern stems not so much from your more precarious position as from the fact that you have so much more to lose if you fall.

[14] Harry Levinson, Charlton R. Price, Kenneth J. Munden, Harold J. Mandl, and Charles M. Solley, *Men, Management, and Mental Health*, Harvard University Press, Cambridge, Mass., 1962, p. 130.

Try for Greater Utilization

Although there is considerable evidence that businessmen are underutilized, I am increasingly convinced that many management men in large measure set their own level of underutilization. Here is some evidence. Historically most management observers have preached more delegation at all levels of management. Still managers tend to hold on to their decision making even on small matters. How have you handled your decision making?

Start with the power seekers. When these people get into top management positions, it is axiomatic that they attempt to perpetuate and increase their power and its rewards. Their euphemisms about power not only serve to screen the consequences of their own power drives from themselves but also serve as a rationale for their behavior. They are incapable of seeing the deleterious impact of their behavior on the intellectual and emotional structure of subordinates and the consequent lowering of effectiveness.

Centralized control in the hands of the relatively few in top management demonstrates their increasing anxiety about being sure that they are obeyed. They focus more and more on how to make their authority more effective. In the main, they want people to do more—to speed up, accomplish more, work longer hours. It appears that most top management men continue to seek to bring to themselves more of the organization authority—decision making on smaller matters. With the mechanization of communication and data processing equipment, the trend is found to be toward the recentralization of power. Top management can now secure more detailed information faster than ever before. Many people are maintaining that top management is getting so much information that it does not know and cannot determine how to use it.

Take a wide variety of presidents with whom I have become well acquainted in the past several years. In the main they are not power seekers. Some manage and build their companies effectively with apparently little time and effort. Some, however, never seem to get on top of their operations. They put in long hours and get into an enormous amount of detail. They try to quarterback all department heads. I have seen these differences in other management men in these organizations. Failure to delegate all but the big decisions and do the planning is in part caused by the desire for as much control as possible. It may stem from insecurity and inability to trust people. More important, I believe, they have not thought out what they want from their work and what is important and unimportant for them. They lose themselves in hyperactivity over a lot of trivia.

The Measure   Here you have had listed the major work needs of the normal man. You are the "measure," as man is the measure of all things concerning himself, of these work needs. How important is each one to you? This will give you a good indication as to whether or not you have normal work needs. In summary, intrinsic needs include intrinsic job satisfaction, achievement opportunities, decision making, a good boss, good peers, and good subordinates. Extrinsic needs include compensation, status, a fair organization, an effective organization, good working conditions, and job security.

Then you face three questions. First, if these needs are important to you, how much of them are you getting? Second, how much are you able to get in your present job? Third, how do you try for more? From my consulting I am convinced you have more of a chance than you think to achieve greater utilization at work without the power struggle of empire building. As you will find in Chapter 12, you must try for it. Let your boss know what more you can and want to do. Keep in frequent contact with him. It has been found that higher performance occurs only when there is much interaction between you and your boss.[15] Unless you have a boss who is a weak sister, chances are that he will say go ahead and try it. Then you are on your way to self-actualization and autonomy at work, two of the main facets of the maturation concept of success.

[15] Rensis Likert, *op. cit.*, p. 24.

4

Build Your Own Career

> It is assumed that everyone aims for the top of whatever career he enters, and then if his mental health remains in moderately good repair, he goes through a succession of reality adjustments as objective results fail to match subjective expectations.
>
> —WILBERT E. MOORE, *The Conduct of the Corporation* [1]

IF YOU WANT TO SURVIVE the business rat race, face the realities not covered by most management articles, speakers, books, and business schools: bureaucracy in business, nepotism, favoritism, organization politics, power struggles, and building a career. Most management people, I find, have naïve expectations about themselves and their organizations. These unrealistic expectations frequently adversely affect their careers—and worse, their emotional health. There is too much sentimentality promoted about "how lucky I am." How "if I work hard and do my job, I will be rewarded." Many phrase it as "paying the price to get ahead" as though there is a conscious, objective choice rather than a rationalization for the compulsive anxious need to get ahead regardless of the consequences. There is too much naïveté, a refusal to face the realities of working for a

[1] Random House, Inc., New York, 1962, p. 173.

business organization. We are extolled with such fine, but essentially empty phrases as "our team," "our people," "our management family," "loyalty," and "security."

Face some basic questions which are determinants of your career:

Is your company likely to offer you a more successful career than other organizations?

Are those who are moving forward your kind of people in terms of both work and personal attributes?

Do you feel compatible with the people above you?

Do the people above you, in your judgment, feel that you are competent and compatible and have more potential?

Are the ethics of the company your kind of ethics?

Is your company a growing, thriving organization or a conservative, staid outfit? Which do you prefer?

Does your company place primary emphasis on promoting younger people? What are the implications of the promotion practices for you over the long pull?

Do you feel comfortable with the level of personal aggression, competition, or rivalry tolerated or promoted by your company?

Is the power struggle so great that significant management power cliques have been formed? How would these affect your career?

If a boss does not look upon you with favor, what chance do you have of getting one who does?

If you find yourself working for a neurotic, what can you do about it?

Do you have a safe way of letting anyone know if you have an incompetent or incompatible boss?

Are you performing against standards that are both unknown and arbitrarily changed?

Can you try for another job inside or outside your company without the risk of being fired?

Personal Economic Autonomy

To enable you to become more aware of the realities of your work life, I opened this part of the book with a description of the certainties you faced in the school system and its comparative indifference unless you were a top student. You also had the opportunity to think through your kind of success and then how your work needs compared with those of the normal businessman. Now, in order to survive the business rat race, I suggest that you strive for economic autonomy. Hence, here you acquire a worm's eye awareness of working out your career.

Temporary Economic Servant You are only a temporary economic servant. You must, theoretically, earn more for the organization than you are being paid. Otherwise, you are an economic liability, and businesses tend to get rid of economic liabilities. As long as your efforts are viewed as a bargain, not necessarily the best, you will be retained.

When you work for someone else, you must do the job that is given you and accept the terms of the giver. These are found to be different from the normal work needs listed earlier. Although economic man, one who works only for money, was supposedly laid to rest many years ago, research indicates that we have not advanced much beyond the economic servant in the business world. You are expected to accept without question the cult of efficiency with its tribal ritual of group uniformity and individual conformity. Bureaucracy, with its techniques of planning and control, detailed job descriptions and appraisal forms, and standardized practices and procedures, forces an organization to be static and to resist change. To standardize, simplify, and unify in the popular management sense demonstrate that routines are more important than people.

Larger companies maintain a substantial reserve of management talent, perhaps even more than the military. Hence, there is no room at the top for many of their management people. Moreover, the top management currently in power determines the selection of those who offer the most promise according to its standards. As the top management group changes, unannounced standards change.

If schools, as we saw earlier, cannot be other than impersonal, how can a business organization? You must produce in terms of the standards of the organization. It never will be concerned primarily with your work needs and career goals. Top management is usually concerned with organization growth in terms of size, power, and profit. To these ends, the organization develops a set of obvious and not so obvious rewards, sanctions, and ideologies to influence or force individual and group behavior toward organizational ends.

Take the disagreement about staff people. Ever since the terms "staff" and "line" were borrowed from the military, there has been a running argument. One group maintains that staff people should work without authority, helping line management people do their jobs more effectively.[2] Another group insists that staff should act as a super brain trust to top management and do the knowing, thinking, and planning as well as the inspecting for top management.

The continuing profusion of articles pleading for the understanding of the scientist, engineer, and professional offers additional testimony as to how specialists become dominated by management. Professional standing is precarious in big organizations where power and status are the primary influence. The professional's traditional independence and his way of working are being undercut.[3]

You can never feel completely secure in your job and your career. In contrast to school, there is no scoring which will give you any objective indication of how you are doing in various important areas. That performance reviews are highly subjective is commonplace. One day you may be a crown prince in your organization. The next day you may find yourself at your terminal level until you retire. The winds of power can suddenly shift. A new boss can raise havoc with your work and your career. You exist in a continuous state of uncertainty.

Private Law   When you first started work with your company, you may well have been courted. Once in harness, however, your feelings, ambitions, and interests are more often than not of no real consequence to anyone. Gradually you come to realize that you are continuously on trial in an uncertain situation. To a large extent your potential and special talents are ignored.

You find that information is used as a weapon. Information helpful to you is withheld from you with no explanation. There is also some sort of vague, private law in your organization about which you must guess. The law is not always obeyed by everyone. Much of it is not written. And even that which is written more often than not has no announced penalties for violation. Violation gives you

[2] See my book *The Staff Role in Management: Its Creative Uses,* Harper & Row, Publishers, Incorporated, New York, 1955.

[3] Robert Presthus, *The Organizational Society,* Vintage Books, Random House, Inc., New York, 1962, pp. 20–21.

no hearing and no appeal. You can be excommunicated through no further promotions or salary increases without notice or explanation. You may even receive the death penalty of dismissal without warning, usually when the organization has your replacement ready. Worst of all, working hard and doing a good job may well lead to personal obsolescence. No one is likely to tell you that you have probably reached your peak because you have not kept yourself up to date.

No one in the organization can tell you the direction or the nature and progress of your career within the organization. It must be this half-conscious awareness of the fundamental insecurity of work life that causes so many people to feel indebted to their organizations. They are showing expert observers an emotional overdependency which does not and cannot square with the facts of working for someone else.

Yet, you are expected to provide more than a temporary economic service. You are expected in large measure to give up yourself, not give of yourself, to the organization. You are expected to conform, be obedient, be respectful, and be loyal. Many of the trappings of the servant-master, peasant-aristocrat, or child-parent relationship are still found in the subordinate-boss relationship. True, new management words have been invented. Bossing has become leadership. Persuading has become communications. Telling has become coaching. Manipulating has become motivating. As a subordinate you are often forced to respond in restricted or unnatural ways much like a dependent, grateful servant.

Loyalty Take loyalty for example. If memory serves me correctly, "loyalty" first came into the management vocabulary during World War II. I believe it rose out of the Communist hunt and loyalty tests of government employees. It is now common parlance. Most people have no idea of what loyalty is or where it begins and ends. "Loyalty," according to one of the popular dictionaries, means "a faithfulness that is steadfast in the face of any temptation to renounce, desert or betray." Either the dictionaries have not caught up with loyalty to a business organization or the business organization, aside from protecting company secrets from competitors, should not be requiring loyalty.

What then can loyalty mean to you in terms of the organization for which you work? However you approach it, loyalty must finally be an emotional state where you respond with faithful and selfless dedication conforming to expected behavior and values of the business organization. You are expected to have an unquestioning acceptance of the organization and the way it operates. To be loyal ultimately means that you may be expected to engage in questionable, unethical, immoral, and at times even illegal behavior for your company.

We should be talking about integrity. This does not mean unquestioned devotion to an organization. It means to be trustworthy and dependable. Integrity is a two-way street as far as both the organization and the individual are concerned. Integrity means devotion to the organization, a liking for it, still judging it and trying to improve it—wanting the best for it. Loyalty has come to mean that the organization is best, no matter what it does.

Patterns of Prejudice

With the continuous expounding of prejudice against black people and women in business we have lost sight of the basic prejudices against white men.

Even the biggest companies are not agreed as to the determinants of success. General Electric has found that many men who rise to the top 1 percent of the management positions are not paid as real comers by age thirty-five.[4] Sears, Roebuck finds that its successful executives have a preference for orderly thought and number-related tasks and are aggressive, self-confident, and low in aesthetic values. American Telephone and Telegraph finds that the best managers tend to come from the top half of their college graduating class.[5]

Not So Subtle Prejudices   Take the matter of age. "Death begins at age forty" still holds. It is even harder to find a good job at fifty or over. The emphasis is on the young. They cost less and are believed to have higher potential. Experience up to a point is very important. That, plus education, is all that a businessman has to offer.

[4] Lawrence L. Ferguson, "Social Scientists in the Plant," *Harvard Business Review*, vol. 42, no. 3, May-June, 1964, p. 134.

[5] "How Do You Pick an Executive Winner?" *Business Week*, no. 1905, Mar. 5, 1966, pp. 108–110.

Worse, I find many seasoned businessmen at good salaries wanting to break into another field where they have had no experience. They are unhappy and bored and want to try something new. It is hard for them to understand that changing vocations almost never happens in seeking an opportunity with another company. Just as with an actor, they are typecast.

There is good evidence of religious prejudice. Of college graduates in one study, 80 companies were recruiting only Protestant students, 42 hiring only Catholic students, and 14 hiring only Jewish students, a total of 136. Another 188 recruiters hired students from more than one ethnic background. Jews, for example, are conspicuously absent from the management of insurance companies, public utilities, banks, and certain large companies in heavy industry.[6]

Another prejudice is education. Organizations talk about equal opportunity for everyone. But the prejudice against high school graduates or college graduates with certain kinds of backgrounds is self-evident. Some organizations have a well-structured caste system based on education. You should carefully analyze who moves up in your organization. In some companies high school graduates can become foremen or first-line supervisors, but no more. In others, they cannot reach even this level. Therefore, if you are ambitious and have only a high school diploma, or little more, switch to an organization that favors your kind. Among college graduates patterns in various organizations are developing. In some organizations engineers are favored. In others, it is accountants. Look at your organization and its prejudices about education. If it caters to people of educational attainment or specialization other than yours, the odds are against your rising very far.

There is another kind of prejudice which should be evaluated. This is the nepotism that may exist in your organization. Relatives of people in power get ahead faster than others. In family-owned companies this is to be expected. However, in companies where a family does not have substantial ownership, favoring of relatives by those in power is a good clue to the fact that odds are against your being given an "equal opportunity" on the basis of merit, potential, or competence, unless you are a relative.

[6] Lewis B. Ward, "The Ethics of Executive Selection," reprint from *Harvard Business Review*, vol. 43, no. 2, March-April, 1963.

Build Your Career

The kinds of things you have seen here should enable you to gain a clearer notion of your chance for promotion in your own organization. They will also serve as guides should you be considered for a position in another company. In building your career, you should reconsider the various concepts of success. If you follow the maturation concept, you are more likely to face the reality of yourself. You come to terms with your own emotional, physical, and chronological changes. Because you seek to develop more of your resources, you can accept more readily the fact that you will not be able to achieve all the ambitions and dreams of your work life.

Promote Your Career   Do not leave the decisions about your career to others, as many businessmen do. Start with this simple maxim: Compete for advancement but cooperate in getting the work of the organization done. Thus, promote your career. By career, I mean promotions and compensation. Successful businessmen act as agents of their own progress. In contrast to less successful men, the more successful demonstrate that they want to do well in their jobs. Their interests and the goals they set for themselves are realistic in terms of the problems they must solve to get ahead. They are more sensitive to the things that count in their immediate job environment and are quick to adapt their strategy to local conditions.

Still, successful businessmen have more of an attitude of detachment and independence from the organizations in which they work. They work with their superiors not only on the expanding definition of their jobs but also the determination of their futures. They promote their careers by making sure that other people in key positions know what they think their attributes are, know their wishes and their interests. Finally, they are more willing to take reasonable risks, and when they suffer a setback, a reprimand, or a rejection, they do so with relative equanimity.[7]

If you are not part of the young management people in your organization, evaluate their approach and follow it as best you can.

[7] William R. Dill, Thomas L. Hilton, and Walter R. Reitman, "How Aspiring Managers Promote Their Own Careers," reprint from *California Management Review*, vol. 2, no. 4, Summer, 1960.

For example, in one company the young men continued to demand more training. They were critical of what they got, and still wanted more.[8] Polish your personality and appearance. Assume the proper executive stance. In most companies odds favor those who dress conservatively and are neatly groomed at all times. Such things as beards, long sideburns, bow ties, sport jackets, or clothes that are too stylish can be a hindrance.

Pick the right boss, one who appears to have the right contacts with the management above you. You and your potential will be evaluated in large measure as your own boss is evaluated. It has been found that effectiveness of subordinates tends to be classified in the same manner as the effectiveness of their bosses. Management people above your boss actually have very little idea as to your effectiveness. You bask in reflected glory or suffer from tarnishment.[9]

A Prudent Executive "A prudent executive has his résumé in his pocket at all times." If you seek other opportunities, you will be joining an ever-increasing number of management men who are building their own careers. Men are no longer working and waiting for the opportunities in their own companies. Cosmopolitans, they move from company to company. They are interested more in their careers than in a company.[10]

It is only good sense to try to do as well for yourself as you can. Now you find the most outlandish aspect of the business rat race. You must, except in rare instances, make your availability known on a highly secretive and confidential basis. If you are found out, you are viewed as "disloyal" or "deserting the ship." You are summarily discharged or blocked from future promotions. A company openly enters into a variety of competitive activities—both in acquiring things and services and in offering things and services. But when it comes to management people and their desires to explore

[8] Harry Levinson, Charlton R. Price, Kenneth J. Munden, Harold J. Mandl, and Charles M. Solley, *Men, Management, and Mental Health,* Harvard University Press, Cambridge, Mass., 1962, p. 88.

[9] E. A. Fleishman and D. R. Peters, "Interpersonal Values, Leadership Attitudes and Managerial 'Success,'" *Personal Psychology,* Summer, 1962, pp. 127–143.

[10] A. W. Gouldner, "Cosmopolitans and Locals," *Administrative Science Quarterly,* vol. 2, December, 1957, pp. 281–306.

other situations to see if they can do better, the typical company goes into a state of management hysteria. This is well proven by terms applied to those of us who do executive search—such as "pirates," "headhunters."

Build your career as a prudent investor builds his investment program. Periodically test the management market. Some executives continuously keep their résumés on file with executive search organizations and companies they might want to work for. Because older résumés tend to be discarded, it is a good idea to mail out a new one about every six months or when there is new data to add. When you start looking for another job you will usually discover, for all the talk about the shortage of management people, that job seeking is a long, inconsiderate, and sometimes cruel process.

If you use private employment agencies, you may find that counselors use aggressive salesmanship to "soften up" the human commodity. To secure faster placements, and greater income, they deliberately reduce the self-image of an applicant. This makes him more compliant so that he will accept one of the first jobs offered to him. Many job counselors are primarily expert in the role of salesman. The employment agency's main purpose is not to obtain the best job for the man but to make a quick placement and a profit.[11]

From the wide variety of books [12] that are available on how to find a job you will receive much conflicting advice. You also find that your friends and executive search organizations give you conflicting suggestions. Here are my hunches developed after years in executive search work. Sell yourself with a simple but well-prepared résumé which covers your education, age, and marital status. Give a brief description of what you are looking for. Your picture should be a glossy print. As for your work, list the size of each company, its business, what you have done in each job, and the amount of compensation you received. I am skeptical of anyone who claims superior results. There is very little any one man can do alone unless he was hired to reorganize or update a poor operation. And even here, he usually had help. So, be factual. Use plain white bond paper. Leave ample margins and use only one side of the sheet with a total

[11] Thomas M. Martinez, "Why Employment Agency Counselors Lower Their Clients' Self-esteem," *Trans-Action*, vol. 5, no. 4, March, 1968, pp. 20–25.

[12] An example is Auren Uris, *The Executive Job Market*, McGraw-Hill Book Company, New York, 1965.

of no more than two pages. Keep your cover letter brief and have it typed.

You might send your résumé to executive search organizations. However, they cover only a very small portion of the total market. Many of them work only at higher salary levels. In addition, therefore, you should scout companies. Search out the names of firms you think you would like to work for. Do it systematically. Try to find the names of the officials with titles appropriate to your interests. Also follow up on ads in newspapers and trade journals. Do not expect replies. Do not expect generous offers. There are many bargain hunters. You will be interviewed and entertained only to find often that they want to hire you for less than you are making.

Steel yourself to the fact that it usually takes several months for a seasoned businessman to find a good job. Even the truly outstanding ones, and I know of several, find it a trying, anxiety-ridden experience to find a good spot.

part 2

Help Yourself as a Businessman

*What Americans know of their own society, what
they believe about the other 94 per cent of the
species, how they interpret the behavior of men
high, and low, how they size up their own place in
time and space—all have been influenced by
formal schooling, but perhaps as much by default
as by intention. What Americans typically have not
learned in school about humankind is probably
what matters most.*
—ROBERT G. HANVEY, "Social Myth vs.
Social Science" [1]

CONFUSION HAS BEEN COMPOUNDED in management know-how. Books, magazines, and speeches are coming at an ever-increasing rate. Yet, almost every one of the authors, speakers, and experts are unaware of their own biases. (I may be also.) At many management development sessions I appear as the exponent of behavioral sciences management consensus. I often find that the people who put the program together seem unaware of the fact that they have selected other experts whose approaches are diametrically opposed to the behavioral sciences. In some instances they claim this type of program is planned "to give a manager a choice." The assumption that this would help him is

[1] *Saturday Review*, vol. 50, no. 46, Nov. 18, 1967, pp. 80–95.

erroneous, for it leads only to more confusion. It would be helpful if every speaker and writer about management would outline his sources of knowledge, opinion, or research findings.

In many fields, university professors are accepted as thought leaders, especially in economics, sociology, anthropology, and political science. Not so with business schools. Critics claim that the 1959 charges by the Ford Foundation and the Carnegie Corporation of New York still, for the most part, apply: low admission requirements, low academic standards, low-caliber students, superficial teaching, excessive vocational courses, neglect of research, and an atmosphere of stagnation.[2] To these findings I would like to add that I have not found a business school where the students receive a consensus of management, whatever it might be. Courses are not tied together with a common thread. In contrast the economics department can usually be identified as liberal or conservative, and the students themselves generally are aware of this.

A common complaint about the approach of business schools is that they teach a man to look at an organization from the top down rather than from the bottom up where he is likely to start. Aside from what they learn from an occasional professor, students do not get a worm's eye view of an organization. Controversial matters are avoided, such as the win-lose complex, how to get ahead, how to plan your career, how to size up an organization to see if it provides you with what you want to get out of work. The bureaucratic organization with its cold indifference to its people, where you end up as a number, is usually accepted without question. Still, you would probably find in the sociology, anthropology, or political science department in the same school that bureaucracy is treated as a basic problem because of the adverse ways it affects the lives of people.

Finally, there appears to be general avoidance of research knowledge about people. Recently I had the opportunity to address a group of senior professors from several business schools. My subject was "Management Education—for What?" I stressed the need for developing and teaching a consensus of behavioral sciences management knowledge. The essence of this speech was drawn from the materials in this book. At the end, discussion focused on whether or

[2] Robert Sheehan, "New Report Card on the Business Schools," Courtesy of *Fortune Magazine*, vol. 70, no. 6, December, 1964, p. 148.

not students should become "amateur psychiatrists" as one of the professors put it. Some saw the need clearly. One professor said, "A boy becomes an amateur psychiatrist on his first date." The need is to become a knowledgeable amateur psychiatrist with no thought of treating or providing therapy.

You can see that there are several large issues involved. To put them in order, in this part of the book I am going to help you help yourself as a businessman and a management man: first, in wading through the management mess to a behavioral sciences management consensus; second, what it means in terms of policies; third, where the consensus stems from; and fourth, how to develop an autonomous professional stance in your work. Then in the next part, Part 3, you will find some of the keys so that you can develop some hunches as to emotional problems of people and what makes them tick the way they do—and what makes you tick the way you do.

5
Make Sense
Out of the Management Mess

> The textbook principles of organization—hierarchical structure, authority, unity of command, task specialization, division of staff and line, span of control, equality of responsibility and authority, etc. —comprise a logically persuasive set of assumptions which have had a profound influence upon managerial behavior over several generations. Despite the fact that they rest primarily on armchair speculation rather than on empirical research, the literature gives the impression that these classical principles are beyond challenge.
>
> —DOUGLAS MC GREGOR, *The Human Side of Enterprise* [1]

CALL IT A MESS, jungle, chaos, or what you will. Fantastic concoctions of management ideas cause confusion and add to your business rat race. Therefore, the next task is to make sense out of the present management mess. As an observer and a student of management, I find it helpful to classify the various types of management philosophies. There are basically five:

Common sense
Scientific management

[1] McGraw-Hill Book Company, New York, 1960, p. 15.

52

Personal opinion
Personal experience
Behavioral sciences

These in various and sometimes inconceivable ways influence the five basic operations of almost any business: general management, financial management, manufacturing or service management, marketing management, and staff services. Each basic operation may have a variety of subfunctions. General management consists of those concerned with the total operation of the company. Financial management usually includes such functions as accounting, auditing, paying, and collecting. Manufacturing management may include, in addition to production, purchasing of materials, industrial engineering, research and development, quality control, and shipping. Marketing management includes sales, public relations, pricing, and market research. Service functions are those staff activities designed primarily to service all the basic functions—personnel, legal, and management information systems. Accessorial staff services include a multiplicity of activities from cafeteria to messenger service.

Common Sense

Did you have any training, education, or informal help in how to manage before you moved into your first supervisory position? Chances are only about one in a hundred that you did. At least that is what I find in my informal polls.

Your Biases   What is your philosophy of management? Men usually say "common sense." If you have supervised, you may say "experience." You may even indulge in the clichés about leadership and communicating. Odds are you cannot expand on these. No wonder you feel you are in a rat race.

Most businessmen cannot verbalize to any degree what they are doing, the approach they are using. They go along day after day, year after year, working and trying to solve their immediate problems with little thought of what they are striving to achieve in their particular endeavor or how best to go about it. Some have picked up some of the management vocabulary. For example, almost all believe that they must "motivate" their subordinates. Motivate for what? To work harder? Press them to be specific and they are lost.

On what basis do you pick and choose the best for your managing? You are undoubtedly using your unconscious biases in your reading and learning about management. You select what you like and reject what you dislike. For the most part you pick clichés and phrases which appeal to you. Probably you are unable to apply them. You may talk and believe one way and behave another. At least that is what the research has shown. Moreover, as you go on, you tend to rely more and more on your experience, rejecting new findings.

To make sense out of the management mess, you face a major test. It is a test of your ability both to become aware of your own biases and to modify them in light of research. To repeat, you *unlearn* in order to learn. To get through the stereotypes you hide behind and to accept the consensus of behavioral sciences management findings require rigorous self-discipline. You constantly and continuously seek the *common* findings which are interrelated.

How-to Silent testimony to our anxious search outside ourselves for common sense is the how-to books. They offer all-too-simple answers to complex questions, personal power and prestige, success and status, security and certainty. Racks of paperbacks promote panaceas on how to win friends, how to make love, how to diet, how to secure release from nervous tension. Management books tell you how to be a leader, how to be a success, how to get your way, how to motivate people. Most of these appeal directly to the power concept of success discussed in Chapter 2. Still, they are too superficial to work. As you see here, knowledge and awareness come first.

Short how-to-supervise courses are used almost exclusively by trade and management associations and by companies. These courses, based on common sense, use most of the current popular management stereotypes of communication, motivation, leadership, and the like. Their appeal is that they are short and appear "practical." They require no substantial reading. Nor do they offer basic findings about people at work. There is little genuine learning.

Scientific Management

The popular principles of management, even though they are inconsistent and conflicting, are usually cited as the basics of scientific management.[2] Late in the nineteenth century, long before any research about man at work, F. W. Taylor started his scientific management, more accurately termed "management engineering." Taylor had several things going for him. First, cheap, eager immigrant labor. Second, the Puritan ethic of serving God by making money or economic man who worked only for money. There was no expectation that people should get satisfaction out of work. Third, the industrial revolution in this country. Fourth, few labor unions. Fifth, an expanding economy. Sixth, the rise of the engineer. Taylor's basic contribution was work simplification and time study. Money is an incentive to produce more. His disciples and industrial engineers have now worked out a diversity of conflicting approaches to time study.[3] Moreover, time study claims generally ignore the behavioral sciences' well-documented negative effects of incentives on the behavior of people.[4]

Management Engineering Today, there is the traditional management engineering with many principles and techniques. Everything must be formalized into a procedure or a practice. Both managers and workers are expected to fit into the system—under the organization concept of success discussed in Chapter 2. Man is induced to work and produce more under incentive systems and pressure, the carrot-stick motivation. The traditional PODCC—plan, organize, direct, coordinate, and control—appears to have been changed. There are now seven basic operations that a manager does: set objectives, organize, innovate, motivate, communicate, measure, and

[2] See my *Managing the Managers,* McGraw-Hill Book Company, New York, 1965, pp. 4–6.

[3] Solomon Barkin, "Diversity in Time Study Practices," *Industrial and Labor Relations Review,* vol. 7, no. 4, July, 1954, pp. 537–549.

[4] William Foote Whyte, *Money and Motivation,* Harper & Row, Publishers, Incorporated, New York, 1955.

develop people.[5] Both motivating and communicating are viewed by behavioral scientists as part of the human relations fad of a few years ago.[6]

Behavioral scientists who are critical of scientific management are castigated for giving new meanings to old scientific management terms.[7] Still, whether under duress or not, Taylor, when called to testify in the halls of Congress around 1900 regarding efficiency and speedup, suggested the need for scientific investigation of the motives which influence man.[8] But Taylor died before there was any study of the motives which influence man at work. Management engineering errs in underutilization of man by the organization of work into simple motions with each motion performed wherever possible by an individual worker. A second erroneous assumption is that a human being should fit in as a cog in a machine.

Behavioral Myths versus Sciences   The first behavioral scientist, I know of, to bring together the comprehensive research of the negative impact of scientific management on the blue-collar worker starts with the findings about healthy workers. They need jobs where, among other things, they can be more active than passive, be more independent than dependent, and be able to express their deeper more important capabilities. Under scientific management, this cycle has occurred:

First, the formal organization stresses work simplification and use of only a few "skin-surface" abilities.

Second, individuals tend to feel frustration, conflict, and failure and "adapt" negatively through a variety of means. Some of these are giving up, fighting the system, becoming apathetic, and gold-bricking.

[5] Phillip W. Shay, executive director of the Association of Consulting Management Engineers, "The Emerging Discipline of Management," in H. B. Maynard (ed.), *Handbook of Business Administration*, McGraw-Hill Book Company, New York, 1967, pp. 1–39 to 1–40. See also Sampson, "Management and the Behavioral Sciences," in *ibid.*, pp. 11–3 to 11–15.

[6] Chris Argyris, *Personality and Organization*, Harper & Row, Publishers, Incorporated, New York, 1957, pp. 139–149.

[7] The meaning of "organization" appears to be the concern of Lyndall F. Urwick, in "Have We Lost Our Way in the Jungle of Management Theory?" *Personnel*, May-June, 1965, pp. 8–18.

[8] F. W. Taylor, "Testimony," *Scientific Management*, Harper & Row, Publishers, Incorporated, New York, 1947, p. 26.

Third, seeing these kinds of reactions, management concludes that the employees must change. Pressure is used by supervisors under "dynamic leadership." More controls are added.

Fourth, workers tend to unite against management, the informal cliques.

Fifth, management tries the "human relations fad" to motivate these lazy and apathetic employees—pseudo participation, communication programs, being nice, and the like. It does not work.[9]

Personal Opinion

There is a wide variety of people who write in the "I know" or "I say, therefore, it is" philosophy. Whether their utterings are wise and profound or shallow and superficial, they are really personal opinions. You can spot these authorities usually by infrequent footnotes and limited bibliographies.[10] Much of the popular literature written for the businessman, regardless of how cleverly it is stated, plays up to the prejudices of managers. Management medicine men stress how you can have your way with subordinates, peers, and bosses. Some of it very clearly points to manipulation, to how you can win; hence, its fatal attraction for many businessmen. Because man is a rationalizing animal, much of the opinion should be classified as folklore, in that it stems from the past; "powerlore" in that it appeals to power needs; "fakelore" in that it has no scientific basis; and "traplore" in that man cannot go on taking advantage of others without himself in turn being trapped more deeply in the business rat race.

Academic Opinions   Academicians without any significant comprehensive research, and this includes many members of the behavioral

---

[9] Argyris, *op. cit.*

[10] A writer with management experience is J. D. Batten who appears to support the salvation concept of success and its Puritan ethic with "work is life and life is work" in his *Tough-minded Management*, American Management Association, New York, 1963, p. 145. "I will believe that the Ten Commandments are the supreme laws that should guide and inspire me," occurs on p. 145 of *Developing a Tough-minded Climate for Results*, American Management Association, New York, 1965.

sciences, get into print.[11] Apparently the "publish or perish" edict does not include research—or even recognition of the mainstream of the new behavioral sciences research on such matters as business organizations, people, their work needs, and emotional problems. A vast number of academicians add to the management mess with their personal "armchair" philosophies using their college degrees as the bases for their claims to expertise. They proliferate many different viewpoints when what a thinking businessman who wants to learn so desperately needs are some well-founded basics.

Personal Experience

Have you noticed how frequently the word "experience" is used in management literature? Most management men who write seem to rely on what they call their experience as their management philosophy.

Only a few appear sympathetic with the behavioral sciences research.[12] There is a growing number of businessmen and academicians who make clever but extreme statements against people, management, managing, and businesss schools. Some of them call their opinion a law or a principle. You wonder if they are not spoofing when the statements are so extreme.

There are also innumerable successful businessmen who are deadly serious when they write from their experience. They write from an autobiographical viewpoint—with the usual limitations of

[11] As one example, Peter Drucker, notable economist and famous management writer, seems to "pick and choose" from some aspects of scientific management while disagreeing with other aspects. See p. 282 of his *The Practice of Management,* Harper & Row, Publishers, Incorporated, New York, 1954. Evidently he feels much the same about the research of the behavioral sciences. On p. 124, in discussing the need to focus on what the job rather than the boss demands, he maintains, "To stress behavior and attitudes . . . cannot solve the problem." On p. 158 he states, "The earliest writers . . . in ancient Greece or ancient Israel knew all that has ever been known about leadership." Take one of his latest books, *The Effective Executive,* Harper & Row, Publishers, Incorporated, New York, 1966. On p. 18 he states, ". . . the only person in abundant supply is the universal incompetent." On p. 173 he apparently terms one facet of the behavioral sciences approach "the new romanticism."

[12] For example, Chester I. Barnard, *The Functions of the Executive,* Harvard University Press, Cambridge, Mass., 1938.

personal interpretation.[13] As a case in point, recall the frequent articles by presidents on how they make their own decisions, now known as "the lonely art of decision making." [14] Yet most presidents are found to use committees to make decisions.

Behavioral Sciences

Until well after World War II, management was one long amateur hour. It still is for almost every businessman. Only in the last fifteen years has there been enough research about people at work to provide a basis for moving forward on a truly research-based scientific consensus. The significant contribution of the behavioral sciences consensus is the *commonly accepted* findings about man. His behavior, needs, drives, emotional makeup, and his relationships with others become the focus of a wide variety of specialties through research and clinical observations. My consensus is made up of innumerable "bits and pieces" buried in several articles and books which fit together and come from more than one or two sources.

The eight specialties which make up the behavioral sciences— psychiatry, psychology, social psychiatry, social psychology, sociology, anthropology, economics, and political science—are outlined in the next chapter. They all deal with data of essentially the same order, the exercise of man's powers, but the focus of each field is different. In general the behavioral sciences are concerned with the study of (1) human behavior, or how people act and why, (2) human values, or what people want and need, (3) their institutions, or what kinds of organizations people need and get, and (4) their power structures, or the nature of power and how it is used. Basically, research is that of systematic inquiry into what people are like in and as a result of their family, school, church, society, and work. The behavioral sciences consensus replaces the personal philosophies of common sense, personal opinion, and personal experience, as well as scientific management.

[13] Robert Townsend, *Up the Organization,* Alfred A. Knopf, New York, 1970, a book written in terse and dramatic fashion that appears to be highly critical of just about everything in business; and Alfred P. Sloan, Jr., *My Years with General Motors,* Doubleday & Company, Inc., Garden City, N.Y., 1964.

[14] See my *Managing the Managers, op. cit.,* p. 133.

Internal Differences   There are some specialists at one extreme who believe that "love flees authority" and others who stress the need for friendly relations. Then there are those who limit themselves to the individual with no reference to the group. Others stress the group almost to the exclusion of the individual. Some appear to ignore people with emotional problems, and others find a pathological problem in almost every personality. Some claim to follow the behavioral sciences (in the plural) yet continue to be limited by their own specialty. Some practice behavioral science (in the singular), whatever that may be. Worse, some people not trained in any facet of the behavioral sciences find it convenient to embrace them in toto with no real understanding or knowledge of the basics of human behavior. This is the patent medicine time of the behavioral sciences. There are so few on the leading edge and so many others who want to profit from the new developments. I hope that what you are getting as background and guidelines here will enable you to sort out the main line of the behavioral sciences consensus from the offshoots, the more popular oversimplifications, and outright distortions.

Research can range all the way from the journalistic approach [15] to the single-purpose research of many academicians. Some scholars are wrestling with the problems of being a leader or rising in the management hierarchy.[16] Many behavioral scientists are doing much the same as other management theorists. They are unable to get together. Resistance by scientists with half-closed minds to the newer findings of others is the pattern of history.[17] Research on the development of intelligence tests illustrates how psychologists may try to validate the impossible. What started out to be straightforward

[15] Vance Packard, *The Pyramid Climbers,* Crest Reprint, Fawcett World Library, published by arrangement with McGraw-Hill Book Company, Inc., New York, 1962, and *The Status Seekers,* David McKay Company, Inc., New York, 1959.

[16] For example, Ernest Dale, in *The Great Organizers,* McGraw-Hill Book Company, New York, 1960, appears to be an exponent of the great man or the superior man ideology, leadership as a gift. Eugene Jennings is concerned about the man who does not quite make it to the. top: *The Executive in Crisis,* Graduate School of Business Administration, Michigan State University, East Lansing, 1965.

[17] Ian Stevenson, M.D., "Scientists with Half-closed Minds," *Harper's* Magazine, November, 1958, pp. 66–71.

measure of intelligence has now been found to involve not only ge-
netics, but also childhood environment, parental influence, schools,
and schooling. Little was known about intelligence when testing
was first experimented with early in this century, and less appears
to be known now.

Cruelty to the Human Animal Not all behavioral scientists are dedicated to humane consideration of man. Some are guilty of cruelty to
the human animal. Many psychologists and personnel people assume, without a shred of evidence and with no concern for invasion
of privacy, that the methods they use are right. Testing, training,
appraisal, and salary administration have come under a cloud.[18]
The old "stress interview" has come back. This consists of a series of
sticky, anxiety-producing questions through which, it is claimed, an
applicant can be judged as to whether or not he can successfully
cope with the stress of top-level corporate life.[19] Yet, stress interviews were abandoned because they were inconclusive. Even stress
test situations were dropped by the United States Office of Strategic
Services during World War II when they were found not to be pre-
dictive.

Some members of the mental health professions continue to em-
ploy useless and even harmful treatment and diagnostic techniques.
In teaching, too, educationalists hide behind academic freedom,
spewing platitudes about the art of teaching while rejecting new scientific evidence about the learning process. College students, without knowledge or consent, are put under stress tests as a part of a
general psychology course. Many practitioners and experimenters
on humans avoid the question of ethics, the responsibility they
have to the people with whom they experiment or on whom they
foist their outdated and unproved tactics.[20]

There is concern as to whether or not many behavioral scientists
are servants of business power. Some, through such things as testing
and sponsoring the human relations fad, demonstrate their willing-

[18] Douglas McGregor, in his *The Human Side of Enterprise*, McGraw-Hill
Book Company, New York, 1960, offers a critique on each.

[19] Chris Welles, "Test by Stress," *Life* Magazine, vol. 63, no. 7, Aug. 18, 1967,
pp. 69–74. Those who used this technique were not called behavioral scientists.

[20] Ray H. Bixler, "Ostracize Them," *Saturday Review*, vol. 49, no. 27, July 2,
1966, pp. 47–48.

ness to serve power and increase the rat race. It is feared that as they come closer to controlling conduct they may put these means into the hands of managers. Then some researchers will be guilty of manipulation by consent.[21] Hence, they must finally face the question of purpose and ethics.

Behavioral Sciences Management Consensus   The differences among behavioral scientists make it difficult if not impossible for a businessman to know how to fashion a behavioral sciences management consensus for his organization. Hence, not too many companies or businessmen, as near as I can determine, are attempting to apply the behavioral sciences on a broad scale. Some are encouraging research. Others are encouraging some sort of behavioral sciences training even though they are not sure what they are buying. Still, I have seen little evidence that the behavioral scientists are reaching out to help the businessman with a consensus of findings put in his language. Thus far I have found no general consensus on a behavioral sciences management system.[22]

Realistically, I believe that those companies which are locked in with a heavy investment in assembly-line hardware are not likely to try the behavioral sciences approach. But they could use this consensus for their people who do nonrepetitive work and management work. Above all, you can use the behavioral sciences consensus in your managing and reduce your own rat race.

Because we are concerned with more than the new consensus management system, let me list what I believe are the rudiments of the system. Based on research about people at work, you build your organization to capitalize on those approaches which make for greater job satisfaction and productivity. Some differences between the old ways and the new are dramatic, such as the need for gaining a knowledge of people and their work needs. Then you build and manage your organization based on these findings. Other differences are more subtle, such as leadership and budgeting. Here

---

[21] This idea is discussed by Loren Baritz, *The Servants of Power*, published as a Science Editions paperback, authorized by Wesleyan University, Middletown, Connecticut, 1965.

[22] Except for this book and my earlier one, *Managing the Managers, op. cit.*

leadership is helping. Instead of using a budget as a weapon or a limiting, controlling device, you use it here in a positive sense. Your organization plans with the collaboration of the key members. The budget consists of these plans. Members get feedback to enable them to know how they are doing in terms of the plan.

Briefly, the rudiments form a ten-step program:

First is you. Just as you must start with knowing yourself if you want to survive the business rat race, so too must you start with yourself in applying the new management consensus. What are you like? What are your attitudes toward others? What do you have to learn and to unlearn? What do you want to accomplish in managing? Parts 1 and 3 of this book enable you to become more aware of yourself.

Second is a businessman's first-order knowledge of emotional health. You need some understanding as to the differences between normal emotional health and abnormal. Part 3 gives you clues not only to awareness of yourself but also to your understanding of those you can help and those you cannot.

Third is knowledge of the work needs of the normal or average man. These are detailed in Chapter 3. In addition, Part 1 provides you with knowledge as to the kinds of careers people tend to follow as the result of their early conditioning by their parents.

Fourth is knowledge about universal transactions and their goals, outlined in Exhibit 10 in Part 4. The transactions are behaving, communicating, participating, and counseling.

Fifth is becoming aware of your various organization roles in *authority over people* and *authority over actions* and your *no authority* roles. Exhibit 13 in Part 4 indicates where each role is covered.

Sixth is understanding the dimensions and how to be helpful where you can in your *no authority* subordinate, staff, service, work-flow, and group roles as well as your *authority over actions* of approval and inspection roles.

Seventh, in your administration, your first *authority over people* role, you learn to evaluate and to supervise each subordinate individually. Try to provide the work needs for your normal subordinate as listed in Chapter 3. Those with emotional problems, once you have tried to help them, may have to be policed, coerced, pampered, or "dehired," as discussed in Chapter 13.

Eighth is integrating—building those subordinates who have the potential to work together into a cohesive work group—in your second *authority over people* role (Chapter 14). Those who do not have the potential may have to be isolated or "dehired," for they may work against building an integrated group.

Ninth is a general plan-budget-feedback system for your organization whatever your special function may be at any management level, outlined in Chapter 14—and a job-man budget for those who do nonroutine work, covered in the next chapter as well as Chapter 13.

Tenth is a continuing reorganizing process where you help your people secure greater utilization through the job-man budgets and thereby upgrade your organization and keep it viable.

6
Use the Consensus

> The proper study of mankind is man.
> —ALEXANDER POPE, 1733

IN ORDER TO HELP YOU understand the consensus, I am going to suggest major management and personnel policies for an organization. They are the logical extension of the behavioral sciences management consensus. Some organizations with which I am consulting are working out these kinds of policies and gradually putting them into practice. In your managing others, you can put much of them into practice for both your own benefit and the benefit of your subordinates. After the suggested policies, you will find the eight specialties that make up the behavioral sciences, with a thumbnail sketch of each.

Suggested Personnel and Management Policies

Bread-and-butter items such as hours of work and fringe benefits are excluded. Here are my suggested policy statements.

Introduction Our big leverage, as an organization, lies in establishing a climate that permits people, at all levels, to become more involved, and thereby make greater contributions. We want individuals to learn to work with each other in such a way that our human system assures a sense of well-being, where work is fun. There is a greater sense of joint accomplishment in getting more out of work while getting out more work. Your supervisor is responsible for helping you improve your work and grow beyond your present job toward your full potential. Only when all of us are growing and improving our functions can we maximize our effectiveness and thereby maximize total corporate effectiveness. To these ends our personnel and management practices have been established. They are idealistic and, therefore, not always carried out. But they do signify intent for which all of us should strive.

Your Feelings   Your feelings are important to us. They influence directly such key factors as behavior, reasoning, thinking, decision making, drive, and relationships with others. We need your positive and pleasant emotions, such as your identification with the organization, your commitment to organization goals, your feeling of accomplishment, your feeling of acceptance by others, your self-confidence, your self-actualization, and your creativity. To enable you to express these and cultivate them, we must be aware and prepared to accept and help you, if you so desire, with your negative and unpleasant emotions which dwell in greater or lesser degree in all of us. These include competition, rivalry, domination, anger, envy, jealousy, hurt feelings, antagonism, resistance, hostility, getting even, having "my way," uncooperative attitudes, manipulating, selfishness, and slowing down.

Emotions are too important for the well-being and effectiveness of an individual to be dealt with lightly or critically, to be ignored or abused. Therefore, we shall try to work with each other in such a way as not to cause negative emotions or repression of them. We shall also try not to retaliate or punish a person for his negative emotions, but instead help him do something about them.

Your Personal Security   People need a firm foundation of personal security from which to work. You will be informed by your superior within the first three months of your trying out a new position as to whether or not you are competent and compatible. Hopefully, competence should indicate high performance, and compatibility should demonstrate friendliness. With basic personal security, you can, we believe, reduce such negative emotions as fear, anxiety, worry, and tenseness. Your every action is not to be a testing ground on which you win or lose. You are to be informed when there is any question as to your basic competence or compatibility. If you have doubts at any time and want to learn how you stand, you may ask your supervisor, his superior, or a member of the personnel staff.

Your Personal Freedom   We want to help you watch out for your own interests. We expect that you should, in the interest of your personal freedom, be able to go to your supervisor or beyond him without fear of retaliation or being considered disloyal. Feelings are facts. Negative feelings should not be "swept under the rug" but explored with a superior in the hope of working them through before they become a major problem or a barrier to working effectively together. We want to be open and aboveboard and do our best to resolve negative feelings.

At times emotions disable people. Because we are concerned about emotional health and want to be helpful, we encourage you, if you feel under prolonged undue tenseness or are emotionally disturbed, to seek help from anyone in the organization. Letting someone know about it early might prevent a more serious disturbance. If you prefer, consult your physician but let your supervisor know how you feel and that you are trying to do something about it. He should adjust your work load to give you temporary relief while you work your problem through.

You should feel free, too, if you want some prognosis about your future—usually it will be highly speculative—to explore the matter without any fear of adverse consequences. We encourage you to seek or explore openly and freely any opportunity that might appeal to you in other parts of the organization or *other companies* without fear of negative repercussions.

Communicating   People communicate when they listen in order to understand others and speak freely, deeply, and meaningfully to each other. There is lack of communication when they try to persuade or manipulate others or withhold information that could be helpful to others. To help you do your job and become part of this organization, we expect your supervisor to share with you all the information you may reasonably want about our operations, problems, plans, and hopes, as well as compensation of others.

Moreover, we hope that you take the initiative to communicate openly and accurately to help your supervisor. Only through full and undistorted communications can we provide a feeling of confidence and mutual trust. No organization has ever communicated enough to satisfy everyone's interest. And we shall never communicate enough. So, ask when you want to know about something.

Leveling If we are going to work together more effectively, we must try to level with each other to improve our interpersonal skills, developing ways to work together in mutual trust and support. Leveling is not a critical attack, not responding with emotion such as anger, not an intellectual observation, and not a probing of the motives for another's behavior. Rather, it is an authentic expression of how another's behavior affects you, either positively or negatively. Improving our own interpersonal skills is a slow, difficult, uncertain, emotionally charged process. We need to become acutely conscious of how we work with or fail to work with others. We must learn the impact of our behavior on others. Leveling with another person about how his behavior affects you is encouraged if the individual is interested and able to understand and modify his behavior. Leveling may enable the other person to see the discrepancies between what he thought his behavior was and what actually took place. He may then be able to make a better choice of behavior the next time when faced with a similar situation.

Helping Helping others with *their* work and having them in turn help you with your work goes beyond participation where we collectively work together on *our* work. To be helped means that another individual wants to help you *your way* do something that is your responsibility. It may mean assisting you to get your work out, providing information you need, suggesting a solution to a problem you have, thinking something through with you, reacting to an idea you have, or lending a friendly ear. Because we want helping to be part of our way of life, we would expect that you too would be alert to opportunities to help others in the organization. In turn, then, you should be helped.

Participating Ideally, we want your job to provide opportunities for decision making, for freedom to innovate, for participation in work decisions, and for greater responsibilities so you can grow on the job. We believe that many of you want the opportunity to participate in shaping high goals and standards for your organizational unit. You want to be committed to the success of your organization, not be forced to comply or acquiesce. You want to link your own aspirations with those of your organization.

Because our success depends on successful group effort, decisions about the work of your organizational unit should be based on group participation and group consensus. Every individual is expected to try to develop his group skills so as to help: (1) his fellow workers arrive at decisions by consensus rather than domination, competition, or manipulation; and (2) the group function better together. Through our continuing to learn to work together, we grow individually and collectively in a deeper, more profound way, a more open and a more effective approach toward genuinely cooperative working relationships.

Job-Man Budget Our goal is to enlarge as many positions as possible to provide varied work which will offer more interesting and stimulating opportunities for you. If you do varied rather than repetitive work, you and your supervisor should work out a job-man budget for you.[1] Repetitive work has well-established routines which are followed. Varied work where no routines have been established may range from clerical and blue-collar to management positions if there is a strong element of discretion. Secretarial work can be a clerk-typist or a "true" assistant.

Your job-man budget is part of the total corporate plan-budget-feedback process. To enable us to grow and operate efficiently and effectively, we do extensive planning at all levels to determine what we want to accomplish and set up appropriate feedback so we can see how well we are progressing. We emphasize the positive aspects of budgeting so that we work together to accomplish our goals with the maximum amount of individual freedom and the highest possible utilization of every member of our organization. Budgeting is

[1] See Chapter 13 for details.

not a means for putting pressure on people to do more or to put in long hours. It is an integral part of the management process. You should take the initiative in developing your own plans. Your supervisor can then place himself in a helping, counseling role. Rather than job descriptions which are essentially static, the job-man budget is your plan of operation. In addition to your own job-man budget you have the opportunity to participate in the plan-budget-feedback process for the organizational unit of which you are a member, along with your supervisor and your peers.

Managerial Development   Those of us who manage need continuing education on how to manage. Members of management are encouraged by continuing study to learn how to manage others better and to work more effectively with each other. Managers are requested to form, with or without a behavioral sciences resource person, small groups to study and discuss on a regular basis an adult book (not a college text) from the behavioral sciences and its application in improved supervisory knowledge and skills.[2]

Eight Specialties

The suggested policies just outlined are based on eight specialties. The behavioral sciences consensus of management draws from the interrelated findings of these specialties. Exhibit 4 lists the business behavioral consensus. The treatment aspects of psychotherapy and counseling for individuals are covered in greater detail in Chapter 10. There you will also find group counseling and sensitivity training. Your personal counseling of others is outlined in Chapter 11.

Psychiatry   Psychiatry not only supports the idea that you can help others in order to help yourself but goes beyond this. As I have said, psychiatry maintains that you can do no better for yourself than helping another with no thought of personal benefit. Psychoanalytic theory, stemming from medicine, is concerned with total man—instinctive, emotional, cultural, and physical. Freud, for example, is reputed to have said that in our Western culture man must have both love and work. Psychoanalysis is also a method of psychotherapy. A psychoanalyst, by nondirective therapy, helps a

[2] Some of the books are listed in the next chapter.

Exhibit 4   BUSINESS BEHAVIORAL CONSENSUS
               (Drawing from Eight Behavioral Sciences)

The Individual
  1. Psychiatry:
       Psychoanalysis
       Nonanalytic psychiatry
  2. Psychology
       Industrial
       Clinical

The Group
  3. Sociology
       Group behavior
       Social work
  4. Anthropology
       Cultural
       Physical

The Individual and Group
  5. Social psychology
  6. Social psychiatry

Systems
  7. Economics
       Economic behavior
       Business administration
  8. Political science
       Government of men
       Public administration

---

person deal with unconscious materials through many "fifty-minute" hours of free association based on dreams. Nonanalytic psychiatrists, generally referred to as psychiatrists, use mainly three approaches: drugs, shock treatment, and therapy counseling on conscious matters.

Psychology   Basic to psychology is personality. There are at least seventeen theories of personality. Although each school defines personality in a different way, many have this basic notion: personality represents an individual's usual motives and his usual responses to them, independent of any other individual, object, idea, group, or institution.[3] Many practicing industrial psychologists test for indus-

---

[3] Calvin S. Hall and Gardner Lindzey, *Theories of Personality*, John Wiley & Sons, Inc., New York, 1957, p. 548. "Psychology," as a term is used by some psychiatrists.

try. Industrial and clinical psychologists who both counsel with individuals in industry and evaluate them for the management are a new development since World War II.

Sociology   Sociology has openly evinced concern about the abuse of man. It focuses on group behavior. The first and still the greatest single study of people at work is the classic Hawthorne experiment in the late 1920s. Here the sociologists made two basic findings. First, within the formal organization are small informal organizations of workers who unite to protect themselves against exercise of authority. Second, when workers are allowed to participate in decisions about their work, their productivity tends to increase.[4] Social work has its counseling with an increasing emphasis on social psychiatry.

Anthropology   Physical anthropology is searching out the evolution of the human animal. It is no longer a simple, straight-line affair. Recent fossil discoveries in East Africa tend to indicate that there were at least three types of manlike creatures living side by side. One was a vegetarian, one was carnivorous, and one ate almost everything. One of these three types survived to produce the human animal, although no one is quite sure which.

Through cultural anthropology we learn of the development and spread of technology, customs, faiths, and tools not only to satisfy the needs of man but to serve to keep society together. Man's significantly human traits are essentially the same for all varieties of man. Anthropologists agree that our racial differences—some claim there is no such thing as race—have nothing to do with our culture differences, which are "socially" rather than genetically inherited. There is no universal drive to achieve. Some cultures such as ours and the northern European cultures are much more achievement-oriented than Eastern cultures with the notable exception of Japan. Hence, one-half of the people in the world never have a square meal. One-half are growing up illiterate. Four-fifths never see a physician.

Social Psychology   Combining sociology and psychology, social psychologists appear to outnumber any other specialty in industrial be-

[4] F. J. Roethlisberger and W. J. Dickson, *Management and the Worker*, Harvard University Press, Cambridge, Mass., 1947.

havioral sciences research. Social psychologists also seem to share the concern of sociologists for the better utilization of man at work, not only for his own well-being but for his greater productivity.

Social Psychiatry Social psychiatry, of all the psychologies, examines the total functioning of a person in his environment. Most of the people problems you face stem from people who have emotional problems. Social psychiatry draws from the several fields of the behavioral sciences as well as medicine and some of the hard sciences. In contrast to the therapy of psychiatry, it is concerned with those things that make for "healthiness" in both the environment and the individual.[5] There appears to be a common concern that the family, school, religion, business, and society force man to conform, to reduce his faculty for critical thought as well as personal growth, and to lose his capacity for awareness and profound feeling.

Economics A good shorthand definition of economics is "getting the most for your money." Economists, in the main, however, tend to ignore the human factor such as producer behavior, financial behavior, and worker and consumer behavior.[6] That the behavioral sciences are the "inexact sciences" is well-illustrated by economics. Take two illustrations. Economists cannot agree on annual business forecasts. After years of scarcity economy, they are having a rough time developing new theories to cope with our affluent economy. Farming, our first case of abundance through technology, though many years old, has no good solution. Business administration has its roots in economics and accounting.

Political Science There are two parts to political science—the governing of men and public administration. Schools of public administration for government agencies appear to be no further along than business schools in the behavioral sciences management consensus. Yet, the federal government alone is undoubtedly providing

[5] Psychiatrists Eric Berne, Erich Fromm, Karl Menninger, and Theodore Reik are all interested in social psychiatry. Some of their works are included in the Bibliography.
[6] Stuart Chase, in consultation with Edmund de Brunner, *The Proper Study of Mankind*, Harper & Row, Publishers, Incorporated, New York, 1963, p. 198; and John Kenneth Galbraith, *The Affluent Society*, Mentor Books, New American Library, Inc., New York, 1958.

grants to support more behavioral sciences research in management than is industry.

Governing of men can be divided into two basic types—autocracy and democracy. In an autocracy people are ruled by a self-appointed king or dictator. In a democracy people govern themselves. Because the business system and the governmental system are so interdependent today, economics and political science are again becoming what they once were, political economy. The new economics is one of political planning for business.

There are two basic forms of business ownership and operation —private and public. Public ownership of business is socialism if the move toward state ownership is gradual, or communism if the move is through revolution. The public schools, postal service, as well as a variety of other government activities demonstrate that we do not have a purely private ownership economic system. The only socialistic endeavor in recent years is TVA, a community rehabilitation project.

During the Great Depression, we added personal welfare to business welfare. We now provide assistance for people who are outside the economic stream. This is welfare, not socialism, for unemployables. Hard as it may be for many businessmen to acknowledge, this country started with the welfare of its businessmen. At the time of the Revolution, four-fifths of the men were individual entrepreneurs. One of the first acts of Congress was a tariff to protect infant industries. Government also regulates business, but oftentimes the regulatory agency becomes the defender of the business.

7

Develop a Professional Stance

The nurturing of growth requires the long patience of the husbandman rather than the hasty intervention of the mechanic.

—ROBERT W. WHITE, *Lives in Progress* [1]

THAT ONLY PEOPLE are the cause and the victims of the business rat race is a truism. Unless you do something about it, it will get worse. Whatever may be your career goal, to become a generalist or stay in your specialty, you work less and less independently and more and more with others. To survive in the rat race, seek a professional stance:

1. Develop your professional approach.
2. Work for your personal autonomy.
3. Avoid the management development traps.
4. Learn about yourself and others.
5. Diagnose a particular situation or relationship.
6. Realize that another will make his choices wherever possible.
7. Make some educated hunches about the people involved.
8. Acquire skills to help where you can.

[1] The Dryden Press, Inc., New York, 1952, p. 364.

It is to these ends that this chapter and Parts 3 and 4 are devised. For you these are steps not only to increased proficiency in working with others and possible promotions but also to a greater sense of well-being. You develop greater equanimity in your relations with others. You come to the point where you help those who will accept your help and help you in turn. You do not try to help those who are unable to accept it. You have the knowledge to know the difference.

Professional Approach

The professional approach includes your management education, re-creation for your business life. You see the importance for today and tomorrow of the behavioral sciences consensus of management. It is not a highly complex approach once you have the basic framework. You can use it in bureaucracies. Their rules and practices do not prohibit it. At least in my many management conferences I have found no one who felt that he could not practice the basics of the behavioral sciences approach in his company.

Your Autonomous Stance   A professional autonomous stance, I believe, is the one thing most lacking in the practice of management. This is not to suggest that management is a profession, even though it is so claimed by many. At least it cannot come to be a profession until there is, among many other things, a professional stance. Caring about others in a professional way is the key. Still, this is not recognized in management. To care does not mean being sympathetic or desiring to be liked. You need to care about helping others to the extent that you are willing to risk changing yourself. Helping others also requires that you in turn are willing to be helped. Gratitude is not to be expected from responsible adults. The help received creates an obligation which must be discharged by "giving" something to the helper; otherwise, the learner may withdraw from or even resent the helper.

To help means to care enough to contend with negative feelings, frustration, tensions, and hostilities of another as part of the growth process. Our lack of understanding about interpersonal relationships and the low level of our interpersonal skills increase our normal anxiety in facing the unknown and often unfathomable feelings of others. Take the matter of anger. What is your first thought when someone loses his temper? You wonder, "What did *I* do wrong?" not "Why did *he* lose his temper?" A person loses his temper when a situation gets beyond him and he does not know how to resolve it. Rather than feel guilty and try to smooth over the situation, sit calmly by until his emotional storm blows over. Getting your own ego and emotions involved only compounds the situation rather than helping it. Help him talk out his feelings.

Think of the stance of a physician, lawyer, social worker, or psychiatrist. Each one in his professional dealings helps people who have many more serious problems than does the average businessman. Most of the professionals deal with considerable amounts of hostility, open conflict, and major crises. Yet, they act out their professional roles in such a way as to get the best results. It is a studied role. It is an impersonal role with a background of substantial formal education and ethical standards. They know what they are trying to do to help.

If they work with you, they try first to establish your acceptance of them and then come to understand your situation. They believe that you are doing the best you can. And they generally try to help you make your decision—not make it for you. In this nonemotional approach of theirs they are empathic rather than sympathetic. They try to see things from your standpoint.

As another step toward your maturation concept of success, try to cultivate in your work relationships a similar professional stance. Many management men become so emotionally involved with others that they get hurt, anxious, or angry. Empathy is the ability to see things from another's viewpoint without becoming emotionally involved. People should be important to you, but so too is keeping your ego and emotions from involvement in the problems of others. If professional people allowed themselves to become emotionally involved with clients or patients, they would be lost.

Your Personal Autonomy Not only is developing a professional stance a way to your personal autonomy, but also achieving autonomy enhances your professional approach. Develop an awareness of what goes on within yourself, your own intrapersonal transactions. What makes your mind do what it does to make you behave as you do? For example, if you lose your temper when most others do not, you can conclude that your emotions have taken over more for you than for others.

In managing your inner conflicts, have you been able to develop enough awareness to accept the diversity of your motivations, both the good and the bad ones within yourself? How well do you really know your own mind and yourself? Do you have a firm sense of identity, the autonomy of knowing who you are and who you are not? In your relations with others are you consistent in presenting yourself? Do you continue to try to learn to communicate better? Are you selective in your activities and relationships? Do you maintain a consistent pattern in your life? [2] Learning about yourself and others as well as management should enable you to develop your professional approach and personal autonomy through knowledge and self-awareness based on that knowledge. Start with management education.

Management Development Traps

But avoid the management development traps. Trap number one is the management mess, examined in the previous chapter. Trap number two is the smattering trap, learning a little bit about everything. Pick up almost any management magazine. Examine the management development program of any management association. Both are designed for the broadest popular appeal with a variety of topics ranging all the way from "leadership" and "how to motivate others" to new techniques and electronic data processing. It is futile to try to learn something about everything. It is fatal today to try to master the technical aspects of each basic field in management. This would not make you a generalist. As you work up in business you hire technicians. Yet, I find outstanding young businessmen, some with an M.B.A., still planning to take technical courses when they should be working toward becoming generalists.

Trap number three is to rely on your organization for your management education. I have never found an organization that is continuously engaged in long-term management development. At best, there are sessions which are open to only a few people and then on a highly irregular basis. Some men are sent to management confer-

[2] Summarized from Abraham Zaleznik, *Human Dilemmas of Leadership*, Harper & Row, Publishers, Incorporated, New York, 1966, pp. 40–43.

ences, which may or may not be a company activity. For the man who really wants to learn, a typical management development program poses special problems. Too often he sits with a group of executives whose learning barriers are so high they accept only what they want to hear. Moreover, most companies, as we saw in the previous chapters, favor a management philosophy other than the behavioral sciences consensus.

Your Desire to Learn   Trap number four is the experience trap. You may feel that you are learning from experience. Still, when you rely on your experience, you demonstrate that you are not genuinely interested in learning. Five, ten, or twenty years of managing people does not mean that you have learned anything about people. As you will discover in subsequent chapters, your knowledge about people is, in all likelihood, very limited and often erroneous.

Trap number five is to pretend to yourself you want to learn. In my management conferences, the clearest signal of a closed or disinterested mind is the failure to take notes. Research on regression after learning is such that even though a participant may deny it, he is unconsciously saying, "I brought my body, but I am not interested enough in learning to take notes which I shall review later to reduce the regression."

Trap number six is to assume you know. For the many who are underutilized at work, this is an easy trap to fall into. If you are a college man, according to my informal polls, you use about 10 percent of your education. If you are just out of business school, you can feel sure that you have had more mathematics, statistics, economics, computers, and systems than most of the men in management. You may well feel that you have most of the knowledge you need. Most, but not quite all. Odds are that you are not well versed in management. As we have seen, it is too much of a mess. If you have been out of school for some years, or did not get through business school, you may rely on your common sense and get caught in the trap of assuming you know.

How to Learn

Learning about people is compounded by the fact that you must become aware of what you think you know about people and yourself. Examine what you think you know from a scientific stand-point. Only then can you build skills on knowledge and awareness. If you seek to use experimentally the common findings from the be-havioral sciences, you no longer blindly charge ahead. You can, through the behavioral sciences, work not *against* but *for* yourself and others.

What you really need from the behavioral sciences is a *first-order* knowledge and skills in the behavioral sciences. This means that you should have nontechnical, nonacademic materials. Hence, I have translated a considerable amount of the writing which is in technical language. Finally, you should be able to draw on compe-tent staff people who need to acquire a *second-order* knowledge of the behavioral consensus. They should be able to translate and inte-grate the findings of the behavioral sciences in counseling with you, much as I do in my consulting work.[3] We must still continue to look for guidance to researchers, clinicians, and academicians who pos-sess an individually specialized *third-order* knowledge. With their specialized pioneering, we cannot look to them for either a consen-sus or a translation into your language.

A Lesson from Theory X and Theory Y   The difficulty which many businessmen and management experts have in understanding and learning is well illustrated by the confused reaction to Theory X and Theory Y. Though these have been hailed as a major break-through, they are generally misunderstood. I shall try to clarify them for you. Theory X, the traditional view of direction and con-trol, is a set of assumptions about human behavior implicit in most of the current literature of organization and management practice: [4]

—The average human being has an inherent dislike for work.

—Hence, most people must be controlled, coerced, or threatened with punishment to get them to produce.

—The average human being wants to be directed and to avoid responsibility.

The assumptions of Theory Y are as follows:

[3] See my *Staff Role in Management*, Harper & Row, Publishers, Incorporated, New York, 1955.

[4] Douglas McGregor, *The Human Side of Enterprise*, McGraw-Hill Book Com-pany, New York, 1960, pp. 33, 34, 47, and 48. See also my discussion of Argyris's earlier version of Theory X on pages 56 and 57 of this book.

—Work is as natural as play or rest for the average person.

—Man will use self-control toward objectives to which he is committed.

—The average human being learns to seek responsibility.

—The intellectual capabilities of the average person are only partly used.

Now, to which do you subscribe? Do you "use" a little of each? This you cannot do, for the two theories are antithetical. In well over a hundred of my management sessions where the participants have read the book about X and Y, no one has ever volunteered the significant word. Can you? These two theories are assumptions about the *average* person.

Writers also have difficulty with the two theories and their implications. For example, one writer, after an excellent piece supporting the implications of Theory Y, says that as a last resort a supervisor may have to use Theory X and tell a subordinate to change his plan.[5] Actually, there is nothing in Theory Y that says one cannot change the recommendation of a subordinate, disagree with him, criticize him, or fire him.

Basic Questions Answer some basic questions about yourself. How sympatico are you with the behavioral sciences consensus? You have had a chance to find out by your reactions to what you have read thus far. Do you favor Theory Y?

How interested are you in really learning? The best indicator is your own actions over the past few years. You have the evidence as to your current learning habits. These may provide hard-to-face clues. The trick is to start a new *studying* habit on a small scale and gradually expand it. By *studying* I mean reading analytically rather than casual or classroom reading to parrot back. Do you want to study to learn? Research indicates that the best way to learn is by *studying a book*. Next best in descending order are reading a book, watching a training film or slide presentation, listening to a lecture, and using a teaching machine or a programmed textbook.[6]

[5] J. P. Barger, "The Managing Process," in H. B. Maynard (ed.), *Handbook of Business Administration*, McGraw-Hill Book Company, New York, 1967, pp. 1–11 to 1–14.

[6] Coolie Verner and Gary Dickinson, "An Analysis and Review of Research," *Adult Education Magazine*, vol. 17, no. 2, Winter, 1967, pp. 95–100.

To read analytically means not only that you build a reservoir of knowledge from which to draw—previous readings—but also the ability to think with the author. Studying also means to avoid popular management materials, especially magazines. To learn, you need tougher material, books. Books drawing from the behavioral sciences written for the businessman are a fruitful source of knowledge. Exhibit 5 lists a few that should be most helpful to you, including my own on management. These are the most popular among the members of the several management book groups I have conducted. You become a student of the behavioral sciences. As part of your management education, you continue to learn more and

Exhibit 5   COMPARISON OF EXPERT VIEWS *

Apparent Primary Areas of Focus	Sampson, Managing the Managers	Argyris, Personality and Organization	Levinson, Emotional Health in the World of Work	McGregor, The Human Side of Enterprise	Likert, The Human Organization	Moore, The Conduct of the Corporation	Whyte, Money and Motivation	Palmer, Understanding Other People	Berne, Games People Play
Management level	x		x	x	x	x			
Worker level		x	x	x	x		x		
The individual	x	x	x	x		x	x		
The work group	x	x	x	x	x	x	x		
Supervision of:									
One subordinate	x			x					
Group of subordinates	x			x		x			
Nature of work	x	x		x					
Emotional health	x	x	x					x	x

* See Bibliography for publisher and other details.

more about people, much like a physician engaged in a continuous learning process. If you cannot accept your need for continuing personal growth, I suggest that you not start. For, without an increase in knowledge about human behavior at work, you have no basis for personal growth. Unless you grow, you have no means for moving much beyond where you are now. You cannot buy, imitate, beg, borrow, or steal someone else's system. You have to develop your own tailor-made approach, stemming from your own personality.

Are you able to change? If, as a result of your reading, you hold the same viewpoints, attitudes, and values, you have not learned. To learn means to change. You face a basic hurdle in learning how to change yourself. André Gide said that "the only real learning comes from what goes counter to you." Change, for all that it has been discussed over the last several years, is still a difficult process. It is increasingly difficult as one grows older. In adulthood, the easiest period of change comes before age thirty or thirty-five. People at forty or fifty are usually less able to change. After a man has passed fifty he is rigidly molded generally.

Finally, can you think with the normal young people? For an adult this is perhaps the greatest challenge of all. How else to avoid obsolescence? Cultivate the curiosity, enthusiasm, and learning attitude of young management men. Accept the young, and help them help you. Your challenge is to manage them. Place your emphasis on learning about these young men and how to work with them so that you can help them contribute their maximum—both to your organization and to you.

part 3

Help Yourself to Personal Awareness

This bewilderment—this confusion as to who we are and what we should do—is the most painful thing about anxiety. But the positive and hopeful side is that just as anxiety destroys our self-awareness, so awareness of ourselves can destroy anxiety.
—ROLLO MAY, *Man's Search for Himself*[1]

THE BUSINESS RAT RACE is basically emotional. The structure and the certainties of beliefs and values of the eighteenth and nineteenth centuries are gone. Only the accelerations of diversity and change are taking their place. No wonder it is difficult for a man to find himself. Because he does not know what makes him anxious, he can be easily paralyzed by his anxiety. Because he does not know what he is trying to accomplish, he can work at it frantically.

Although he is more comfortable and better fed, housed, and clothed, and suffers less physical pain, his feelings increasingly turn and twist him out of physical and mental

[1] W. W. Norton & Company, Inc., New York, 1953, p. 44.

shape. Although he may not see it, he exhibits evidences of anxiety, guilt, fatigue, frustration, and tenseness. Boredom is his worst enemy, and may well project him into recurring feelings of uselessness, futility, and depression. He falls into the trap of believing that events occur in spite of what he tried to do.

Take charge of your own total development. And I mean more than management development. It includes the re-creation of your emotions through your mind, among other things. The maturation concept of success is personal growth: to grow toward the full realization of your endowment, to expand and enrich your concept of yourself, to discover who you are as a person. The issue for you is life, not as a biological fact, but as a process of personal growth and development toward maturity—*if* you make it so. All your resources should focus not only on your work and career, but more important, on your total life.

You need first more knowledge so that you can get some measure of where you are now and the best means for your own development. To these ends I am going to consolidate in this part of the book the behavioral sciences consensus of findings about yourself and your achievement tendencies. In addition, I shall use the consensus to suggest means to help you in relaxing, working, and re-creating yourself at work.

8

Discover Yourself

> The individual tends to assume that he is in full
> control of his thoughts and actions. It comes as a
> shock when he discovers that his thinking and behav-
> ior can often be traced back to very early experiences
> of which he is now totally unaware. He finds it hard
> to realize that within his own mind are submerged
> forces—mental forces—which can drive him against
> his better judgment (or even against his will) to act
> in an unreasoning and unreasonable manner.
>
> —JAMES A. BRUSSEL, M.D., *A Layman's*
> *Guide to Psychiatry* [1]

THE HUMAN ANIMAL spends a good deal of time attributing to himself lofty but frequently phony motives which have been developed
for only a few thousand years. Yet, you would be far less anxious
and guilty and a more mature person if you would face your animal
impulses. These have been with us for millions of years and are still
major moving forces within us.

It is a good bet that your ancestral apes moved first from the tree
ape to the ground ape, second to the killer ape and the hunting
pack ape, third to the naked ape and the infantile ape, fourth to

[1] Barnes & Noble, Inc., New York, 1967, p. 1.

the apes with very obvious visible sexual differences, fifth to the territorial ape, and sixth to the cultural ape.[2] Both the hand and the brain gave your ancestors substantial evolutionary advantages. At some still unknown stage in these moves, your ancestral ape acquired a brain and with it the abilities not only to think and to create but also to be anxious and become neurotic.

In the business rat race you see rugged "naked apes" in their gray flannel suits. They seem more self-confident than you. They appear to know where they are going and how to get there. Quick decision makers with objective reasoning minds. Cool, calm, and without emotion or anxiety. Yet, they are as anxious and unaware of themselves and others as your are. You spend more time trying to convince others that you are self-confident and happy than facing yourself. It is a common finding that people generally feel more inadequate than they should.

"Know Thyself"

Man is highly complex. Socrates' dictum of over 2,500 years ago, "Know Thyself," was premature. Only now is there enough knowledge about man to enable you to help yourself by developing awareness of yourself. This is re-creation through your mind, the most important step in self-awareness. Recall the three lives—business, personal, and family. Recall the three activities—relaxation, work, and re-creation. Recall the avenues—mind, body, and other people. Here, for two chapters, the focus is on the re-creation of your mind, developing greater awareness of yourself through knowledge and guidelines. This is not a psychiatric treatise, but rather an everyday-language, first-order knowledge for the businessman. Hence, it is both incomplete and oversimplified. As I have done before, I shall draw together interrelated common findings and make them as specific as possible. Even so, they will require a good deal of reflection on your part, for they go well beyond what you think you know about yourself. Moreover, at first reading you may feel that you have most of the emotional problems.

Known and Unknown   Although there appears to be more that is unknown than known about people, there is enough that is known to

[2] A recent popular treatment is Desmond Morris, *The Naked Ape*, McGraw-Hill Book Company, New York, 1967.

help you secure increased self-awareness. Here is a convenient guide for separating the known from the unknown.

Known to yourself and others includes the many things that you think you know about yourself, as do others. These may be inaccurate, for they stem from folklore and common sense. Willpower is a good illustration. You and others believe that you can exercise willpower. As another example, you believe that you are an objective, rational person. Most experts reject this.

Known to you but unknown to others is what you successfully hide from others. You wear a mask. If a person you want to please has opposing political views, for example, you conceal yours.

Known to others but unknown to you are those things about you believed by others but unknown to you. It is highly unlikely that anyone will tell you about what he sees as your bizarre behavior. Examples might be your being too effeminate, too suspicious, too secretive, too hostile, too arrogant, too pushy. Under the right circumstances, you might be told about your more acceptable "off limits" behavior, such as when you lose your temper over what appears to be a trivial matter, when you try to ramrod something through, or when you are resisting too much.

Unknown both to you and others are those items deeply buried within you which neither you nor others perceive, yet have a major impact on your behavior and feelings. This is the beginning level of self-awareness of the deeper things you conceal. Included are your normal feelings of anxiety and guilt, to be covered later.

Known and knowable to you contains a vast amount of behavioral sciences knowledge, much of which you are finding here and will accept.

Known but unknowable to you includes those behavioral sciences findings which are not acceptable to you. They are not knowable to you because you reject them. Recall the need to unlearn so that you do not pick what you like and reject what you do not like. The more you can accept in this area in terms of yourself, the more self-awareness, and hence maturity, you achieve.

Still unknown and, therefore, unknowable to you brings us finally to what at this stage of our knowledge is not knowable either to you or the behavioral scientists. Take the mind.

The Mind

Although there are many theories, we do not know how your mind works, how it remembers, how it learns, how it thinks, how it decides, how it solves problems, and how it is creative. There is much more to the mind than intelligence. Whatever you do, you believe you do first with your mind. Your mind at the conscious level is an organ of survival, the receiving, feeling, and thinking part of your being. It is now commonplace that your mind thinks continuously and constantly. You use your mind mainly to find ways of getting what you want or need and to avoid what you do not want. In your intrapersonal transactions your mind produces rationalizations and explanations to yourself to justify or cover up your feelings. Your mind can recall some of the past and think, wonder, and worry about the future.

It is man's mind that makes the human animal so different from other animals. Still, the mind is hardly an effective and efficient instrument. It deals with specifics, but only with a few at a time. It

Exhibit 6 THE MIND'S TRIANGLE OF TRIADS

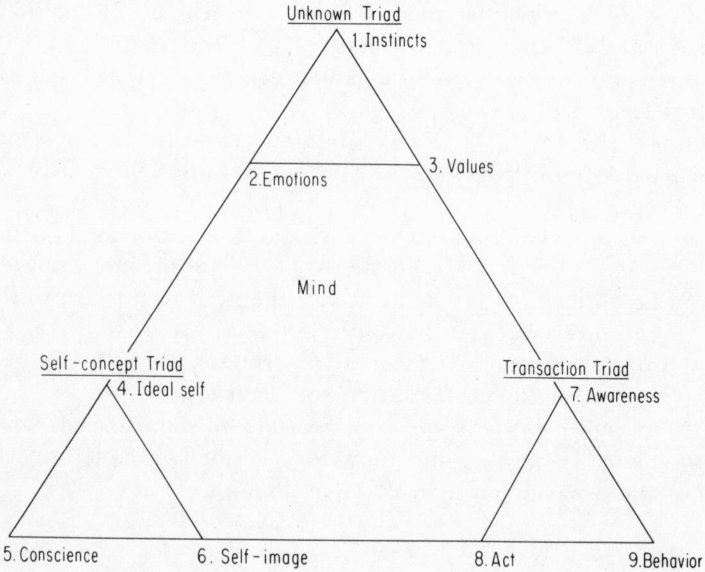

Unknown Triad
1. Instincts
2. Emotions
3. Values
Mind
Self-concept Triad
4. Ideal self
5. Conscience
6. Self-image
Transaction Triad
7. Awareness
8. Act
9. Behavior

prefers certainty and order. It cannot easily handle numbers of more than three digits. Moreover, your mind is enclosed in a Triangle of Triads, as shown in Exhibit 6. Accept the fact that your transactions within yourself are essentially threefold: your Unknown Triad, your Self-concept Triad, and your Transaction Triad. The Unknown Triad, the unconscious inner self, includes (1) instincts, (2) emotions, and (3) values. The Self-concept Triad, the outer and generally conscious self, includes (4) ideal self, what you would like to be; (5) conscience, what you can and cannot do; and (6) self-image, what you think you are. The Transaction Triad contains (7) awareness, what you think you see and what you think you should do in a particular situation or relationship; (8) act, what you think you are doing or how you are acting; and (9) behavior, what you actually are doing as perceived by others.

Unknown Triad

Your mind is imprisoned by a tenacious network of instincts, emotions, and values, much of which you are unconscious of.

Instincts Man's instincts have caused and still cause much controversy among the experts. Of the many innate tendencies of man, he has three open-ended instincts of primary concern to us here—sex, status, and aggression. In other species these instincts are closed; they are followed blindly. Sex is considered in Chapter 16.

Status as an instinct is best typified as the pecking order. Animals determine their relative rank in terms of "who pecks whom." The human animal is compelled by the status instinct as are the other animal species. With very rare exceptions, every other species instinctively protects its weak, once the pecking order is established. There are elaborate rituals for avoiding destructive conflict with their own kind. Once the human male animal gains supremacy, however, he tends to abuse, misuse, and even kill members of his own species. Some psychiatrists, not all, accept Freud's destructive drive.

Some natural scientists believe that man's aggressive instinct, the wanton killing of his own kind and other species, stems from his evolutionary experience. Among our prehistoric ancestors there was little possibility of seriously injuring or quickly killing another.

The potential victim had time to make submissive gestures to show acceptance of a lower rank in the pecking order. Suddenly, in the evolutionary sense, for man alone, came the hand. The use of weapons to kill his own kind emerged without enough time for the development of suitable submissive gestures.

With our country founded on the ideals of democracy, justice, and equality, we maintain the mystique of a peace-loving people. Actually, we have always been a violent country. Some of us cherish our larger violences such as rebelling from Mother England, killing Indians, and the Civil War. We forget farmer rebellions of both yesterday and today, the continuing union bloodshed, the anti-Catholic riots, and the Civil War draft riots in the middle of the nineteenth century. Our propensity for murdering national figures is well known. In the second half of the twentieth century we have the race, peace, and university riots.

As a nation we exceed all other nations by far in the death rate caused by firearms. Since the early 1900s when the first count was recorded, firearms have claimed the lives of over 750,000 Americans. Yet, in all the wars in our history including Vietnam, a lesser number of some 530,000 Americans have been killed.[3] Physical aggression against other persons has generally gone out of fashion. Still, hunting offers an opportunity for direct aggression for a minority of men who get a thrill out of the pursuit and violent destruction of wild animals for no constructive purpose other than amusement, whatever the rationalization may be.[4]

In spite of man's violence to himself, his kind, and other animals, it appears that anthropologists, in general, support the nonaggression theory. Prehistoric man, they claim, was cooperative, peaceful, and unaggressive. Civilization has made us aggressive, hostile, and less cooperative in our relations with others.[5] Aggression begets aggression. An aggression-laden environment makes for aggression in individuals. Individuals take their cues from the boss.

[3] Carl Bakal, *The Right to Bear Arms,* McGraw-Hill Book Company, New York, 1966.

[4] Karl Menninger, M.D., with Martin Mayman and Paul Pruyser, *The Vital Balance,* The Viking Press, New York, 1963, p. 214.

[5] M. F. Ashley Montagu, *The Direction of Human Development,* Harper & Row, Publishers, Incorporated, New York, 1955, p. 196.

Emotions   I include emotions in the Unknown Triad because, while you are aware of your feelings generally, you have little or no knowledge of your unknown emotions, of the sources of your emotions, of their extensive ramifications and the great impact they have on your life. Emotions include anger, joy, pleasure, surprise, excitement, fatigue, hostility, resistance, defiance, conflict, fear, anxiety, neuroses, and many others. To help you get some understanding of the elemental negative emotions, a most important aspect of helping yourself and one so infrequently and loosely treated in the management literature, I make some distinctions here that are not usually made.

Tension is the usual range of energy to satisfy a normal need in action. It is internal because the tension arises from your wanting or needing something, your drives and desires, your emotional involvement in preparing for and leading a special meeting or in solving a problem or being creative. Tension also occurs when you interact with others in positive ways. General tension is the bubbling over of energy and having, in the main, good feelings. In contrast there are such reactions as indifference or apathy.

Stress suggests negative connotations of your being put under pressure by others through conflict, competition, demands, disapproval, criticisms, threats—all the external factors of the rat race.

Tenseness is your internal reaction to stress, such as emotional fatigue, frustration, exasperation, disappointment, defeat, or worry. Nervousness, covered in the next chapter, is chronic tenseness. There is good evidence that we do our poorest when we are uptight. Tenseness makes a man more active at the lower level of *doing* and less active at the higher level of *thinking*. Rather than think clearly and creatively in the gray areas, he tends to return to earlier, more simplistic black-and-white positions, ideas, and opinions. With too much tenseness or outside pressure, he polarizes his judgments. Extreme tenseness may make a person incapable of functioning, immobile, panicked, angered, or unduly aggressive.

Fear arises when you know specifically what threatens you. When you see a car trying to pass your car in a situation which you judge unsafe, you become afraid. When you make a serious error, you fear the consequences. If you hear a strange noise in your house, you experience fear. These are all tangible, specific events. Your physical reaction gives you additional energy to face the event, to run, or to overcome the danger in other appropriate ways. You feel that you are sharper, particularly your perceptions. You can feel your heart beat faster. Fear, a conscious act, causes release of adrenalin, slows down the digestive process, and dries the mouth. These are the physiological changes in your body.

Guilt occurs when you violate your own standards—go counter to your conscience. It may be a sin of omission, not having done something that you should do, or a sin of commission, having done something which you should not do. A responsibility which you have not met or decisions you have avoided cause feelings of guilt. You find ways of disguising or distorting the actual situation. Whether you are aware of this or not, the discomfort is only temporarily resolved.

Anxiety is called the modern great white plague.[6] Of all the emotions, anxiety, with the painful uncertainty about self and the uneasiness of mind, is one of the most difficult afflictions of man. Anxiety arises over an intangible threat with no objective basis. Hence, you do not know what steps to take to meet the danger. Physiological reactions of anxiety are an increase in salivation and gastric secretions.

Old age, death, suffering, and after-life cause a dim but gnawing anxiety about the significance of existence. More serious are the immediate anxieties. To be anxious about nothing in particular and to feel bewildered are the most painful things about anxiety. Anxiety overshadows and hinders your thoughts and actions. You feel restless, upset, uneasy, nervous, uptight, unhappy, or depressed. You have a higher level of anxiety when you face the various minor and major crises of life. Normal anxiety tends to be at a high level in childhood, rising to higher levels during adolescence, declining in adulthood, and then rising again around the age of sixty.

Anxiety-Guilt Complex   Normal people are blocked from facing some of the negative realities of themselves. Never in my many group discussions about emotional health has anyone even hinted at his little recurring sins. Therefore, near the end of our discussing what a normal person is like, I ask these questions: Has anyone in this room

[6] May, *op. cit.*

never told a lie? (If so, please raise your hand.) *Never* cheated? *Never* taken anything that did not belong to you? *Never* flirted when you should not have? Once we get to talking about these kinds of things, the groups appear to accept that it is normal to be selfish, envious, jealous, and greedy—to be inconsiderate, biased, and prejudiced.

Answer this question: What are the four or five things about yourself that you have never told anyone, including your wife? Put them in writing. I have used this approach with many groups and always with the same basic results. When I ask a group to write these anonymously, there is first much laughter and joking which indicates that this is not an easy experience. When I catalog the results they are surprised that they are not the only ones who feel anxious and guilty.

Exhibit 7 shows the six circles of the normal anxiety-guilt complex, developed from some of the sessions. Below are a few typical comments.

Exhibit 7   ANXIETY-GUILT COMPLEX

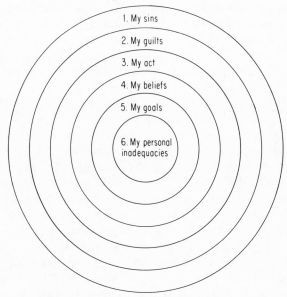

1. My sins
2. My guilts
3. My act
4. My beliefs
5. My goals
6. My personal inadequacies

1. *My sins.* For many groups there is a good deal of concern about premarital and postmarital sexual experiences. Typical comments are: My sexual activities prior to wedlock. Affairs with women. Stealing something.

2. *My guilts.* Acts of dishonesty: I lie about my formal education. I am not always honest in my dealing with others.

3. *My act.* This covers essentially those concerns about how I am being accepted by others as well as my attitudes toward others. There are usually a high percentage of items in this category: Acting superior. Talking too much. Too frank. Feel that I am disliked. Inability to talk with other people about their feelings. Too impatient with others.

4. *My beliefs.* This category usually does not have many items and most deal with religion: Take job more seriously than religion. I am not fully convinced of the existence of God. Cannot believe in life hereafter.

5. *My goals.* Here we come very close to some of what we talked about earlier, that is, one's purposes in life: What am I reaching for? No feeling of personal progress. Grandiose aspirations. No plans for old age. Afraid I am in the wrong work.

6. *Personal inadequacy.* In every group, without exception, the feelings of personal inadequacy outnumber the items in the other categories: Perfectionist. Too skeptical. Too egotistical. Too quick to judge. Impatient. Jump to conclusions. Temper. Worry too much. No self-confidence. Timid. Poor judgment. Feeling of worthlessness. Too emotional inside. Insecure at home and work.

Values   For each of us our values, the third facet of the Unknown Triad, form an unconscious but coherent and stable screen for our instincts and emotions. Whatever we hear, see, feel, or read goes through a screening process whereby we eliminate (overlook or reject) that which threatens to violate or differs from our personal values. If a bit of information gets into our memory which is inconsistent with our value system, we tend to forget it or adjust the facts to fit into the value system acceptable to our memory.

Your values, taught for the most part in infancy, are so much a part of you that the mind is usually a prisoner of your basic assumptions, blind to your biases and prejudices. That your values may be set apart from you and looked at is itself an "enlarged outlook." [7] To illustrate, in contrast to those in the lowest classes, middle-class American children are taught cleanliness, good manners, hard work, accomplishment, and avoidance of open expressions of hostility.

Do you think man is basically good or evil? Your answer will tend to indicate whether you have fundamentally liberal or conservative values. About 80 percent of those who think man is basically good are humanistic and liberal even though they may believe they are conservative. And about 80 percent of those who think man is basically evil hold to the conservative belief that man needs to be governed by external standards. Liberal and conservative values exist in all fields of knowledge. They affect creativity. Liberal mathematicians approach mathematics imaginatively, attracted by novelty; right wingers seem to want the security of the correct answer. In child rearing there are those of the left pole who believe in permissive love; the right pole, control. In education there are those on the left who believe in the importance of the child as opposed to those on the authority-oriented right who stress obedience. Those on the left are interested in people and helping them while those on the right tend to oppose "do gooders." [8] These have direct implications for managing,[9] creativity, curiosity, and helping.

The many paper-and-pencil "value" tests generally differentiate the businessman—and provide clues to his rat race—from others. In these tests he tends to show a high *practical* value, control of money and goods, rather than a *theoretical* value of intellectual curiosity. Generally he has a high *personal power* value over the *social* value, wanting to use people for his own ends rather than helping them toward their ends. Typically, he has a low *aesthetic* value, with little interest in art and music. Nor does he usually score high on the *religious* value of ethics and beliefs.

Unknown Intrapersonal Transactions An unconscious intrapersonal transaction of the Unknown Triad of instinct, emotion, and value is

[7] James V. Clark, *Education for the Use of Behavioral Science*, Institute of Industrial Relations, University of California, Los Angeles, 1962, p. 22.

[8] Sylvan Tompkins, "The Psychology of Being Right—and Left," *Trans-Action*, vol. 3, no. 1, November-December, 1966, pp. 23–27.

[9] For example, see William D. Guth and Renato Tagiuri, "Personal Values and Corporate Strategy," *Harvard Business Review*, vol. 43, no. 5, September-October, 1965, pp. 123–132.

best illustrated by a prejudice which the mind contains without being aware that it is a prejudice. Although all Christians make up less than 30 percent of the world population, many of them feel that theirs is the only true and valid religion. It can be reasoned, though not accepted by devout Christians, that their religious stance stems from the pecking order *instinct,* with a *value* supporting it, and an *emotion* which tells the mind to be wary of other religions. Among the Christian religions, there is much prejudice. Values cannot be divorced from emotions and instincts. Just as a person under stress feels threatened, so too may a person whose values are threatened feel a crisis or even panic. People who have no cherished values but feel threatened tend to experience uneasiness.

Self-concept Triad

Your Self-concept Triad provides you with an internal configuration of the sum total of perceptions of yourself which are admissible to your awareness. Your self-concept consists of ideal self, conscience, and self-image. It is the basis for your self-esteem, what you think of yourself.

Ideal Self   Ideal self, normally a positive facet, consists in large measure of your parents' aspirations for you at your ultimate best, as well as things about other people you have admired. It is toward your ideal self you tend to move. Many people, for example, cannot go beyond the status and success which their parents dreamed for them. They slow down to the point where they are no longer effective because they do not have within them higher levels of achievement. On the other hand, there are people who are "false failures." The ideal self established by their parents is substantially beyond what they are really capable of. They may overrely on status and other outward symbols of success to prove to themselves that they have come part way.

Conscience   For most of us our conscience is a rigorous, inescapable taskmaster telling us what we can and cannot do, a major facet of the anxiety-guilt complex. It is generally believed that the conscience is formed before the age of five or six by parents. A conscience is reinforced by teachers and clergy. Generally, the conscience permits some forms of behavior, prescribes others, and prohibits other kinds of behavior. These are internalized into "thou shalt not" behavior. A constrictor of our activities, conscience is so strong that it operates almost automatically.

As part of growing up and breaking away from parents, there is a considerable amount of trying to modify the conscience. Still, an individual cannot become self-governing unless he develops a conscience as a child, living by rules, prohibitions, and taboos. Some have been able to block it off almost completely and are usually viewed as ruthless. Some have never been able to grow up, to break away from the unduly rigid standards of their parents. Typically, an individual is uncomfortable, guilty, and anxious if he does not live by certain rules, although he is no longer aware of why he must do so. Some few may even have a need for punishment. This need may become so strong that an individual may get into a serious situation through what appears to be carelessness but is really the need to be punished. Some few never get over the credibility shock. Both father and mother typically stress the need for a high level of integrity, selflessness, and respect, with no premarital sex. Children are usually shocked when they find that their parents have not lived up to the standards they establish for their children.

Self-image   Self-image reflects the level of your self-esteem, fluctuating from low to high opinions of yourself. The degree of basic divergence between the ideal self and the self-image is a measure of your emotional health. If you have an unrealistically high ideal self and a low self-image, you are likely to have more emotional problems and anxieties than a person whose ideal self comes closer to his actual self-image. How you stand with others also has a direct bearing on your self-image. When you are depreciated by people who are important to you, your self-image is lowered. When, however, your standing is enhanced by others, you tend to have a more confident view of yourself and your capacities.

The intrapersonal transactions within and between these two triads, Unknown Self and Self-concept, are highly complex. One facet helps or hurts another, some of which the mind can become aware of. Much of it is unconscious even though there is a direct effect on the mind in terms of what is thought and felt.

Transaction Triad

The Transaction Triad consists of (1) your awareness, the degree of your perception of reality or your evaluation of what you should do in light of the circumstances; (2) your act, what you think you are deciding or doing; and (3) behavior, what you are deciding or actually doing as perceived by others. Underlying the three phases of the Transaction Triad are the expectations of others, the needs of the immediate situation as perceived by you, your personal ways of behaving, and your ways of resolving the interplay of the forces within yourself in the situation and the expectations of others. However, almost everything you do involves no conscious analysis, for you follow patterns which you have come to feel are the right ones. Only in an unusual situation do you think about how you should try to behave.

Awareness   Your perception of reality is your awareness—your evaluation of a particular situation and the determination of what to do. In most cases this is not a conscious process, but rather a habit pattern. You plan and direct your actions, restrain your impulses, and act in terms of your perception of reality—your view of your various situations and relationships—not in terms of the way they actually are. It is a mark of awareness and maturity to be able to perceive a variety of situations or expectations of others and then to make analyses that square more with reality. One evidence of your growing understanding of others and yourself is your moving from being able to act in only a few ways to being able to act in many different ways. That awareness is the culmination of the Unknown Self Triad and Self-concept Triad is evidenced by your conscience. There is always the conflict of personal integrity, guilt, and anxiety. Do you say what you really think? Do you express your true feelings? Do you do what you really want to do? What mask do you choose?

Act   Act includes deciding, doing, or acting out what you think is the best in light of the circumstances. To act is to use the techniques of an actor in shaping your speech and manner to secure the desired response. In your professional stance you form a protective screen to ward off and protect yourself from both real and imagined threats from others and to help those you can. Some cultivate a manipulative screen to get what they want from others. Acts are universal, and once learned provide convenient routines. For example, if you are a typical subordinate, you usually wear three different masks, one for superiors, one for peers, and one for subordinates. You wear an "I aim to please" mask for your superiors. For your peers you are not as considerate. Your Sunday manners fade into a more guarded "I keep my own counsel" mask. Often you drop your manners with your subordinates. This is where you come closest to acting just as you feel, thus directly satisfying your need to dominate, for this is where you have power as "head of the family."

Behavior   Your behavior is almost never a direct response to objective reality—things as they really are—but rather your perception of that reality and your response to it. Behavior is observed by others. For example, you may make a decision which in your eyes is sound but which is bad in the judgment of others. You may even think that you are a good decision maker though, according to others, you are viewed as indecisive. You may feel that you are doing the right thing in a certain situation but it is wrong in the judgment of others. The gap between what you think you are doing, your act, and what you are observed to be doing, your behavior, may be so great that you may be viewed as a problem by others.

9

Check Out
Your Achieving Tendencies

Gone forever is the notion that the mentally ill person is an exception. It is now accepted that most people have some degree of mental illness at some time, and many of them have a degree of mental illness most of the time. This should not really surprise anyone, for do not most of us have some physical illness some of the time, and some of us much of the time?

—KARL MENNINGER, M.D., *with* MARTIN MAYMAN *and* PAUL PRUYSER, *The Vital Balance* [1]

BY NOW YOU SHOULD BE ABLE to acknowledge that your behavior is governed not by your mind, your reasoning, your willpower, your common sense, or what-have-you but by a complex of inextricably intertwined facets of your personality, many of them unknown to you. You are a "product" of your Unknown Triad of instincts, emotions, and values and of your Self-concept Triad of your ideal self, conscience, and self-image.

Emotional Health

To enable you to get some knowledge and awareness of your primary behavior at work, I have introduced a consensus of achieving

[1] The Viking Press, Inc., New York, 1963, p. 33.

Exhibit 8 TYPES OF ACHIEVERS
IN SEVEN STAGES OF EMOTIONAL HEALTH

Emotional Stages	Types of Achievers		
1. Mature	Superior Achievers: Enterprising Self-actualizing Autonomous Helpful Physically fit		
2. Normal	Low Achievers: Conformist Adapted	Average Achievers: Practical Win-Lose	Undue Achievers: Competitive Impulsive
3. Nervousness	Underachievers: Indecisive Apathetic		Overachievers: Hustler Eager beaver
4. Psychosomatic	Underachievers: Hypochondriac Functional neurotic		Overachievers: Sickness prone Twitcher
5. Neurotic	Underachievers: Worrier Sideliner		Overachievers: Work addict Neurotic competitor
6. "Prepsychotic"	Underachievers: Moody Alcoholic		Overachievers: Egotist Suspicious
7. Unemployable	From temporary or chronic unemployment to institutional care		

tendencies at work listed in terms of seven stages of emotional or mental health.[2] The approach is summarized in Exhibit 8.

[2] As yet there is no agreement among psychiatrists as to whether mental or emotional health is preferred. Classifications of emotional health and the varieties of cases abound. My primary sources are Menninger et al., *The Vital Balance;* Stuart Palmer, *Understanding Other People;* Eric Berne, M.D., *A Layman's Guide to Psychiatry & Psychoanalysis;* James A. Brussel, M.D., *A Layman's Guide to Psychiatry;* Edward Weiss, M.D., and O. Spurgeon English, M.D., *Psychosomatic Medicine;* and Roy Heath, *The Reasonable Adventurer* (see Bibliography for publisher).

You do not quickly slip into a stage and then slip back to normal. You have the symptoms and the suffering of the stage generally for some time. Each stage also has a range and may phase gradually into the next stage. Moreover, a person, especially when he gets into one of the lower emotional stages, may have a combination of emotional difficulties. I know of one obese neurotic underachiever with an ulcer, high blood pressure, insomnia, a violent temper, and an authoritarian personality. (The last is described in Chapter 13.)

Achievers   Most important to you is the general agreement among most psychiatrists that through greater knowledge and self-awareness you can move forward. You can reduce the negative impact of your emotions on you and on your achieving. As you review the achieving tendencies, resist the usual impulse to find yourself in every category. All of us have a moderate amount of some of the extremes, as we saw in the previous chapter. Remember, too, that this classification is a highly simplified approach designed for you, a businessman. It has been viewed as acceptable and appropriate by several psychiatrists who have sat in on some of my management conferences where I have presented it. There is not much point in getting into causes, for in spite of all the clues and theories of psychiatry, there is still no known specific cause of any emotional or mental disorder.[3] Some start with relatively severe emotional problems in childhood. Others go beyond their emotional breaking point because of some stress from the outside such as the business rat race.

With the introduction of the achiever concept into management, it has come to be used in a variety of ways. It has also been used in other fields, especially education. My use of average, low, and undue achievers for the normal stage of emotional health indicates a range.

Under- and Overachievers   Under- and overachievers are two extremes of people who are below the normal range of emotional health. There is no middle ground here. The achieving tendencies are extreme.

It is in school where the underachiever has been studied. As a

[3] James A. Brussel, M.D., *A Layman's Guide to Psychiatry*, Barnes & Noble, Inc., New York, 1967, p. 223.

student he tends to show neurotic tendencies and may also have a psychosomatic disorder. He is the student who is capable of achieving considerably higher grades than he does. He is low in study motivation, sense of responsibility, dominance, self-confidence, and capacity to work under pressure. He shows disinterest and boredom as well as little concern for others.[4] The underachiever usually has high goals but he does not strive to attain them. He is the one who does just enough to "get by" and frequently just enough to get into a college. Contrary to popular belief, the underachiever cares about his grades and is disappointed with himself, his parents, and his teachers. His primary interests are sports and girls. He finds his homework discouraging. He usually comes from an average or better home where he receives much urging, pushing, and nagging. Parents are discouraged, and teachers view the underachiever as lazy and trying just to get by.

The adult underachiever is much like the student. Work may go on after a fashion. There are absurd fears, guilty thoughts, ridiculous notions. He keeps doing things he does not want to do and thinking things he does not want to think. He fails to do and think what he wants.

Overachievers try too hard with no outstanding results. They are unrealistic. They may or may not be hard workers. Usually they are not effective workers. Moreover, they tend to be emotionally cold or alienated from others. Typically, you find an overachiever dissatisfied, bored, and unhappy. He has a sense of futility with a vague feeling that life is meaningless. He may be in a frantic flight into escape activities or into work. He may crave more money, power, and prestige. The overachiever is trying to compensate for his inner vacuity.[5] His ways of behaving are more or less unrealistic, unpleasant, offensive, and handicapping. He suffers not only from the conflict he has with others, but also from internal tenseness.

Under- and Oversocialized   There is an explanation which may enable you to get a better grasp of emotional health and its many ramifications. It is maintained that very young children who were

---

[4] C. Burleigh Wellington and Jean Wellington, *The Underachiever: Challenges and Guidelines*, Rand McNally Curriculum Series, Rand McNally & Company, Chicago, no date.

[5] Erich Fromm, M.D., *The Sane Society*, Harper & Row, Publishers, Incorporated, New York, 1955, p. 295.

oversocialized by their parents tend as adults to aggress against themselves. Those who were undersocialized tend to aggress against others. They do not relate in normal ways with others. Their needs for securing approval, avoiding disapproval, or aggressing are unacceptable to others. Few would be viewed as helpful in the business world. Some try too hard to secure approval—the attention getter, the boaster, or the he-man. These unwittingly turn people against them because they come on too strong. Others seek approval in more acceptable ways—self-depreciation, habitual lying, social climbing, work addiction, and being unusually kind. Some people try at the same time to seek approval and avoid disapproval— verbally extreme, enigmatic, pompous, snobbish, self-righteous, reforming, scrupulously honest, and doing good. Others try to avoid disapproval by staying on the sidelines—shy, reclusive, and lazy. Poor avoiders of disapproval are the worrier, indecisive person, chain smoker, and overeater. Odd avoiders include the man with some sort of phobia and the perfectionist. Escapists are the alcoholic and the homosexual.

Then, there are those individuals who act in ways to satisfy the need to aggress and the need either to gain approval or to avoid disapproval. These are the arguer, complainer, gossip, disquieting one, humorist, petty officious one, race hater, jealous one, bombaster, and the thief who disobeys laws such as a tax consultant who recommends tax evasion. Those who are not in the work world usually are the juvenile delinquent, pickpocket, convicted murderer. Finally, there are those who need to aggress. The small-timers are the surly, poor loser, and wife beater. Extremists are the rapist, sadist, and arsonist.[6]

Stage One: Mature

To be mature is a relatively rare occurrence. Maturity does not mean perfection or total equanimity, for even the few people who achieve it have emotional hangups such as smoking, temper, or moodiness. To work toward maturity is the maturation concept of success of Chapter 2. Of all the success concepts, only this one has a

[6] These cases are all described in Stuart Palmer, *Understanding Other People*, Premier Books, Fawcett World Library, published by arrangement with Thomas Y. Crowell Company, New York, 1964.

positive goal. The salvation concept can lead to a religious fanatic. The organization concept can lead to a yes-man. The power concept can lead to a neurotic competitor. Moreover, consciously striving to become more mature through the "three by three by three" formula is one of the best means to increase your sense of intellectual, physical, and emotional well-being and your survival in and beyond the business rat race.

The goal of maturation is to become an enterprising, self-actualizing, autonomous, helpful, physically fit achiever. The program for physical fitness is covered primarily in Chapter 15. The program for self-actualization and autonomy in management was covered earlier in Parts 1 and 2. Beyond business, self-actualization and autonomy are outlined in Parts 5 and 6. Self-awareness for autonomy is covered here in Part 3. Being helpful is described in Part 4. The mature achiever is listed in Chapter 2. Another version of the mature achiever is the reasonable adventurer. Adventure speaks of your inner self, reasonable speaks of your outer self; both interwoven to enable you to function as a whole. Though you are spontaneous in your behavior with others, you are far more spontaneous in your inner life, impulses, and thoughts. Your spontaneity is simple and natural, with a lack of artificiality. You may have average mental endowment but you use it well.[7]

Stage Two: Normal

Are you normal? Can you describe what a normal man is like? People in my conferences are dumbfounded by this question. Even if you have delved into psychiatric and psychological literature, odds are against your being able to describe a normal person. If my experience with management groups is any indication, you have no "handles" or guides to aid you. Yet it is not so difficult. In the previous chapter, you learned the basics of the normal man. In Chapter 3 you learned about his work needs.

Vital Balance   From a psychiatric standpoint a normal person (1) has a satisfactory working capacity, (2) is able to love someone other than himself, (3) is not hampered by mental conflict, and (4) is free

---

[7] Roy Heath, *The Reasonable Adventurer*, The University of Pittsburgh Press, Pittsburgh, 1964, pp. 35–37. Recall Berne's "spontaneity."

from physical symptoms of anxiety.[8] To be normal is a question of emotional balance within a range. Almost all of us who are normal will occasionally have a bout of emotional ill health of some sort which may throw us off balance for a while. Most of us who are normal have some continuing emotional hangup such as smoking, car sickness, or overuse of sunglasses. We may be inhibited, irrational, or even irresponsible in some ways.

Normality is the ability to hold to the vital balance. It is the ability to stop when satiated, to change when necessary even with difficulty, to influence and be influenced, to accept and be accepted, to be interdependent and independent, to be counted on and to count on others. Normality is to try and fail, to try and partially succeed, and to compromise, to step aside, to fight back, or to run away.[9] It is to seek approval and avoid disapproval and when frustrated in either of these or any other need to aggress in acceptable ways.

Average Achievers   The key to the normal achiever is adequate work capacity. Typically he is a practical man with the win-lose complex.

As a *practical* achiever he is a doer rather than a thinker. He obtains satisfaction not from problem-solving so much as from finishing a task. Industrious, he usually works at everything more or less indiscriminately. Without an intense urge to achieve, he does not seem to care very much about doing things better. Not creative or curious, he usually views learning as a threat to himself. Yet, he welcomes opportunities to advance in his work.

As a *win-lose* achiever, he may be a follower of the salvation, organization, or power concept of success. As outlined on page 4 of Chapter 1 he does not know how to cooperate or be helpful because he has never been schooled or counseled to these ends. For him it is to win or to lose; there is no middle ground.

Normal Low Achievers   Though they may think they strive to please their bosses, normal low achievers fall just a little bit short.

The *conformist* is the true organization man. Afraid to be different, he seeks approval of others. He places more value on the opin-

---

[8] Stated by Edward Glover, M.D., in Edward Weiss, M.D., and O. Spurgeon English, M.D., *Psychosomatic Medicine*, W. B. Saunders Company, Philadelphia, 1943, p. 27.

[9] Menninger et al., *op. cit.*, p. 126.

ions of others than on his own judgment. His need to be with others he likes is stronger than his desire to excel at a task or work hard. He prefers the sociability of organization life.

The *adapted* normal low achiever has reacted negatively to his underutilization at work. He may give up, goldbrick, or try to regulate his aspirations and adjust his ways of thinking to the expectations of the organization. The part of his life which is left over from work is used to be with others, to play, to be entertained, to have fun, and to consume. He does not realize that, being alienated from work, he usually is also alienated from true leisure, autonomy, and genuine relationships with others.[10] If finally he becomes alienated from himself, he becomes a neurotic.

Normal Undue Achievers Typically normal undue achievers are followers of the power concept of success. There are two classic types, neither of whom may work very diligently because they are too self-centered.

The *competitive* achiever has stretched but not broken the bounds of the normal win-lose complex. A power seeker, he competes to beat others, to climb the organization pyramid. He keeps alert, avoids missteps, and attempts to show up well. In his own work, he makes modest progress neither by doing nothing nor by doing anything exceptional. A status seeker, he joins the right clubs and thinks the right thoughts. He entertains the right people.

The *impulsive* undue achiever is another classic. At first, with the way he generates ideas, he appears to be creative. As soon as he gets a new idea he tries to sell it. When the possibilities of the idea are exhausted, he does not have to wait long before a second and very different idea pops up. It too is worth a try. He views himself as a good idea man and does not like to be criticized. He tends to follow the impulse of the moment, at the mercy of his feelings.

Stage Three: Nervousness

In nervousness, the third stage of emotional health, you see a man who is slightly off his vital balance. Because of too much anxiety on the inside, he cannot effectively deal with stress from the outside.

[10] C. Wright Mills, *White Collar: The American Middle Classes*, Oxford University Press, New York, 1951.

Again, a normal or a mature person may have some aspects of nervousness beyond the normal range—as he may well have several but mild symptoms of the more severe stages of emotional ill health. He may even slide into one of these stages temporarily. All of the findings are affected by an important ingredient—age. As you grow older, you may well have to strive harder to keep the normal but rising anxieties under control, use more "relaxers" to reduce the anxieties, exercise much harder to reduce the debilities of old age, and strive more to "keep in touch with the times." To relish the "good old days" is a sign of personal emotional defeat.

As self-centered, selfish, and anxious as a normal person is, nervousness is indicated by the fact that an individual begins to show that he feels he is the center of the world rather than a part of it. Nervousness is chronic or continuing tenseness—a small but definite impairment of his own intrapersonal transactions with a distinct failure to.cope with other people and situations as the normal person would. Changes in body functions and organs may appear, such as headache, tremor, flushing, nausea, diarrhea, palpitation, itching, or sweating. The sexual function may also be affected, ranging from diminished potency to undue sexual excitement.[11]

Chronic listlessness, indifference, apathy, indecisiveness, or fatigue may be one kind of clue to nervousness. Chronic fatigue is the most frequent complaint physicians hear, according to various studies. Rest and sleep do not help. The second most frequent complaint is chronic restlessness, such as overactivity, straining, impatience, unrealistic expectations, too little time for family or personal life —or any significant kind of relaxation or re-creation. Both chronic fatigue and chronic restlessness may indicate a more severe stage of emotional ill health.

Another symptom may be in the heavy use of tranquillizers and sedatives. It would appear to be a good guess that a very heavy smoker (two or more packs a day) is in the nervousness stage at least. The same applies to the heavy constant drinker until he becomes a "prepsychotic" alcoholic who drinks to get drunk. Continuing and overwhelming feelings of unhappiness, boredom, worry, insecurity, being "put upon," being ignored, or impatience may well be clues to nervousness. To be either too thin or too fat may be clues. Both the unduly thin and unduly fat man may need more

[11] This stage is described by Menninger et al., *op. cit.*, pp. 153–173.

than the normal amount of reassurance, love, consideration, and support. Low self-esteem seems to make them unusually sensitive. Physically they may not be able to stand much pain or disapproval.

Chronic dissatisfaction covers most of the symptoms. Chronic means "of long duration or frequent occurrence." Dissatisfaction, with no positive striving to do better, includes basically yourself, others, time, and work. In your case, with the additional information you have acquired, go back and check yourself out again on Normal Work Needs, Exhibit 2, page 28. Are you sure, for example, that you are getting intrinsic job satisfaction? You might take each of the items and try to think them through in terms of you and your work situation and see whether or not you have normal work needs, with normal frustrations when these needs are not satisfied. Do you have chronic or recurring dissatisfactions beyond normal? Hold off on thinking through whether or not you have a good boss, good peers, and good subordinates. Later you will have additional means for determining your attitudes toward others.

Nervous Underachievers   The *indecisive* nervous underachiever cannot decide. For some it is a way of avoiding disapproval. For others it is an emotional inability to decide. The individual may be a pleasant, intelligent, often talkative person, or he may be reserved and diffident. For all the many commonsense formulas or special training programs on how to solve problems or make decisions, it still seems to be primarily a matter of emotions. One of the most common indicators of chronic tenseness is indecisiveness.

The *apathetic* nervous underachiever appears dull and bored. His complaints are usually few, for he is not aware that his life could be more interesting. He works below his capabilities. He may talk about his aspirations for greater success but he does nothing about them. For him life after working hours is usually one of apathy too.

Nervous Overachievers   The nervous overachiever is not an outstanding person of unusual accomplishment. Rather, he is under emotional tenseness which results in something less than effective work. Although he may appear calm, he usually tends to talk too much, argue too often, laugh too easily, lose his temper too frequently, or be erratic and restless in his movements. He may lie awake at night stewing over problems more or less real, and dream of various ways to correct situations which he regards as unpleasant for him.

The *hustler* is highly competitive. He has an intellectual rigidity, a social insensitivity, and an obsessive drive for hard work. With strict adherence to his values, he enjoys a good fight. He has an inordinate need for achievement in the concrete sense. Each new situation gives him an opportunity to demonstrate his worth and superiority over others. Not creative, he wants to stay away from himself. He prefers to discuss the personal difficulties of others. Research reports show the heavy smoker to be restless, compulsive, and thrill seeking, to change jobs more often, to hustle more than the nonsmoker, and to be more frequently hospitalized. Moreover, he tends to weigh more and to consume more alcohol, candy, fats, and coffee.

The *eager beaver* expects too much too soon. He may be verbal and personally aggressive, the "squeaking wheel." He may constantly press for more salary, promotion, or special privileges. He feels he "deserves" more. Though demanding and exploiting, he can give nothing in return, for he needs so much for himself. He resents any demands on him.

Stage Four: Psychosomatic

A psychosomatic is a neurotic whose unduly anxious mind has generated a bodily reaction. It may be functional in that there are no organic or physical changes in the body. There may also be organic changes. Asthma, hay fever, and allergies are usually viewed as psychosomatic.

Psychosomatic Underachievers The *hypochondriac* is the best-known psychosomatic underachiever. He has numerous vague aches and pains with no organic changes. Both his work capacity and work relationships are limited by his depressed feelings. Although he believes he is depressed because he does not feel well, actually he does not feel well because of repressed hostility. On his boss, as on his physician, he may place the responsibility for his health in an unsuccessful attempt to satisfy his dependency needs.

The *functional neurotic* has some organ which misbehaves in a functional way without any organic or physical change. He may have, among many things, chronic nervous indigestion, colitis, an anxious stomach, or an anxious heart. Cardiac neurosis is found in people who have all the discomforts of a person with high blood pressure, but none of the physical symptoms show up in the examination.

Psychosomatic Overachievers The *sickness prone,* whose badge of business is often an ulcer or high blood pressure, is a psychosomatic overachiever. Other organic diseases include such afflictions as diabetes and chronic arthritis. There is an organic or physical change for the sickness prone. While he appears to be all business, keen, and highly competitive, he really is tense and rigid. There are also relaxed types who are not overachievers. The ulcer prone is on the horns of a dilemma. He wants to dominate and yet be dependent, to be cared for.

Hypertension can exist for a long time with no symptoms beyond those in a typical emotional disturbance: headaches, dizziness, insomnia, and fatigue. Once inner tenseness finds an outlet in high blood pressure, rest and reassurance offer little hope. The high blood pressure personality strives for position, prestige, and economic success. He is highly competitive and hard driving. Yet, he is usually unsuccessful when he does compete and restless if he does not.[12] He tends to be aggressive and hostile. Because these feelings are intense and near the surface, he goes to great lengths to deny or keep his hostility under control.

Then there is the *twitcher,* who bats his eyes, bites his nails, has a tic, twitches, or blushes. In addition, he has the more common nervous digestive disorders, such as diarrhea, cramps, and vomiting. More extreme manifestations are amnesia, hysterical blindness, or lameness. The twitcher tends to be emotionally unstable and erratic. He is easily influenced by suggestions of others but is unpredictable, reacting emotionally rather than logically. He may be a poor worker but he usually tries hard.

Stage Five: Neurotic

Rational as he may appear to be, the neurotic usually suffers from deeper tensions and anxieties than the psychosomatic. He may be

[12] Sydney Pell and C. Anthony D'Alonzo, "Acute Myocardial Infarction in a Large Industrial Population," *Journal of the American Medical Association,* vol. 185, no. 11, Sept. 14, 1963, pp. 831–838.

aware of his troubled state but not of its hidden elements. A few definitions are in order. A neurotic has lost communication with himself.[13] He tends to pain the environment almost as much as he pains himself and requires both expensive compensatory living and tension-reducing devices.[14] He needs *power over* others to attempt to satisfy his neurotic needs.[15] Although a neurotic hurts himself and others, he may channel his crippled and less efficient personal attributes into acceptable work channels.

Neurotic Underachievers   The *worrier* is one of the most common neurotic underachievers. He is a man in search of something to worry about. He may well have some psychosomatic problem as well. He worries during the greater part of his waking hours, often suffering from fitful or persistent insomnia. There may be exaggerated perceptions such as undue sensitivity or alarm about events to the point where some things become painfully overdrawn. Worrying to the point where it becomes repetitive thinking is common. More effort is exerted than the results warrant. Worrying and perfectionism appear to go hand in hand. Even though the worrier appears friendly, he tends to be skeptical and distrustful of others. Although he may appear confident, he finds it difficult to make decisions. He is inclined to be moody and irritable. His free-floating anxiety is apprehensive, pessimistic, and dreading.

The *sideliner* has withdrawn from life. He may be lazy, shy, or an odd ball. A lazy person suffers from chronic fatigue, lives in his own preoccupied world, lacks drive, or procrastinates. If you look beneath the surface, you find that he is afraid of disapproval and is very insecure in social situations. The shy neurotic underachiever has a marked tendency to avoid involvements. Commitments might reduce his freedom to get out of the way when trouble threatens. He tends to take a passive role in any conflict. The odd ball usually has been subjected to much ridicule earlier in life. He may be the seclusive individual who has retreated into a world of his own and views others with dislike or hatred. He is not like the rest of us and

[13] F. J. Roethlisberger and Carl R. Rogers, "Barriers and Gateways to Communication," *Harvard Business Review,* July-August, 1952, pp. 18ff.

[14] Menninger et al., *op. cit.,* p. 162.

[15] Erich Fromm, M.D., *Man for Himself,* Holt, Rinehart and Winston, Inc., New York, 1947, p. 88.

does not want to be. If he is a lone wolf, he may be a lonely, wistful outsider who wants to get into the swim but cannot because of illusions of inferiority. He may be a ne'er-do-well, the executive who seems to have almost everything, yet does not quite make it. Or, unable to accept responsibility, he may be a buck passer using malingering or tricks to cover up his undependability or inefficiency.

Neurotic Overachievers The *work addict* is a contagious overachiever who expects his subordinates to overwork too. He is the one who takes on more than he can really handle. He usually cannot meet deadlines, make decisions, or be creative. Moreover, he is unable to delegate and unable to learn. Although he says he loves his work, he has fled from life and himself into his work. He puts in unduly long hours to escape from his family, his community, and himself.

The *neurotic competitor* is another common overachiever. He wants to get recognition, command attention, and control others. Following the power concept of success, he sets his sights upward, using each new job to show proficiency for a higher position. He does not enjoy the plateau of the current job. He is never satisfied with himself or his success. He adds a neurotic acceleration to his basic competitive drive. Realizing how unhappy he will be if he does not win, he works at it night and day and weekends. If he is not too impolitic, his emotionally driven, single-minded devotion to domination enables him to win.[16]

Stage Six: "Prepsychotic"

Of all the terms used to describe the incipient psychotic, "prepsychotic" appears to be the best. Even though "psychotic" is not accepted by some experts, it continues to be used. The people in these categories have never reached adulthood emotionally, or if they have they are regressing to childhood. The prepsychotic is able to function in the business world unless he becomes a psychotic. Then he is unemployable. Prepsychotics tend to hold rather bizarre beliefs which enable them to ignore or avoid others, require excessive

---

[16] C. Knight Aldrich, M.D., "The Neurotic Competitor in the World of Business," *Executive Behavior, Selected Papers*, no. 5, Graduate School of Business, University of Chicago, Chicago, 2d printing, April, 1966, p. 9.

behavior of them, hurt them, or blandly violate all the rules of the game.

"Prepsychotic" Underachievers The *moody* underachiever has long periods of depression. For him, life's burdens make cooperative working relationships and job satisfactions almost nonexistent. Among the moody is the talkative, dynamic, brilliant, hard-working man with a sunny disposition who often exhibits bad judgment and overbearing behavior. Often he becomes a hothead, impatient and belligerent, even irritable and pugnacious. Or, he becomes pessimistic, seeing only the dark side of life. He may become so despondent that it is nearly impossible for him to do his job. He gets no ideas; he cannot make decisions. He seeks the advice of others on the smallest pretext. Suicide is the danger for the moody man.

The *alcoholic* is an all-too-common underachiever. When a man drinks to get drunk, he is an alcoholic. (Or he may use drugs.) He is anxious about his relationships with others because of his own low self-esteem. He turns to alcohol to dull the pain of reality and to give him gratification in fantasy. Although he tends to be a lovable, charming fellow on the surface, he can love no one but himself. Hence, he gets little real satisfaction from associating with others or in achieving.

"Prepsychotic" Overachievers The *egotist,* loving only himself, cannot have any affection for others. A large number of egotists are playboys who cannot keep their work and their play separated because they never really learned how to work. The Don Juans need to be loved but can give no love in return. They use the sex act to promote their self-esteem, or to cover up anxieties about homosexuality or virility. The romantic Don Juan was not primarily a lover. He had unyielding pride, a need to subjugate others, a provocative love of fighting, a need to dominate. Sex was of secondary importance. An egotist is a disrupting force in the work world. He must dominate and requires much admiration. Wanting to be the center of attention, he is a show-off. He is too self-centered to accept or understand anyone else. Basically amoral, he has contempt, even hatred, for others. He can hurt anybody without a twinge of conscience. He can be ruthless, calculating, demanding, aggressive, ornery, or bullying. He may be an opportunist, climbing the ladder of success over the knives he has slipped in the backs of others. He may be a troublemaker, razzer, teaser, prankster, gossip monger, stool pigeon, rowdy, gambler, or liar.

The *suspicious* overachiever has chronic distrust of others. The suspicious individual is unable to put himself in another's place or understand another's feelings. Yet, he is easily hurt and frustrated by others. Nor can he think clearly, because he is tortured by doubt and suspicion. When a person holds persistently to his suspicions, he may be in the beginning stage of a slowly developing system of false beliefs. Delusions of persecution may start him on the subtle path to the paranoid.

Stage Seven: Unemployable

There are psychosomatics and neurotics whose conditions have become severe enough to make it impossible for them to work. Some suffer from the so-called nervous breakdown. With professional care, which might include shock treatment, they may rather quickly return to the work world. Some may do so without professional assistance. The psychotic has a rougher time. Not only does he cease or fail to develop, he tends to regress toward babyhood. Meanwhile, if he is unduly aggressive, he can do damage to himself or others. Each of those outlined in the prepsychotic stage become psychotics if they exercise overly aggressive tendencies. They may indulge in assaults, social offenses, or outbursts to such an extent that they are unemployable. Their behavior is featured on television but not tolerated in business life. Aggression is frequently directed against self. In the United States there are two times as many suicides as murders. It is among the top ten killers—highest among the rich and almost unknown among the very poor. As for murders, four-fifths of them are committed by close relatives.

Professional Assistance

If you think you have an emotional problem, consider professional assistance. The kinds of help generally available are outlined in the next chapter under special aids.

10

Work, Relax, and Re-create Yourself

> My experience is that the more the phony self evaporates, the more the real self becomes invested with interest and the more unbridled an incentive emerges to unfold by becoming free from internal bondages, to live as full a life as given circumstances permit.—KAREN HORNEY, M.D., *Self-analysis* [1]

IF YOU ARE ABLE to think through the knowledge of the last several chapters in terms of yourself—it will require study and reflection—you should have substantially more self-awareness. Here the emphasis is on how to help yourself survive the business rat race with more peace of mind through

1. Activity aids—new habits for old
2. Mental aids—mental moves toward autonomy
3. Special aids—therapy and counseling
4. External aids—others

If you can face yourself at all, you should now be able to think your way through these stages of self-awareness: success, work needs,

[1] W. W. Norton & Company, Inc., New York, 1942, p. 23.

career, some of your intrapersonal transactions, your stage of emotional health, and your brand of achiever. A pattern should emerge for you. How close are you to the ideal of the maturation concept of success and the mature achiever?

For many of you who are, in the main, normal achievers, the great problem is underutilization at work. You have these choices. Get another job. Try to help others more, as I shall suggest shortly, and thereby try to enrich your job. At least you can enrich your personal and family lives, as I shall also suggest later, so that being underutilized is offset by fuller utilization outside working hours.

Very few of you, I suspect, are essentially low or underachievers. If you are, it would be highly unlikely that you would read this book or any other of this type. But if you are, the place for you to start is to help yourself move to more normal states of achievement. Helping others to help you, as outlined in Part 4, may be a good way. You might seek special counsel, suggested later. At least you might try to do more for yourself off the job in terms of utilizing yourself. Managing your total time for not only work and relaxation but also re-creation might well be the answer if you start slowly.

For those of you who lean toward undue or overachieving, the moral is clear: slow down your business rat race and live! And let others live. Help others as much as possible so as to reduce your striving for aggression, domination, recognition, status, and power, the marks of the power concept of success.

Activity Aids

In whatever stage of emotional health you may find yourself, move toward autonomy and reduce your own rat race.

Relaxed Behavior Pattern   For many of you the basic problem is tenseness. Go back to the hurrying habits of those afflicted with chronic tenseness or nervousness. Check yours off. Develop new relaxed habits for the hurrying habits you have. Start gradually and on a small scale. Otherwise, you will have just another set of New Year's resolutions.

A key to evidence of tenseness is impatience with yourself and others. Make a studied practice of a leisurely pace at work. This is especially important as the demands by others for your time increase. Avoid where you can those situations where you are likely to receive disapproval. Avoid, too, when possible, people with whom you feel incompatible. Try to avoid unpleasant people and unpleasant situations. Conflict, competition, and pressure from others are all forms of disapproval of you. External stress causing tenseness abounds. Competition, struggle for power, blame, unreasonable demands or deadlines, underutilization, and a feeling of being continuously on trial are some of the many devices which are used knowingly or unknowingly by management to "motivate" people, to keep them under stress. Actually, they are detrimental to your emotional health. It does not mean that you must become a yes-man or an organization conformist. It does mean that you give deliberate thought to those times when you must have a difference of opinion with others and where feasible reduce the number of opportunities.

Plan and Budget Your Total Time   One of the worst things about the business rat race is that work for many men is unlimited in time. Work, as we have seen, does not make unusual physical or intellectual demands, but does make emotional demands. You have seen where a man can escape from everything else into work and become a work addict. For many men their emotional needs compel them to put too much time into too much detail. They claim that it is fun. You, too, can claim that you are having too much fun at work to want to slack off. Still, when you put in more than regular hours at work and work-related effort, you are sacrificing other things which over the long pull are vital to your survival and emotional health. Both the number of hours you work and the way you put in your work time are manifestations of either your own thoughtlessness or lack of emotional security, or both.

Start to budget your time for work to the normal hours plus a few more for work-related matters, such as reading trade journals, emergencies, entertaining, and management development. Start by leaving your briefcase at the office every so often. Increase the number of times you do not take your case home. Do not mix work and play to the point where you can no longer distinguish between the social times you spend with personal friends (who cannot help your business) and business friends (who can). Budget your time as you budget your money. If you cannot budget your money either, I urge you to start there, for that is easier than budgeting your time.

If you feel you cannot budget your total work time, you have not faced the reality of survival any more than those who say they do not have enough money to get the things they want. For all but a few men, money is limited. Those who budget and spend carefully end up in better financial shape and have more than those who go on impulsively, emotionally buying what they want and never having enough. As with money, there are definite and surprisingly short limits to time. You cannot afford to make many missteps with your time. It is your life.

Relaxation and Re-creation at Work   When you think through most of the articles about how better to use your time on the job, you must conclude that they are another device for the speedup and the stretch-out—namely, how to gear yourself up to do more each day. Plan your work time, including that away from the office, so that you consciously and conscientiously follow a balanced plan for your job —relaxation, work, and re-creation, as shown in Exhibit 9. These are some suggestions on how to help yourself through your mind, your body, and other people. Walking and other noncompetitive exercises are multipurpose: (1) they can maintain, or if vigorous enough, rebuild your body; (2) they can reduce undue, periodic tenseness; (3) they enable you to have more energy and work with greater sense of well-being. Walking as much as possible at work slows down the work pace. Walking with awareness is a special kind of re-creation for the mind—going slowly enough to cultivate awareness of the environment where you are, the here and now and not somewhere else. Within the office building it means to be aware of what is going on around you, the people as human beings and their need for others, the artistic efforts of good pictures and decor if your office building is blessed with such. When you walk outside, if your building is in a downtown location, get to a park. Then think only of your present environment. Try to see things through your own eyes as you did as a young child. Then you are aware.

Plan Your Work Your Way   Accept the fact that you can do only a few things and do them well. Trying to do too many things builds tenseness from pressing too hard and from disappointing results.

Exhibit 9   RELAXATION, WORK, AND RE-CREATION IN YOUR WORK LIFE

	Relaxation	Work	Re-creation
Through: Your Mind	Varied work pace (Chap. 3)	Chaps. 3 and 4	Management and technical growth (Chaps. 5–7)
	Daydreaming	Leisurely work pace	Walking with awareness
	Relaxed behavior pattern Goofing off mentally	Near normal work hours	Mental aids
	Taking a walk when tensed up	Modest daily goals	
Your Body	Consciously resting, stretching	Walking whenever possible	Long, fast walks before or after lunch; using stairs
	Napping, if possible, when tired	Walk, don't phone within office	Exercise at noon: swimming, jogging (Chap. 15)
Other People	Coffee breaks with no shop talk *	Helping others (Chaps. 11–14)	Helping others to help you (Chaps. 11–14)
	Lunching with friends, not co-workers	Stopping the win-lose complex	Counseling or therapy
	Joking with associates	Avoiding conflict where possible	Learning from others
	Looking for humor in situations		
	Keeping in touch with family, friends		

* Some physicians are concerned about the negative effects of "caffeine addiction."

Crisis management is self-defeating. Plan your work day, but set modest goals for what you personally want to accomplish. Allow much time for the increasing demands of others—your boss, peers, and subordinates. Because everyone approaches his work, as everything else, in a different way, I can only outline some general suggestions. There is no *one best way*. Do some of the obvious things: (1) Do not do anything that does not need to be done. (2) Set priorities, the more important things first. (3) Delegate to others what they can do and at the same time enrich their jobs. (4) Try to reserve long periods of time when you can do your own work with as few interruptions as possible. (5) Give time to others to help them.

When faced with a new task either small or large, examine your work load. It is easy to assume that you can handle almost anything that comes along. Remember you have only so much time, energy, and capacity. Do not sow the seeds of your own destruction. More often than not men founder and slip emotionally on the little extra pressures they encounter rather than on the big pressures.

Remember, too, that you are evaluated on everything that you do. You are always on trial. If you do something well, you probably will be asked to do another assignment. And then another. You are expected to do them all well. Too often a man who performs brilliantly in one field is believed to have the aptitude to do everything. Yet, if you do just one assignment poorly, you may be branded a failure. Discover your own interests and strengths and capitalize on them.

Suit the task to your mood. Do what comes naturally after you have thought through how you work the best. For example, if you are not creative, do not attempt creative work. Tackle the difficult or unpleasant when you are at your peak. Each of us has a cycle of energy. Some of us do our best the first thing in the morning. For others, morning is torture. For some, the first of the week is the time for work; for others, the last of the week. In addition to the fluctuations in mood, you will have times when tenseness piles up. An obvious way to help you relieve that tenseness is to get away for a little while. But keep active so that you do not sit and brood. Help comes from a change of scenery and a change of pace. Walk or exercise your tenseness off.

Mental Aids

Behavior, values, emotions—none of these occur by chance, though the cause may be very obscure. What have you done for yourself lately? Ask yourself such questions as these:

During the past decade what significant views I once held have I changed?

Do the little things on the job now bother me?

Do I feel that I am no longer getting enough attention from others?

Do I wonder if I boast too much? Or belittle myself too much?

Do my disappointments crush me? Do they obsess me?

Do I feel that I now talk, complain, or gossip more?

Do I have a chip on my shoulder?

This sample list of questions offers you the opportunity to determine if you have been slipping emotionally. These kinds of questions are another approach to your becoming more aware of yourself. The questions enable you to think through the trend of your own emotional and mental direction. Is it downward?

The hard fact is that no one can help you *unless* you can help yourself. Autonomy is possible only when you accept your aloneness and take those steps which will lead toward maturity. In order to mature emotionally, you learn to suppress some impulses, to endure some frustrations, and to resist some temptations. In making conscious constructive choices, you renounce discipline from the outside and emotional dominance from the inside for your own self-discipline. For example, you can renounce a dependency, a phony aspect of yourself or a neurotic strategy, and then discover that you can live as a freer self. You then can choose with greater freedom what you want to do with your own life.

If you can accept your feelings as facts, you may well be able to gain some control over your negative emotions. If you have repressed your feelings as many have, work to rediscover them, to become more aware of the intensity of your feelings. It is generally conceded that negative feelings cause tenseness. The key to their resolution lies in your bringing them up to the conscious level so that you can think them through or talk them out with yourself and others. To enable you to become more aware of your true feelings, to accept them as facts, here are some constructive choices.

From Organization Dependence to Autonomy The feeling of loyalty for a company often is a euphemism for unwarranted dependency upon a company. Dependency may satisfy a longing to be perpetually taken care of. But its promise of happiness is almost always fictitious. A feeling of job insecurity may be the result. On the other hand, some corporations all but dictate the circumstances of most management people's lives. Choices which are against the expressed or unexpressed ways of corporate life tend to make an individual feel guilty or insecure. Many people avoid facing the realities of corporate dependence. They talk the "independence game" and may even be quite critical of corporate life. Autonomy requires that you do not become dependent on the corporation.

From Standards of Others to Your Own If you are going to mature, you need consciously to drop the standards your parents set for you and develop your own. Move away from "oughts" or "ought to be," "I ought to be good," or "I have to be good." [2] It is primarily a struggle against one's own childhood dependency. This is a long process of personal growth to a higher level of maturity, conscious re-education, finding new insights, making conscious decisions, and self-discipline.[3]

To accept and try to live by standards of the business world and society means to meet the dictates and expectations of others. Surely you need people. You may err by placing too much emphasis on "fitting in." In contrast, autonomy means to live fully in each moment as an individual who cares greatly about inner integrity and freedom. You accept the necessity for your own decisions about yourself. Only in this way can you become a more fully functioning person, learning to live in the reality of the present moment.

From Loneliness to Solitude To be in contact with many people and still be lonely is a form of retreat or withdrawal. Fear of self-expres-

[2] Carl R. Rogers, *On Becoming a Person,* Houghton Mifflin Company, Boston, 1961, p. 168.
[3] Rollo May, *Man's Search for Himself,* W. W. Norton & Company, Inc., New York, 1953, p. 136.

sion is a good case in point. A severe form of loneliness is to withdraw physically by avoiding friends. Autonomy is to be interdependent, recognize it, and still seek solitude on occasion. There are distinct differences between loneliness and solitude. Active people who have good relations with others must periodically withdraw, seek solitude, in order to re-create themselves. For example, it has been found that book readers have a surprisingly great number of contacts with other people. Lonely people do not read books. There are also creative people who seek solitude for contemplation, to think and create. They like and need to be alone at times because they have to think things through.

A mature person can sit alone, apparently doing nothing, and enjoy it. He distinguishes the real from the false, the important from the trivial, realizing that his stability depends on how much he can find counsel in himself. Search for meaning is through continuous and critical self-questioning.

The lonely person is caught and bored. For many, loneliness is such a painful threat that it is frightening. John Donne was right in stating that no man is an island. But Thomas Wolfe was right, too, when he said that every man is an island. Because of differences in intelligence, capacities, interests, and anxieties and because aloneness is so peculiarly an individual thing, no man should ever expect to be fully accepted by others. By the same token he cannot relate totally and effectively with them.

From Boredom to Curiosity   If you can regain some of the curiosity you had as a child, you appreciate the common things of life. You have an uncommon awareness about the commonplace. You find a sunset beautiful, a flower lovely, your wife still surprisingly lovely. Then you have a better awareness of reality and are more comfortable with it than others. You are able to see concealed or confused realities swiftly and correctly. You accept your own human nature with its shortcomings without real concern. Still, you will handle one situation well and be highly emotional in another. Autonomy does not mean that you are free from worry and difficulties any more than it means that you are happy all the time. For you, however, the least likely problem is boredom.[4]

[4] These points are a consensus from authors cited earlier, such as Maslow, Berne, and Rogers.

From Opinion to Reflection When something happens with which you disagree, think of those conditions which might make you react favorably. Or try to see both sides of the issue. Develop facts, knowledge, and reasoning, not emotions or stereotypes. All of us say that we like people; yet many of us do not and do not know it. To hold prejudices, for example, is to hate. The person prone to hatred has a considerable amount of hostility, using some racial or religious group as the means for discharging deep feelings of aggression. He tends to spread his hatred to anything alien to his values.

Moreover, the less you understand and accept people as they are, the more you tend to expect of them. To demand too much of people means that you will eventually distrust them. Only when you have modest expectations about people can you be tolerant. It is an elementary principle that feelings of guilt, often irrational in origin, can make you want to find and punish in others what you most fear in yourself. Strong convictions make it difficult for you to see others as they really are. You construct a false perception of them. You then see in others what you expect to see; you hear from others what you expect to hear.

Special Aids

Almost every book or article on securing help with your tenseness recommends that you "talk it out." [5] You should have someone who can listen skillfully to you, counsel with you. Contrary to popular suggestions about the use of your secretary, friend, wife, or boss in this capacity, not just anyone will do. The listener should be a "good" listener. He will not make value judgments about you or inadvertently hurt you. He can listen skillfully and maintain confidences. With his help, you come to think objectively about your problem and the relationship between your actions and attitudes. Skills for lay personal counseling are discussed in the next chapter.

[5] The treatment phases of the behavioral sciences, described in Chapter 6, are discussed in more detail here. As for my biases, I side with psychiatry. I went through psychoanalysis. Also I tried sensitivity training in its early years. Finally, my own education in "professional" counseling, or therapy, came in my graduate work in sociology where I specialized in social work with a few months' work as a trainee before I went into management.

Counseling or Therapy   Beyond securing true lay counseling where you can, there are trained counselors: clinical psychologists, social workers, psychiatrists, and psychoanalysts. But here again you face a confusing situation. Let me try to outline for you my findings.

Many kinds of psychologists are not educated to be counselors. Hence, when you think about the help a particular psychologist might provide you, ask him about his training in counseling. For example, as near as I can determine, industrial psychologists and social psychologists are not usually formally trained to be counselors. The same applies to economists, anthropologists, political scientists, sociologists, and behavioral scientists. Some of these specialists may have secured formal training in counseling. Social workers are trained to be counselors. Psychiatrists with their medical training as a base view themselves as practicing a higher form of counseling, psychotherapy. Yet, both psychologists and social workers maintain they practice psychotherapy.

Start with the inescapable fact that it is all therapy, even the lay counseling mentioned earlier, if the purpose is to help you become more aware of your real self with no thought of your helping in return. Still, accept the fact that there are strong differences of opinion not only between the specialists but also among them. Even the counseling services offered by your company may not be the best for you. Hence, if you want some special assistance, you might do well to investigate the resources available to you in your community. You might start with the family welfare agency or a local mental health association. In all likelihood they would suggest individual counseling resources in the community and give you some idea of the nature of their services. You might start with your physician, perhaps by asking him to recommend a therapist.

Psychoanalysis and Psychiatry   Psychoanalysis is primarily concerned with the treatment of emotional ill health stemming from the "unfinished business" of childhood. People are at the mercy of their dated emotions. Psychoanalysts help a person deal with unconscious materials and thereby resolve his problems. You do free association on a couch for many fifty-minute hours. You focus on dreams. You say whatever comes to your mind, be it improper, unconventional, or impolite. The analyst detects unconscious thoughts and emotions through connecting the random associations.

Psychiatrists, as well as some social workers, behavioral scientists, and some psychologists, go through analysis as part of their training. Most of these consider analysis one of the greatest helps they have ever had. At least this is what many analysts have heard from these normal students. They achieve a greater sense of well-being, and a higher level of happiness and knowledge about themselves and others.

The nonanalytic psychiatrists, generally referred to as psychiatrists, practice psychotherapy or counseling on conscious material. There are other forms of therapy such as shock treatment. Drug therapy has enabled many people to be outside of institutions, even though they may not be cured. Seeking psychiatric help for temporary emotional problems is becoming increasingly accepted. Psychotherapists are generally agreed that their goal is no longer only to help a person become a happy man, nor even to achieve a "cure." Psychotherapy does not free a man to ignore the conventions of our society. Nor does a psychiatrist decide which life activity a man should choose. It is a case of growing to the point where he has sufficient knowledge about himself to make choices closer to the realities of himself and his situation. About two out of three people improve, according to the estimates from the profession. They come to feel better without necessarily solving their internal problems completely.

Clinical Psychologists and Social Workers Psychiatrists and all but a very few psychoanalysts are physicians first. Hence, they consider not only the emotional or mental health of a person but his physical being. In contrast clinical psychologists and social workers are not physicians. Social workers typically work with the family. They may aid a psychiatrist by helping a patient "adjust" to the outside world. The clinical psychologist in a mental hospital usually reports to and is supervised by a psychiatrist. In the community, clinical psychologists have their own counseling practice.

If you dig deeper, you will find claims and counterclaims not only between the various specialist groups but also among the specialists of the same group. Yet if you find someone who really listens to you, accepting you for what you are, you gradually become more aware of yourself. You drop your defensive rationalizations and work through the barriers to your genuine self. You learn, for example, to recognize more clearly when you are anxious, depressed, tense, or even angry when you have no good basis for being so. Or you may become aware of these kinds of feelings which you may have denied or repressed. You accept more of yourself.

Group Therapy   Group therapy is essentially a group of patients trying to work out their problems together under supervision of a group therapist or counselor. The groups usually consist of from four to ten people. Before he enters the group, a patient's physical condition is checked, and he has an interview with a psychiatrist. Most groups meet once a week. This type of treatment is still considered experimental.

There is also the popular sensitivity or T-group training.[6] Some of the sensitivity trainers want the sessions to be reworked to use true group counseling. As of now the training tends to emphasize the group aspect of learning. Individual behavior at the conscious level is explored both in terms of (1) learning in a "laboratory" training session how to relate to each other so the group can move forward, and (2) "leveling," where a person learns how others feel about his actual behavior. However, there are now all kinds of sessions, including "encounter" sessions, put on by all kinds of people.

Sensitivity training, in the main, consists of taking a group of executives from various companies to an out-of-the-way, resort-type setting. They are stripped of all the status-bearing accessories that get in the way of open relationships. Unstructured groups are formed, generally under the loose direction of a behavioral scientist. Interpersonal inquiry, informality, and expression of feelings and comments on the behavior of participants are all encouraged. The idea is to "open up" the executive, to enable him to go home and level with his fellow workers, thereby performing better as a person and as a producer. Individuals are expected to learn from each other rather than from the trainer. The group determines its own learning goals, method of operation, and the nature of the "feedback."

Although the total effectiveness of sensitivity courses has not been measured, the longer courses should be helpful *if* a person is emotionally capable of handling this type of often stressful experience. However, there is usually no screening or preparation as in

---

[6] I went through a helpful three-week session in the early years of the program.

group therapy. Except for some reportedly limited, partial experiments, sensitivity training experiences do not involve the power relationship of the boss and subordinate.

Sensitivity training, which got its start after World War II, has always had its critics and still does. Some view it as a dangerous plaything. Some observers feel that it may do more harm than good. As yet there are only arguments for and against but no significant impartial research. With what you are finding out about people here, you can well ask: Am I likely to learn more readily when I am under stress? After what you have seen about the business rat race, and the power struggle which is not only condoned but encouraged in many companies, you may well conclude that for your company sensitivity training is inappropriate. It might be better to start by working toward a behavioral sciences management system for your own organization. Outline to those involved the essential differences—there are many—and then help the management people to see the differences and gradually go through a transition process whereby they practice behavioral sciences management, much of which is outlined here.

part 4

Help Yourself
by Helping Others

*Our businesses are so close to us, so much a thing
of our daily work life, that only with difficulty can
we see the awkwardness of our working relationships.
We are accustomed to the present system of clumsy
relations which reduces inherent and spontaneous
cooperation to competition, or at best, reluctant
acquiescence. What we like to do is to think that
with extensive controls and complex organization
structure, organizations function harmoniously, or
at least as harmoniously as possible. Actually it is in
the dysfunctioning of organizations where one of the
greatest productivity potentials exists.*
—ROBERT C. SAMPSON, *The Staff Role in
Management* [1]

UP TO THIS POINT you have been presented with ways and
means to survive the business rat race. You have had
suggestions as to how you can help yourself in your work
life through your mind and your body. Here, you can now
directly reduce the business rat race for yourself and others.
The prescription is that you help yourself by helping others. I propose a selfish kind of helping. Help others where
they in turn help you directly or indirectly.

You can use what you have already learned about people
for guidance—now, however, in terms of others. From what
you have discovered, you should be able, with some experi-

[1] Harper & Row, Publishers, Incorporated, New York, 1955, p. 67.

menting, to determine those you can help who will in turn help you, those you cannot help, and those who will take advantage of you if you try to help them. Start with the assumption that however a person may be behaving, he is doing the best he can. You have seen enough evidence as to how inflexible man's personality is, how fragile is his emotional structure, how highly anxious and insecure normal man is. You know now how adversely a man reacts to domination, pressure, manipulation, stress, or disapproval.

You will probably find more people than you may think who will respond positively to your being helpful. Remember that man generally wants approval and wants to avoid disapproval. He wants to do work that will utilize his capabilities. With an egoistic need for friendship and acceptance by others, he is anxious. I find that many people have great interest in learning how to be helpful. They are hurting and they do not know how to stop. Remember, too, that relationships between people are viewed by behavioral scientists in the main as difficult and sometimes even harmful. Hence, one of the greatest boons for you is improving these relationships. Moreover, helping your boss, subordinates, and peers get the business done efficiently and effectively is the essence of an organization. An organization is the basis for mutual collaboration where everyone has the opportunity to make his contribution.

Accept emotionally dependent relationships with meaningful people, but accept them as an adult, not as a child. It is not a question of competition or the win-lose complex. Rather, your primary question is, "How can I help?" As part of developing your autonomy, strive to relate yourself spontaneously and intimately with others, freely expressing your own feelings and accepting, without threat to yourself, the feelings and thoughts of others. You understand them for what they are without praise or blame, seeking to help them because some of them will help you.

11

Help Where You Can

Instead of being critical about the other person's behavior, search out the good points and help him develop them. This will give both of you satisfaction,
and help you gain a better perspective on yourself as
well.   —GEORGE S. STEVENSON, M.D.,
How to Deal with Your Tensions [1]

HELPING YOUR BOSS, your subordinates, and your peers calls for special considerations. In each chapter in this part you will find four
basic conditions for helping: (1) whether you are able and interested in helping another because you will benefit from it; (2)
whether the other person is able and interested in being helped and
helping you in turn; (3) your organization roles; [2] and (4) the ways
you help—and can be helped—in your interpersonal transactions.

Transactions

There are four universal transactions: how you behave, communicate, participate, and counsel. [3] Exhibit 10 lists these four plus the

[1] National Association for Mental Health, New York, 1958, p. 7.
[2] See Chapter 14, Exhibit 13, for the summary listing.
[3] These are an extension of the Transaction Triad in Chapter 8.

Exhibit 10   Transaction Goals

	Universal Transactions			
	Behaving	Communicating	Participating	Counseling
1. Present stage	Maskmanship	Talk to persuade	Win-lose complex	Advice
2. Claimed stage	Openness	Listen to understand	Cooperation	Problem-solving
3. Ideal stage	Help	Level or feedback	Consensus	Personal counseling

	Key Organization Role Transactions *			
	Subordinate-Boss (12)	Boss-Subordinate (13)	Boss-Subordinate Staff (14)	Peer-Peer (14)
1. Present stage	Comply	Control	Coordinate	Rivalry
2. Claimed stage	Conform	Interdependence	Teamwork	Diplomacy
3. Ideal stage	Commit	Job-man budget	Integration	Mutuality

* Numbers indicate chapters where these role transactions are covered. The other key organization role transaction, staff, is discussed in this chapter. All the organization roles are listed in Exhibit 13, Chapter 14.

key organization roles. Note the three stages: (1) the present stage, where almost all of us are, according to behavioral sciences research; (2) the claimed stage, where most of us believe we are; and (3) the ideal stage, the ultimate goal in each transaction. Because many of the words and phrases of each stage are often used loosely, I shall describe each stage.

The Human Side of Your Organization   A major barrier to going beyond the first stage in any of the transactions is determined by the nature of the human side of your organization. Take a reading so that you can see how far you can generally go in being helpful— and being helped, not hurt, in turn. The key is the level of aggressiveness and competition within the company. If the level is high, not only are people hurt, but the organization also suffers in efficiency and effectiveness.

As another major hurdle in your own situation, you may well find that the present ways of thinking, behaving, and working are so deeply entrenched that, as students of anthropology know, they have become rigid cultural patterns. The relationships of the individuals have become so fixed, as students of sociology know, that the individuals may perpetuate them against any odds. The behavior of individuals may be so molded by personal habit or so compulsive from chronic tenseness, as students of psychiatry know, that individuals must repeat them over and over again even though they serve no useful purpose.

To move to stage two and eventually to stage three requires trust. You cannot start trusting others unless you have evidence that you can trust them. You need to feel that people are trustworthy and trusting. Research has rediscovered the axiom that distrust and lack of confidence lead people to "play it close to the chest."

Behaving   Maskmanship, stage one of behaving, the first transaction, is almost always used in business transactions. If you are in an uncomfortable situation, you consciously keep your guard up, using more maskmanship than is normally used. A person with low self-esteem has been found to practice a high level of maskmanship. He cannot talk about himself with others. On the other hand, a person who has high self-esteem tends to be more open with others. To put it another way, the more you try to be open, stage two, to be genuine in the acceptance of the feelings of others and expression of your own feelings where circumstances permit, the greater will be your own self-esteem. To learn to be open with others means to accept them for what they are and how they feel. Only then can you practice one of the best means to self-awareness, to talk about yourself and your feelings, your own problems and concerns. When you work to get others to accept you for what you are, you accept them for what they are. In turn, when others open up about themselves, the greater insight gained leads to an understanding of them. The intimacy of the maturation concept of success is essentially the same as openness. The ideal, stage three, helping is our basic concern in this and the next several chapters.

Communicating   At the first stage of communicating, you talk to persuade another. You want to be understood. Because what you know or think is right, your view should predominate. You unthinkingly start with the giving end and are frustrated when your message, based on your attitudes, values, feelings, and needs, is not getting across. If your recipient does not like the content of the message or the way in which it is issued, he feels threatened. Then he resists, by replying with something totally irrelevant, by arguing, or by ignoring. Resistance implies criticism of your message and results in a communication deadlock. You undoubtedly do the same.

What most of us do not realize is what poor listeners we really are. As touched on earlier, almost no one has had any training in how to listen. Not only do we not want to listen, we are not able to listen. We become bored when the subject is not of immediate interest. We let our minds wander, looking for distractions. We avoid feelings and emotions. We hear what we want to hear, interpreting what we hear our own way. We let emotional words block us, and we challenge that with which we do not agree. We prepare our answers instead of listening. We interrupt because we would rather talk than listen.

The second stage of communicating, listen to understand, is where you try to be sure that you really understand another. This is not simple, for, at best, you communicate from your awareness of yourself, the particular situation, and the other person. Effective communication is molded not to what you logically want to say but to the attitudes and perception of the listener. Only when you give him an opportunity to tell you what his understanding is, his way of seeing things, can there be effective communication.

The third stage of communicating, leveling, is also known as feedback. Based upon openness, the ideal is to develop where possible those relationships where you can help another person by revealing the impact of his behavior on you and how you feel about it and vice versa. Each of you, then, can test your awareness and your resulting act against the reactions of the other and so modify your behavior. A high level of confidence, trust, openness, and authenticity is required. There can be no manipulation, competitiveness, or desire to dominate. If you can find someone who will level with you, you become able to be more aware of yourself. You rediscover behavior, attitudes, values, and feelings which are blocked off from yourself.

Participating　Participating in decision making is one of the major intrinsic work needs. The first level, the win-lose complex, was described in Chapter 1. Cooperation, the second stage of participating, is almost beyond our comprehension. As we have seen, most of us have grown up with nothing but competition which feeds the status and the aggressive instincts. Cooperation is misunderstood and misused in management circles. Some managers think a man is cooperative when he is submissive: "Now I want you to cooperate." Some say a man is cooperative when he is subservient, inferior, or obsequious in servile compliance. Note how all express an inferior-superior personal relationship as opposed to an adult-adult relationship. Cooperation is *active* participation, not *passive* submission. To cooperate means to operate jointly with another for mutual benefit. Notice the expectation of differences of opinion. Rather than the win-lose complex, there are connotations of mutual benefit and common agreement.

The ideal, or third stage of participating, is consensus or a unanimity of feeling through which the best decision is reached. The true *we* spirit is best demonstrated by the age-old practice of the Quakers. Consensus is arrived at by the thoughtful process of speaking quietly and thinking, not for the benefit of those who agree with you but for what is best for the organization. The modern approach to consensus stems from a new phrase, "group dynamics," where those who are participating are concerned not only with what is accomplished, the "product," but also with helping the group to move forward effectively, the "process." These will be covered in Chapter 14.

Counseling

Another badly misunderstood and misused word, "counseling," also has three stages. At stage one it consists simply of giving advice. But telling someone the answer to his problem has been found not to be helpful. In the boss-subordinate relationship, counseling is a euphemism for the appraisal interview about which the behavioral sciences consensus has many reservations. One is the need of a subordinate to avoid disapproval. Research indicates that the subordinate blames the boss. Another is the false notion that you can "strengthen a person's weaknesses." You may be able to strengthen a special technical skill or provide the means for a person to increase his knowledge. But weakness, for the most part, as we have seen, has an emotional base. To try to practice psychiatry or even to express psychiatric judgments to an individual is at best a losing game. It may well be the unconscious reluctance to play psychiatrist that results in another finding. Bosses tend not to tell their less adequate subordinates what is wrong with them and not to hold the appraisal interview.

Staff Role But counseling in a staff role where you help someone work out something for which he is responsible is one of the potentially greatest forms of helping. Think of the times you have talked over one of your problems or some of your strong feelings with an associate, a boss, or a subordinate. Think of the times that others have come to you with their problems. This is the staff role in management. It is practiced in greater or lesser degree by many management men where the other person is responsible for the decision. (There is no joint decision making.) You practice the staff role whenever you help someone who has a problem, be it work, personal, or emotional. You counsel when you leave the decision making with him.[4]

Stage one, advisory or directive counseling, has many of the aspects of the first stage of communicating, persuasion. You believe others are helped when you take over their problem for them. You work out a solution, and then try to convince them that your plan is best. You give advice, impressing another with the logic of your arguments. Surely there are many times when you have information or knowledge which another needs. And if that is all there is that needs to be done, provide it. But all too often we try to solve another's problems for him.

Problem-solving Counseling At stage two, problem-solving counseling, you look upon yourself not as an advice giver but rather as a counselor. Whenever you have an opportunity to help someone with a work problem, subscribe to the fundamentals of helping him to learn. Keep the decision making in his hands. His self-development requires that he clarify his thinking, define his problem, work out his solution. He learns by thinking through his problem with your counseling.

In your staff role you represent a point of view on the way to

[4] My book, *The Staff Role in Management, op. cit.*, describes staff work in a no-authority counseling role. Here we shall examine the staff counseling role as one of the several roles of a management man.

solve problems. This type of counseling, on the one hand, has as its purpose not to do things *to* or *for* another. On the other hand, you do not allow the man to take all the initiative while limiting yourself just to questioning or mirroring back. Problem-solving counseling is *doing* things *with* another. You help the individual discover his real problem. Often the problem a person starts with is only an obvious, superficial difficulty. Below this there is a deeper, more general problem, often not recognized.

It is almost axiomatic that a man who has been in the same kind of work for a few years finds it difficult to see his fundamental problems. Frequently, you will find that getting him to define his problems factually, after wading through opinions, prejudices, blaming others, and pat solutions, is a more difficult process than working out a solution. Only after disguises have been cut away and the real problems uncovered can there be any hope for achieving a sound solution.

The *way* in which you work is paramount. Using no authority even if you have it, you leave the decision making to the man. Call your approach "planned opportunism." It is planned because it is positive and purposeful. It is not a capricious, catch-as-catch-can activity. It is opportunism because the end is indeterminate. You start with the man's own perception of his problem. If the problem has any real complexity, you find that problem-analyzing is slow and difficult. Unsystematic, it requires covering much of the same ground over and over again, rehashing many of the same subjects with new angles coming to the fore. You cannot push too fast or too far. If issues and facts are critically analyzed, out of the thinking-through process will come sound, realistic solutions.

Remember that learning is a matter of degree as well as kind. In terms of degree, a man resists changes which in his eyes are too radical either for himself or others to accept and which threaten his personal security—functions, interrelationships, ways of working. In terms of kinds of changes, he resists those which he does not understand and which are forced upon him. You are constantly faced with the paradox of what is likely to be accepted and what is likely to work.

In this type of counseling you leave the initiative with him. Sometimes he wants to make a quick decision with something fairly superficial. Such an action may indicate deep reluctance to face changes in his work situation, for work changes are bound to involve behavior changes. If he is willing to go deeper, you can move from your questioning to a suggesting function. Suggestions are made lightly, almost as a casual reference. It is not a case of making an elaborate verbal presentation, but more in the nature of tossing out a possible thought which a man may quickly pick up or ignore.

Personal Counseling   The third stage, lay personal counseling, is, in my judgment, the best of all possible help you can give or receive. Sometime, somewhere, we all have personal problems, upsets, disappointments, and emotional disturbances, and we need someone with whom we can talk. If we can find someone with whom we can talk early enough, the greater are the chances that our emotional crisis will clear up without any basic repercussions. It is different from leveling and openness, which we explored earlier.

If you are like most people, you underestimate your impact on others. You are also likely to underestimate the value of your helpful relationship to another when he wants to talk about personal matters. At first you may be uncomfortable at the feeling level, and therefore, reluctant to help. Perhaps you find it difficult to believe that, at any given time, the other person is really doing his best, and that he really needs acceptance by you, actions by you which reflect esteem for him as a human being.

You may feel that you lack time to be concerned about others. As a consequence, you may appear unfriendly to him to the point where you may reject his needs. Perhaps you are overly concerned about the rivalry of others toward you. Because you do not talk freely with others, you build barriers to prevent them from talking freely with you. Personal counseling is also limited by the context in which you are working and by the invisible walls with which most men surround themselves. You are also limited by your skill. You are neither a psychiatrist nor a trained counselor. Yet, the need for personal counseling cannot be wished away. If you are interested in helping others in order to help yourself, you must help others to help themselves.

Personal counseling is primarily nondirective. The rules are simple. Do not give advice. Do not try to solve problems. Personal counseling leaves every decision regarding what will be discussed and how much ground will be covered, even the decision to return for another session, up to the individual. Keep these points in mind:

Listen to understand. Use your listening-to-understand skill of communicating to ensure that each person can work out his own problem. It is not "How do I see this? What do I think about it?" but "How does he see this? What does he think about it?" Use the mirror approach with such phrases as "Are you saying that . . . ?" or "Did you mean . . . ?"

Listen with empathy. Be friendly, but not too sympathetic. Let the man know your appreciation of what he says and how he feels without endorsement.

Listen by indirection. Do not try to direct the conversation or control the discussion. Do not probe. Remember that a man answers questions as he understands them. Listen for what he wants to say, what he does not want to say, and what he cannot tell you without your help.

Listen to help. Do not argue. Do not give advice. Do not make judgments. Do not give opinions. You help when you let him make his own decisions.

Kinds of Personal Counseling   Personal counseling covers (1) a sympathetic ear, (2) behavior problems, and (3) emotional problems. As a sympathetic ear, you act primarily as a listener, lending a patient, receptive, friendly ear to let another ventilate his feelings. In the rough-and-tumble competitive relationships of the business rat race, a man needs someone to talk *to*. There is a neat distinction between this and someone to talk *with*. He wants nothing except a chance to talk. Sometimes it enables him to get a better focus on things, to see that things are not as bad as they seem to be. He reduces his anxieties by talking out fears and frustrations. From these confidential sessions, he may discover for himself that he is getting along satisfactorily.

Although almost all people give the impression of self-confidence, we have seen that they feel insecure about themselves and their jobs. Some want a chance to talk out their doubts and to resolve them. There are, of course, a number of men with so much anxiety that they would spend most of their time with you talking about their doubts and uncertainties. You may have to put them off. Distinguish between problems and griping. Try to avoid the latter unless there is a possibility of turning it into a mutual helping relationship. A small shift in attitude or a slightly different focus on values often makes an important difference in a man's values. The more a man wants to do better and the more he becomes aware of himself, looks at himself critically, and becomes concerned about his relationships with others, the greater are his chances of self-development.

People with behavior problems are not likely to come to you and ask for help for their chronic tardiness, bad work habits, frequent loss of temper, and other all-too-numerous problems of conduct. You might be able to help, though, if they do come. If a man starts to gripe about how unreasonable someone else has been, by indirection you may help him crack the door of self-awareness. Do not confuse this with leveling described under communicating. The man may not be able to handle any leveling. Help him to reformulate his feelings, to understand what his deeper concerns are. In a moderate way you do what you can as opportunity presents itself. Where there are deep-rooted and persistent attitudes, about all you can hope to accomplish is to get him to come to a more realistic understanding of himself, or seek professional help.

Emotional Problems   What about people with emotional problems? [5] You cannot help all individuals with their problems, or even a significant proportion of them. You may be able to help an individual whose tenseness results from acute job or family difficulty. However, you cannot be of much help to a person who has a chronic or repetitive problem of long duration. Nor can you do much for a man who is showing signs of severe distress, such as a highly agitated person, one in panic, a person threatening suicide, or one with a marked behavioral change. The odds are also against your helping those we saw earlier who are below the normal range of emotional health. Assist people with these kinds of problems to get to professionals for help.

Be alert to the possibility of early indications of tenseness; do not ignore them until the situation is serious. There are several early

[5] There is almost no information in management books about how a businessman helps people with emotional problems. One exception is Harry Levinson, *Emotional Health in the World of Work*, Harper & Row, Publishers, Incorporated, New York, 1964, from which I have drawn.

signs of emotional distress. A person's usual manner may be overemphasized or he may develop a different reaction. An increase in hostile feelings, anxiousness, and depression are some of the signs of undue tenseness. On the other hand, an individual may overuse his defenses by being unable to perceive accurately some of the realities of his situation. Other symptoms are withdrawal or helplessness.

Do not follow your usual reaction and gloss over the symptoms. Think about the fact that there is an underlying problem to be solved. The first step, therefore, is to strengthen the individual who is unduly anxious. Here you may do such things as accept the dependency needs of an individual to make it possible for him to express to you his anxiety. The individual is likely to identify with you if he feels that you have genuine affection for him and trust him. Reach out for him. Act as a friend. Encourage the individual to feel that it is all right for him to talk with you about his problems and that you will try to help. Encourage him to talk and then listen. Listening to give understanding in order to help is a good approach. Again, do not try to diagnose, label, or treat. Do not make light of a person's discomfort.

Limit what you do. If you cannot help a person resolve an emotional problem in one or two interviews, it is time to suggest he seek professional help. Do it in a matter-of-fact way. Help the person understand that something is wrong and that help from a professional is appropriate. If his distress is interfering with his work, you should expect the individual to do this. Emotional illness should be dealt with no differently than physical illness.

12

Help Your Boss

> The fact that authority and subordinacy conflicts exist within a web of human relationships does not minimize the importance for the individual of learning to assume responsibility for his own behavior.
> —ABRAHAM ZALEZNIK, *Human Dilemmas of Leadership* [1]

HELP YOUR BOSS? Of course you do. You have always done so. At least that is what most subordinates appear to be telling themselves. Yet your relationship with your boss is found by many researchers to be usually not only the most important but also the most confusing and the most conflicting relationship you have at work. The high emotional content of the subordinate-boss relationship is well demonstrated by the vast amount of research on how bosses should treat subordinates. There is almost no research on how subordinates should treat bosses. Granted, there is much that bosses can do. There is also much that you as a subordinate can do to learn about subordinate-boss transactions and what bosses are usually like, as well as your own attitudes toward authority figures and how to help your boss.

---

[1] Harper & Row, Publishers, Incorporated, New York, 1966, p. 35.

Work and Authority

That the relationships of subordinates and bosses leave much to be desired is in my judgment the most common behavioral sciences research finding of the work world.

Basic Disagreements   It has been found that a subordinate and his boss do not agree, differ more than they agree, or often disagree on specific duties, priorities, and the most and least important tasks. They also differ on anticipation of future changes in work, obstacles which prevent a subordinate from doing as good a job as possible, and the standards of adequate performance.[2] How come? Supervisors are apparently being given little or no help to understand the transactional nature of the supervisory process in the many supervisory training courses and management education courses. Those who have had training in how to supervise are usually no better off than those who have had no training. In survey after survey subordinates whose supervisors have had the typical kinds of supervisory training generally indicate that while a supervisor may have acquired a new vocabulary, his behavior has not changed.

Look at Exhibit 11. In the lower right corner is the work to be done. Question: Whose work is it? If you have the typical reaction, you will say it is the boss's work. At least this is the first answer I get when I draw this triangle on a lecture pad and ask this same question in innumerable sessions. This generally prevalent attitude, supported by management engineering, is the cause of much of the conflict and confusion between subordinate and boss. It means that the boss focuses on the work to be done, not on the subordinate who is doing it. As a subordinate, you become secondary to the work. You are a tool or a machine to produce something, not a person. From the boss's standpoint this means he does not have to get involved with you as a person. He can focus on the work which is his, and he tries to control you through the work rather than help you do your work.

Even though you too may believe that it is the boss's work, you

[2] Norman R. F. Maier, L. Richard Hoffman, John J. Hooven, and William H. Read, *Superior-Subordinate Communications,* American Management Association, New York, 1961.

Exhibit 11   THE WORK TRIANGLE

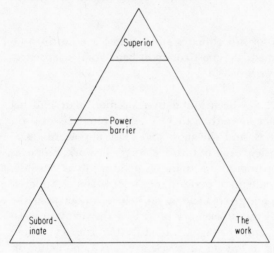

do not behave that way. If you did there would be little misunderstanding and conflict. What you want, according to the research, is for your boss to help you do your work as well as to help you as a person. He should take an interest in you, be considerate of you, look out for your wishes, listen to you, see that you are more fully utilized, and be concerned about you.

Basically, the conflict stems from the boss's interest only in the work and your interest in the boss's interest in you. When two people who should be working together with common interests have different concerns, there can only be misunderstanding and little communication and participation, much disagreement and friction.

Subordinate Self-esteem   Most managers have been found, through research, to be neither helpful nor interested in helping their subordinates grow. Your boss, then, may feel that personal growth and self-actualization goals for an individual are the "utopian view." How does he feel about preserving your self-esteem as a subordinate? [3]

There are so many things that managers unthinkingly do to of-

[3] Zaleznik, *op. cit.*, apparently maintains that self-actualization, to which he subscribes, is a utopian view and distinguishes it from self-esteem—as does Maslow in Chapter 2.

fend your self-esteem. For instance, does your manager respect your integrity and privacy by not prying? Does he want you to make your own decisions, but expect your decisions to please him? Does he disapprove more than he approves? Does he add to your emotional burdens by keeping pressure on you, keeping you off balance, or trying to change you? To threaten, directly or indirectly, the self-esteem of an individual will cause personal tenseness.

Basic Ego States In engaging in transactions with others, each one of us has three basic sets of ego states, a system of feelings causing a related set of behavior patterns for our various organizational roles as well as all our other relationships. These ego states as shown in Exhibit 12 are (1) parent, which are similar to those of parental figures; (2) adult, with some awareness of self and reality; (3) child, with the unfinished business of childhood. With a healthy balance between these ego states where each one makes its appropriate contribution, a person lives a full and productive life. When one or the other upsets the vital balance, a person has emotional ill health.

Games That Hurt Through transactional analysis, it has been found that normal people innocently and *unconsciously* play games that hurt. They engage in games of which they are not totally aware and which are basically dishonest with predictable, dramatic, and unpleasant rather than exciting outcomes. Unfortunately, these games form the most important aspect of interpersonal transactions throughout the world.[4] Things proceed smoothly in our transactions with others as long as the ego states are complementary, such as the parent-child transaction diagrammed in the upper half of Exhibit 12. The parent-child complementary transaction might be a supervisor's expressing a parental attitude toward his subordinate. The subordinate responds as a child would respond.

It is when the respondent does not respond in complementary

---

[4] According to Eric Berne, M.D., *Games People Play*, Grove Press, Inc., New York, 1964, pp. 48–49. Of the thirty-six games described in Dr. Berne's book only a few relate to the work world. Most of them are life, marital, or sex games. In this and the next two chapters, you will find several of Berne's games adapted to the work situation. Disturbed people tend to play more severe games such as Rapo, Cops and Robbers, Alcoholic. The games outlined in this section are first from pp. 143–147, second from p. 94, and third from pp. 88–90.

Exhibit 12   BASIC TRANSACTIONS [5]

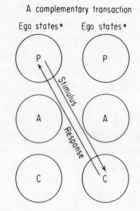

A complementary transaction

Ego states*   Ego states*

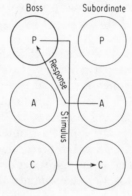

A crossed transaction

Boss   Subordinate

* P—Parent; A—Adult; C—Child.

[5] Eric Berne, M.D., *Games People Play*, Grove Press, Inc., New York, 1964, pp. 30–31. Reprinted by permission of Grove Press, Inc. Copyright © 1964 by Eric Berne.

fashion that a game occurs, for then there is a crossed transaction, as illustrated in the lower part of Exhibit 12. Then a game ensues of which the participants are unaware.

In much of the popular management literature, there is a great deal said about supervisors that is only a thinly veiled parent ego state. Moreover, research reported on earlier indicates that good supervisors, parents, and teachers have common qualities of competence, effectiveness, and supportiveness. A popular term used for a boss is a slang term for father, "the old man." When a subordinate becomes upset with his boss he might say, "Who does he think he is, my father?" Many management preachments convey a strong note of superior (parent) rather than equal ego states in the supervisor-subordinate relationships.

To help you learn to recognize the games your boss may play, here are a few games to illustrate what happens. The game "I Am Only Trying to Help You" results when your boss gives you some advice. You come back and report that the advice did not work. Your boss tries again. He may feel slightly frustrated but he does not question his own motive—people are disappointing and ungrateful. Failing to secure gratitude, but only blame, he gets to the point where, exasperated, bewildered, or inadequate, he says, "I'm only trying to help you." As a subordinate there is not much you can do except to attempt to get your boss to see that people are not like that. If you feel the gamble is not too great, you might gently confront your boss with what he is doing and stop playing the game. There is a legitimate way for a boss to help, an adult-adult transaction where craftsmanship replaces an unconscious ulterior motive. Legitimate help is expressed: "We can do something about it." "Let me help you." "I think I know what you might do."

Then there is the "Dilemma Type of Corner Game." You try to be a helpful subordinate and find that your boss finds fault with what you do. You are damned if you do and damned if you don't. Your approach to help your boss out of this game is about the same as in the previous game.

In the "See What You Made Me Do" game, your boss asks you for suggestions as part of good management. Then any mistake he makes can be blamed on you. His motive is a long-suffering resentment which causes him to want to put others in a position where he can blame them. In addition to the earlier suggestions as to how you might help your boss, try to throw the decision back to him. Expect him to be forlorn or sulky, seldom angry.

Your Awareness as a Subordinate

Although your work situation may not be the best, unknown and unresolved conflicts within yourself about authority figures can make your relationships with your boss even more difficult for you. You may find it hard to bring to the surface your unpleasant values and emotions such as hostility, contempt, rivalry, and dislike. Here are some means for you to become aware of your own conflicts in your subordinate role.

Note the power barrier in the work triangle in Exhibit 11. A boss can hurt as well as help. And he can hurt in ways that organization rules and regulations cannot get at. There is no equality in this relationship. If you are a normal subordinate, odds are your work is important to you, you want to achieve, you want a career, and you want your boss to approve of you, like you, be friendly with you, and help you. Generally he cannot fire you or take other formal adverse actions without others knowing and concurring. But no rules can be written that regulate his distribution of favors and feelings, his pressure and criticism, his little but significant rewards and punishments.

Your Problems with Bosses   If your experiences with bosses have for the most part been more negative than the research findings listed earlier, the problem may well be with you. Recall how your attitudes about various bosses have compared with those of your peers generally. If yours have usually been similar to those of most of your peers, you probably have normal attitudes. If your attitudes differ, check through how they differ. Some of your peers might also give you their impressions of your attitudes toward your boss.

Try to think through and pinpoint one or more common problems you have had with almost all your bosses. What has been the pattern of your experience with bosses? Have you changed bosses frequently because of generally bad bosses? If you have, you may be chronically discontented with bosses. Do you usually want substantially more independence in your work than you usually get? If so, you may be too competitive or rebellious, or need to try to dominate bosses. Have you found that almost every boss you have had is out to get you? If this is the case, you may be hostile toward authority figures. Have almost all your bosses not given you enough support? If this is true for you, you may have unusual dependency needs.

Your Authority Values   Your own basic attitudes toward authority figures should give you additional clues. A child establishes his primary power values in infancy by identifying with (1) his father, (2) his mother, (3) both, or (4) neither. A boy who accepts his father more than his mother sees the father as powerful, wise, and authoritative. Power and holders of power tend to be admired. As an adult such a person tends to be conservative, and having rejected his mother, he is apt to have a relatively low opinion of women.

A boy who accepts his mother more than his father feels that she is the source of love, sustenance, and help. His orientation is more toward minimizing power. Modeling his views after those of his mother, he tends to have a high regard for women and for social values such as democracy and justice. He may well resent authority figures. To the child who identifies with both parents, power has its place, but so does helping and accepting others. He tends to have a high opinion of both men and women. Finally, there is the child who does not identify with either parent, rejecting both, along with authority, society, and its controls. He may be an egotist who has learned to love only himself.

Subordinate Achievement Profile In addition to your achieving tendencies at work, described in Chapter 9, you should check yourself out on your achieving tendencies as a subordinate. You may have mature achieving tendencies, or average, low, or undue normal tendencies, or under- or overachieving neurotic tendencies as a subordinate. Here are some short illustrations of the many varieties to help you gain greater insight into yourself and your subordinate achieving tendencies.

A mature subordinate achiever not only has a high opinion of both men and women, but being aware, he has outgrown most of his childhood problems with authority figures and is not reliving his past history. Hence, he has a ready acceptance of the interdependency of the subordinate-boss relationship. He consciously tries to be helpful, for he realizes that he helps himself by helping his boss. Still, he is autonomous enough to do that which he thinks is important.

The average normal achiever has not resolved the conflicts of childhood. His major conflict tends to be ambivalence toward his boss. Both values and emotions are involved. Ambivalence means holding opposing values or feelings about someone or something at the same time. Most of us have mixed attitudes or feelings which we simultaneously hold, for and against, not for or against. Ambivalence enables us to tolerate our internal conflicts of simultaneously liking and disliking our boss, admiring and condemning, trusting and distrusting, submitting and dominating, being dependent and independent. With his win-lose complex, the normal achiever in his subordinate role still has not successfully resolved, as the mature achiever has, the balance of the polarities about his boss, giving and getting, controlling himself and being controlled, and competing and complying.[6]

A low normal achieving subordinate tends to strive for too much independence. His emotional state is that of the rebellious child or adolescent. As with his parents, he is still trying to free himself of authority figures, a continuation of his adolescent struggle for independence.

An undue normal achieving subordinate is best characterized as dependent, for he admires power figures. He may rely on his boss to initiate matters.

An underachieving neurotic subordinate tries to dominate his boss. He cannot accept a subordinate role and tries to control and overpower his boss often in subtle but unmistakable ways.

An overachieving neurotic subordinate has the passive submission of a little child. He seeks personal approval and support. For the classic yes-man, securing approval is more important than his work or his career. His boss and his organization can do no wrong.

How Can I Help?

Assuming that you have been able to work through your awareness as a subordinate to a positive attitude toward your boss, you face the next major question: Does my boss want me to help, and how? You have seen some of the games supervisors play as well as the basic disagreement as to whom your work belongs. In the next chapter you will find a supervisory achievement profile which you can use not only as your own guide but as a means to getting some other clues to your own boss.

Another means to get some reading of your boss is to take a measure of the kinds of supervisors who predominate in your organization. As a consultant I find that a highly aggressive organization fa-

[6] Zaleznik, *op. cit.*, pp. 24–26.

vors dominating supervisors. A staid organization is inclined to favor paternalistic supervisors. A young, growing organization usually has not developed a pattern, and because it cannot afford at the start to pay for quality, tends to suffer from relatively inadequate supervisors.

You cannot help your boss if his emotional problems stem from the unfinished business of the past. If this is the case, it would be the better part of wisdom to end the relationship. However, this is not always possible. Then there arises the question of how you can work with a boss who must use you to attempt to satisfy his unduly anxious needs. Frankly, there is no good answer. To make the best of a bad situation, about all you can do is recognize that your boss has emotional problems. Sort out his neurotic conflicts with you and the realistic issues of the work transactions, if this is possible. Undoubtedly the greatest test of your frustration tolerance, autonomy, and awareness is to work for a neurotic boss under his conditions and to play the proper role without letting your own ego get entangled and damaged. A truly rare and remarkable feat.

His Concerns If you conclude that there are no emotional barriers which block improved relationships with your boss, your next step is empathy: to see things from his standpoint. Start with the realization that he is doing the best he can. If your boss has not seen the need to acquire some of the basic knowledge of human behavior, he may well have erroneous perceptions about you. You may find, too, that your boss talks one way and behaves another. Of primary concern to him is how he is doing and his relations with his boss. And a major part of that is his having to rely on you and his other subordinates to help him make a good showing.

You may get some clues about his concerns if he supervises management trainees. It has been found that a business graduate's *first* boss, rather than an elaborate trainee program, is the critical factor. This first boss can cast him into rebellion or conformity, job hunting or corporate oblivion, or launch him on a successful career. (Yet companies do not train these bosses to work with college graduates.) So many college graduates get off to a poor start. In one sample of the graduates from M.I.T., one-half of the three-year management trainees have changed jobs, and three-fourths of the five-year trainees have moved on to another company at least once, many three and four times.[7] There are critical company values which a supervisor imparts. These are quite different from what the graduate, at least from M.I.T., learns. A business usually is primarily concerned with such basics as getting a job done, making a reasonable profit, supporting the free enterprise system and competition, and believing that the hierarchy of authority is the best means to get things done. Employees are to be loyal members. The student, on the other hand, thinks in terms of himself, advancement, prestige, responsibility, challenge, creativity, and a high salary.

The traditional views of the company enable a supervisor to hold to and act under the stereotype of the college graduate. He is seen as overly ambitious, unrealistic, immature. He is too theoretical, too idealistic, and too inexperienced for the responsibility he seeks. In your own case you may then conclude that your supervisor is a traditionalist who holds too closely to company values to enable you to secure what the normal person needs from his job. If your boss in supervising college graduates or even recent high school graduates wants to help, his approach is different. He is not threatened by knowledge or competition. He can accept the emotional expressions of a young person who may get flustered easily.

Another good clue to your supervisor is how he reacts to a mistake. In most companies there is a preachment that in order to accomplish something, you must make mistakes. In reality, however, mistakes in many companies become major crises. They are not tolerated. If your boss lets people make errors in spite of this negative company practice, you have a positive clue about him. If, however, he insists on perfection or "zero defects performance," then you have a negative clue.

Finally, if you separate your boss from his position and look at him as a person who is trying to do a job, you may find that in your subordinate role you can adjust more to his ways. It may be easier to support him and work with him on his terms. You may be able to bring things to him that are important to him because they are the things he needs.

Tactics   There are about four tactics which are losers and another four which are winners. Tactics which are losers are:

[7] This research on college graduates is taken from Edgar H. Schein, "How to Break In the College Graduate," reprint from *Harvard Business Review*, vol. 42, no. 6, November-December, 1964.

1. Manipulate—the Machiavellian approach of using any means to gain your own ends. This tactic is a loser not only because you lose your integrity but because you destroy the opportunity for trust. One of the most frequently espoused manipulations is, "I make him think it is his idea."

2. Fight—conflict, rivalry, contention, subtle resistance. No matter how you may rationalize the rightness of your position, this is a loser for you, especially when you are on the short end of the power stick.

3. Escape—emotionally and mentally to withdraw from the situation. In moments of exasperation it is fine to say "to hell with the organization," but escape frequently causes decreased interest and involvement with consequent apathy.

4. Adapt—to be dependent, passive, submissive, and subservient. Adapting occasionally may be healthy, for almost everyone needs to go into the child ego state once in a while. However, adapting frequently or for prolonged periods of time is a result of either neurotic needs or a situation which causes feelings of frustration and failure with consequent disinterest and potential apathy.

Helpful winning tactics are:

1. Avoid conflict and disagreement—try to avoid those situations which cause conflict with your boss. These kinds of situations are difficult for anyone to handle. It is here that it is helpful to strive for the ideal adult-adult transaction.

2. Resolve conflict whenever possible—in both the work and your relationship with your boss. Try to sort out in your own mind the specific nature of these conflicts. Identify them if possible, isolate them, and look at them realistically. Then try to bring them out in the open for resolution.

3. Cope—cooperate with the "we" attitude. Accept the fact that this is the boss's show and not yours. Establish your trustworthiness. Tell him of your errors, rather than cover them up. Try to reduce putting yourself in the most favorable light in your discussions with him.

4. Help—in recognition of your mutual interdependence.

Helping In addition to doing your own work effectively, you can help your boss by trying to be openly helpful. Ask "How can I help you?" "What can I contribute?" Subordinates tend to be overly con-

cerned with their own work, their problems, and what their supervisors should do for them. When they do this, they are helping neither themselves nor their superiors. They are not making a major
contribution to their organization, nor are they doing the best for
their own personal growth and advancement.

When you go to your boss and ask him how you can help him,
do your homework first. Work out some ideas of what you might be
able to do so you can suggest them as tasks. Pick your time, when
you think he is receptive. Build your professional stance. Be empathic. Establish acceptance. Do not be too disappointed if he
seems negative. It may be that no subordinate has ever asked him
this question before. You may have to try two or three times before
you find that you can help him or determine that he does not want
you to help him.

Other ways of being helpful are outlined in the interpersonal
transaction goals in Exhibit 10 (Chapter 11). In view of the authority of your boss, he sets the stage for communicating by leveling,
participating with consensus, and counseling at the personal level.
In the subordinate-boss transaction goals there are two where you as
a subordinate can be especially helpful. First is the subordinate-boss
relationship. Second, to be covered later, is helping your boss develop effective group effort.

In your subordinate-boss role transaction (Exhibit 10), you have
the opportunity, depending on your boss, to work through three
stages: comply, conform, or commit. Rather than use win-lose tactics or other losing tactics to get your own way, you may be
tempted to comply. Here you go along with your boss without
changing your own private view. You contribute very little or you
may even passively resist. If you try to conform to your boss's wishes
you surrender some of your personal autonomy. The ideal stage is
commitment to the plans and goals of your boss through joint participation and working through emotional and intellectual differences rather than ignoring, denying, or repressing them. Then you
will undoubtedly find that there is much you can learn from your
boss.

13

Help Your Subordinates

> Both the behavior of the superior and the subordinate's perception of the situation must be such that the subordinate, in light of his background, values, and expectations, sees the experience as one which contributes to his sense of personal worth and importance, one which increases and maintains his sense of significance and human dignity.
>
> —RENSIS LIKERT, *The Human Organization* [1]

UNQUESTIONABLY, MORE WORDS have been written on how to supervise, manage, or boss a subordinate than on any other subject in the business rat race. You saw the confusion of philosophies of how to manage others in Chapter 5. Managing others from the behavioral sciences consensus is the subject of my earlier book. Here I shall draw on some of the basics.[2]

As a boss, think through this maxim: Just as there are more op-

---

[1] McGraw-Hill Book Company, New York, 1967, p. 48.

[2] *Managing the Managers,* McGraw-Hill Book Company, New York, 1965. You might find such chapters as these helpful: Five Management Conflicts; Superior-Subordinate Underworld; Manager and Authority; Power in Work; Power in Organization; Organizing; Selecting; and Integrating; and Staff Development. These subjects are covered in greater detail than here.

portunities to help your subordinates than in any other organizational relationship, so too there are more opportunities to hurt. You have organization authority. It may not be much in your mind or in fact. But that is not how the subordinate sees it. You have already seen enough of the worm's eye view to accept the subordinate's perception of a boss. Yet, you may, as so many management men do, hold to oversimplified popular concepts, many of which have been touched on. Take a key one, leadership. Contrary to popular opinion, if you do a good job of selecting, your leadership lies in helping. In addition, you can personally practice the personnel and management policies of the consensus in Chapter 6.

Your Awareness as a Supervisor

As the first step in developing your awareness of yourself as a supervisor, recall the last two chapters, but this time from the point of view of your supervisory-subordinate relationship.

Intrinsic Managing Satisfaction   Are you genuinely interested in managing people? First, there is the question of whether or not you are primarily thing-minded or people-minded. In entering managing you leave, in large measure, the world of things and techniques and move into the world of people. Second, even though you have an interest in people, you may really prefer to do the work yourself. You take a management job primarily to move ahead. Third, you find yourself dependent on others for your own success. You are also responsible for them. Fourth, you find you must help your subordinates. Only through helping them can you be assured of successful results. Fifth, you find that it is often a futile process in getting a rather imperfect lot of people to do the things that you think must be done the way you want them done when you want them done. Sixth, you must rely on these people and deal with them when they have work that increasingly you cannot do yourself and cannot know in detail. Seventh, you must expand and raise your own outlook and see things through a manager's eyes. If you moved into managing primarily to make more money and to get ahead, you have little motivation to develop as a manager.

Next you face your feelings about a boss's authority. You find that it is more limited than you imagined. You also face the question as to how you delegate it. Whatever the personnel policies and management practices are, you find that you can keep most of the authority to yourself or you can share it with your subordinates. In the autocratic structure, you always have the right to veto any decision of one or more of your subordinates. You may use your authority irrationally or rationally. Irrational authority rests on motivating, manipulating, intimidating, exploiting, or demanding. Irrational authority seeks to emphasize inequality, a gap between superior and inferior persons.

Rational authority, on the other hand, is used in working with and helping subordinates. It is based upon the essential equalness of boss and subordinate as adults, differing only in the degree of knowledge or skill in a particular field. In fact, subordinates may have more knowledge or skill or both in certain fields. And to the extent that a subordinate takes the lead or acts as a resource, he exercises leadership. To the extent that a subordinate can counsel his boss or help him with the boss's particular problems, the subordinate is helping.

Double Standards Think through your double standards. The most common double standard is that of underutilization. You undoubtedly are constantly concerned about your own underutilization, but you give little or no thought to how you underutilize your subordinates. Recall the work needs of a normal man as given in Chapter 3. In thinking about yourself, you probably agree with most of them. Still, how consciously do you strive to meet the same work needs of your subordinates?

You want integrity from your subordinates. Yet, there are many little ways in which you appear to your subordinates to be lacking in integrity. In some instances, it is thoughtlessness. In others, it is because it is difficult for a boss to handle these emotionally laden relationships. All too frequently I find managers praising their subordinates to their faces and being critical of them behind their backs. Making promises and not keeping them, saying one thing and doing another, causes subordinates to raise questions about the integrity of their boss. Being secretive, evasive, and manipulative are other all-too-common practices which make a boss appear to be dishonest. Surely you cannot tell the truth all the time, and you must tell white lies some of the time. It is understood that you cannot "tell everything" at any given time. But if you are going to ease the relationships for yourself, you strive to develop the highest possible level of trust. You may think you are being clever by being devious, but in reality you are increasing stress for others and tenseness for yourself.

Another double standard centers on the amount and quality of work done by a subordinate. You undoubtedly cannot accomplish anywhere near as much each day as you plan. You accept this for yourself. But when a subordinate does not accomplish as much as you think he should, you tend to think he has fallen down. Yet, you have very few ways in which you can judge what the subordinate's day is like. If you go on feeling that subordinates do not accomplish quite as much as they should, you finally end up thinking that they do not work hard or efficiently enough. (See Theory X in Chapter 5.)

As for quality of work, you often suggest major improvements for some project subordinates are carrying out. You should not forget that you have the advantage of having a larger overview and that you should temper the tone of your criticism with this in mind. Over a period of time you may tend to feel that their work is of questionable quality. Still, if they had your vantage point, they probably could do a higher grade of work on their job.

Another common double standard is the boss's perception of himself as an objective, rational decision maker while holding that subordinates generally are emotional, resistant, unrealistic procrastinators. What kinds of employees do you prefer? Like most managers, you may say that you want people who are better than you. This is seldom the case. In a survey on desirable executive traits, preferences fall into two patterns. One group of managers favors accurate, careful, and precise people rather than those described as courageous, tolerant, and capable. A second group prefers the dull, apathetic, and retiring as against the argumentative, intolerant, and egotistical.[3]

Your Evaluation Sources   As a boss you have an invaluable evaluation source if you are emotionally able to use it—your subordinates. Ask them in a group session how they feel about your working with

[3] Lewis B. Ward, "Do You Want a Weak Subordinate?" *Harvard Business Review*, vol. 39, September-October, 1961, p. 6. Ward used a forced-choice questionnaire on 4,000 executives.

them. Essentially what you want to find out is how you are doing as their supervisor. Expect no candid answers at first. Keep on asking them to level with you on your approach in managing them (another ideal transaction goal). Once you have asked the question, sit back and *listen*. Do not ask the question in the same way each time. Here are some of the ways you might phrase it: How am I carrying out my functions in terms of the needs of the group? What can I do to help the group to work together more effectively? What can I do to help achieve more improvement both in our work and our personal growth? What should I know to be more sensitive to resources within the group and to individual feelings and needs? Am I being too defensive of myself and my position?

You will be informed not only as to what needs to be done but also as to how you can do your job better. The answers, beyond what any single subordinate dares do, are gradually evolved by the group as each member adds a little to what someone else has said to help you see yourself as they see you. Moreover, if you are going to help yourself by helping them, you must come to share your own feelings of uncertainty and frustration with your staff. Open yourself up to them, so that they in turn can open themselves up to you. The opportunity to reduce your own rat race through personal growth in insight and interpersonal skills may well be one of the greatest rewards not only for you but for your staff.

A second evaluation source is to ask a behavioral sciences counselor to take a reading on how you supervise. He will talk on a confidential basis with the members of your staff. He will "filter" the various comments about you to arrive at a consensus.[4] He will give you feedback balanced with his own knowledge of how subordinates are typically hypercritical of bosses. Should you desire to go further with this, you and the counselor might then have a session with your subordinates to explore the means for all of you to work together in a better fashion.

Supervisory Achievement Profile

Finally, check through to find your basic emotional ego state as a supervisor. Basic ego states can be combined with a supervisory

---

[4] In my book *The Staff Role in Management,* Harper & Row, Publishers, Incorporated, New York, 1955, I list four filters: personal context, situational context, social-technical, and change.

achievement profile of mature, or average, low, or undue normal achievers, or neurotic under- and overachievers. Although there are all kinds of supervisory behaviors, the central tendencies of these should provide useful guides.

Mature Supervisory Achiever   A mature supervisory achiever has those qualities of a good boss detailed in Chapter 3. In summary there are three basic qualities: competence, effectiveness, and supportiveness. Competence includes such things as clear thinking, unconventionality, humor, and originality. Effectiveness includes being active, aggressive, confident, enthusiastic, sophisticated, and deep. Supportiveness includes fairness, frankness, informality, good listening, humbleness, kindness, tolerance, sensitiveness, trust, warmth, and helpfulness.

His basic supervisory ego state is adult rather than parent. He might well be termed a "situation-centered" manager. He relies on the needs of the situation, attempting to balance the needs of the organization, his staff, and himself. He tends to be progressive in his thinking, with a strong inclination to seek out the facts on all sides of an issue so as to achieve a balanced solution. Balance is the key. He is a middle of the roader in his primary power leanings. He accepts authority and self-discipline as inherent in any situation. His primary approach is, "Let's examine the particular situation. What does it require? What needs to be done? What kinds of people are involved? How do they feel? What are their needs? What can each one contribute?" He tends to be highly objective and analytical, interested in learning and research, in creative thinking, and in finding the "authority of the situation." He has much interaction with his subordinates both individually and as a group.

Average Normal Supervisory Achiever   An average normal supervisory achiever tends to have a basic parent ego state. In working with managers and management groups, I find that in the main they are quite inconsistent between what they say and how they behave. They indulge in permissiveness at times, paternalism at times, manipulation at times. They want to be more in "control" of their situation than they are. Behind their brave, self-confident front, they are often confused and concerned about how they manage. Even when they have read much of the management literature and can spout so-called management principles, much of what they do is without thought. They are inclined to deal with their men individually, remaining aloof rather than entering fully into active group processes. There tends to be more emphasis on criticism and punishment than on approval and rewards. Because emotional matters are difficult to handle, these are swept under the rug. A person is expected to keep his emotions out of his work.

Low Normal Supervisory Achiever   The employee-centered permissive manager is the low normal supervisory achiever. He dislikes being forced to submit to power or seeing others imposed upon by those in power. He is liberal in his outlook and wants to try new ideas. He believes in honor and gentlemanliness. People are expected to settle their differences in discussion. He views persuasion as the means for getting others to accept his views; it is not important to him that others agree with him. A permissive manager, he has the tendency to become too employee-centered. His staff may dominate him. Morale is up but production is down.

Undue Normal Supervisory Achiever   An autocratic manager, the undue normal supervisory achiever tends to practice paternalism in its literal sense. He would be an exponent of scientific management and Theory X if he could verbalize his basic attitudes. His subordinates are more like children in their disinterest in work and cooperation. He does little or no consulting with his subordinates before making decisions. His emphasis is on punishment and coercion. His typical attitude when faced with an emotional problem, although he may not state it this way, is to say, "Stop crying. Grow up." Happy with the autocratic organization, *direct and control* appeals to this authoritative (but not authoritarian) manager. He makes a good subordinate, for he is dependable, respectful, and compliant. He likes tradition and believes that one should comply with the wishes of superiors. A directive manager, he tends to fear both spontaneity and impulsive pleasure and, therefore, has little open friendliness for others. As a practical, conservative man, he likes details and facts. Suspicious of theories and change, his curiosity and creativity are limited.

Because power is paramount to him, this autocratic manager concerns himself primarily with acquiring authority. He believes that a manager has power and should use it. His authoritative approach fits the popular notion of dynamic leadership, pressure with authority behind it. Much of the material on management that is being written principally by managers assumes that a manager "makes subordinates do." Supervision, counseling, and coaching all get twisted into a sugar-coated old-style bossmanship, rather than creative and helpful management.

Neurotic Supervisory Underachiever It is in the underachiever that we find anarchy, laissez faire, or chaos. He may provide no supervision, with everything and everyone in a chaotic state while the manager goes on his way, oblivious to his management responsibilities. He may be so enamored with his own little world and his anxieties that he is unable to relate himself effectively to others. He does not know how to manage, nor is he capable of learning. He continues to survive and usually gets very little attention from superiors, unless things get too bad, chiefly because, while he is ineffective, he is also innocuous.

Neurotic Supervisory Overachiever The authoritarian manager, the classic neurotic supervisory overachiever, has been well researched.[5] Because ambiguity threatens him, he tends to be concrete in his thinking, sticking close to the details and rigid black-and-white dichotomies. His actions are deceptive. To his superior he appears as an agreeable submissive conformist. However, he completely dominates those below him, believing that no one should express hostility or criticism. An "eight ball" manager, he is a dictator, an omnipotent father. People will produce more "when you keep their feet to the fire." Hence, his primary approach to work with subordinates is through threat and punishment. That he attracts and keeps dependent subordinates is evidenced by the "If It Weren't for Him" game. A subordinate with a child ego state seeks a dominating supervisor (parental ego state) who restricts his activities and thereby keeps him out of anxious situations.[6] Still, the subordinate com-

---

[5] Drawn from T. W. Adorno, E. Frenkel-Brunswick, D. J. Levinson, and R. W. Sanford, *The Authoritarian Personality*, Harper & Row, Publishers, Incorporated, New York, 1950, p. 217. In the management jargon, "authoritarian" is used loosely sometimes to denote the authoritative undue normal supervisory achiever.

[6] Eric Berne, M.D., *Games People Play*, Grove Press, Inc., New York, 1964. Adapted from the "If It Weren't for You" game, p. 105.

plains about the restrictions, bemoaning "if it weren't for him" to his friends and associates.

Your Management Practice

If you have been able to develop a greater awareness of yourself as a supervisor, you now can (1) cultivate a professional managerial stance; (2) develop your supervisory approach; and (3) learn your managerial roles of administering and integrating. In addition, recall Exhibit 3, Qualities of a Good Superior; Exhibit 12, Basic Transactions; and Exhibit 10, Transaction Goals.

Your Professional Managerial Stance   To the professional stance, outlined earlier, add your professional stance as a manager. Caring in a professional way is the key. Once more, in many ways your situation is analogous to that of a medical man. True, he wants to cure a disease, whereas you want production. In your role of "doctor" think what a physician does when he is treating the symptoms of a neurotic. Not only does he prescribe medicants, but he tries to get the patient in a more comfortable frame of mind so as to function more effectively. He knows he cannot remove the anxiety, but over the years he provides the patient with "humours," both verbal and medical. This, too, is your manager's life. You cannot avoid it, any more than the physician can. To try and get your more anxious men to work effectively, you help them get into a comfortable frame of mind. The best hope for an unduly anxious, distressed person is early first aid by you, as I suggested earlier, in personal counseling.

Unless you are able to care enough about your subordinates to help them in a professional way where feelings are paramount, you cannot help. You are neither omnipotent nor impotent. Still, there is an egoistic feeling of power and achievement in helping which you should accept. There is also a lot of the dictator in every one of us, and unless you look behind your self-concept you may use helping to dominate. If you must, because of your own anxieties, use a subordinate to satisfy your personal needs, not help him, you may end up making all the important decisions. This would result in your deciding for a subordinate the way in which he should do his work, expecting too little or too much of him, denying or ignoring his feelings, avoiding spending time with him, viewing him as a functionary rather than a person, pressuring him, or denying mutual interdependence.

In helping a subordinate, accept the power barrier of your authority. You cannot have a totally free helping relationship with a subordinate because he sees you above him with the power to hurt as well as help. Not only is it your power to hire and fire, but it is also your rank, your being in the know, and your right to overrule and mistreat. Your power may be overestimated, and you only appear to occupy an omnipotent role. But too often a subordinate is right. As pointed out before, a manager can make the lives of his subordinates miserable and anxious and allow them no right to get a hearing from anyone. A manager can literally ruin men under him to satisfy his needs.

Your Managerial Approach   Not only to reduce the rat race for yourself and your subordinates, but also to increase productivity, it is up to you as a manager to reduce stress, conflict, and pressure within your organizational unit.[7] Surely you will still have high performance standards. However you may analyze your assignment, you manage people, not things, not production, not results. Ignorance is no excuse. You are responsible for your subordinates' health, both physical and emotional. The more you force or let men become anxious misfits, the harder your job becomes. As you have seen, you cannot change a man very much, and the harder you try, the longer you work at it, the more you may hurt him. But you can make his work more attractive by opening up avenues so he can move, think, and grow. You cannot improve a man's performance, but you can establish the atmosphere for his doing better if he will. You cannot improve a man, but you can help him in his improving himself if he has the internal drive and capabilities. You cannot change a man's personality, so again do not try to be a psychiatrist.

You will add to the anxiety of a subordinate by not controlling your own anxieties and tenseness. You can advance a man's tenseness if you put too much pressure on him, demand too much of him, force him to make decisions, or put him in work that is over

[7] A feeling of high degree of unreasonable pressure tends to be associated with low performance. Rensis Likert, *New Patterns of Management*, McGraw-Hill Book Co., New York, 1961, p. 8.

his head. You can break a man emotionally by loading him with anxieties, building up hostility, and putting him under continuous stress. A man on the road to a neurosis will get there soon enough without your assistance. Only by making his work situation less anxious and by personal counseling can you help him.

Your Managerial Roles   You have two organizational roles as a manager, administrative and integrative. You start by helping each subordinate who will profit from your help, then aid those who can to form an integrated, cohesive group. In your administrative role you work with each subordinate individually, a boss with line authority (Exhibit 10, Chapter 11). In your boss-subordinate transaction in Exhibit 10, your goal is to move from the first stage of control to the second stage where you accept your interdependence with your subordinate. In addition to many of the things already covered, you depend on him for results, help, and support. In some instances you may seek his personal counsel for your own problems. Interdependence is a two-way street. The third, or ideal stage, job-man budget, is to be discussed shortly.

In your integrative role you work with your total staff to turn out what is essentially a group product of your own organizational unit. It is in this area that all the questions about securing effective group effort come into focus—questions about the nature of the relationship a manager should have with his staff, how he should work with them and help them in group development. Your integrative role is outlined in the next chapter. To carry out these two roles successfully, you divide them into two basic functions: managership and leadership. Managership is essentially making decisions about individuals. Leadership is helping those who can be helped.

How Can I Help?

If you have been able to develop a greater awareness of yourself as a manager and are able to accept the behavioral approach, you will find that you can make more intelligent decisions about subordinates and help those who can be helped.

Management Formula   The formula for managing is surprisingly simple. Begin by recalling key things you have learned thus far, but this time in terms of subordinates:

1. Use the behavioral sciences consensus as your policy and practice for your organization (Chapter 6).

2. Practice personal counseling on behavior problems and emotional problems or provide a sympathetic ear (Chapter 11).

3. Accept the work needs of normal man (Exhibit 2).

4. Recall the achieving tendencies and the seven stages of emotional health (Exhibit 8).

Then apply what you learn from the next few pages in your managerial and leadership functions in your administrative and integrative roles:

5. Evaluate your men.

6. Rank your men in terms of good workers, middling ones, and misfits.

7. Treat your misfits and your middling men differently than your normal or good men.

8. Stop the games your subordinates play.

9. Use the job-man budget and the plan-budget-feedback.

10. Help in whatever way you can in both administering and integrating.

Continuous Evaluations Your basic function of managership requires that you make decisions about people. You recommend who gets a raise, who should be promoted, who should be fired, and who should be demoted. I suggest that you make your evaluation of subordinates on four points:

1. Compatibility
2. Technical competence
3. Emotional competence
4. Cooperativeness

Think of compatibility in terms of your feelings about a subordinate. Compatibility may range from disinterest to friendship. But if you dislike a person or feel incompatible with him, the best thing to do, if you can, is to end the relationship.[8] For all the preach-

---

[8] Douglas McGregor, *The Human Side of Enterprise,* McGraw-Hill Book Company, New York, 1960, pp. 142–143. Also recall subordinate achieving tendencies in the previous chapter.

ments about your being objective, there are instances where the chemistries of two people cause friction. It takes two to make a good relationship. And in many ways your subordinate can exercise, if not positive, then negative attitudes which make it impossible for you to establish a constructive relationship. The behavioral sciences approach to managing is not soft; it is tough.

As for technical competence, this should cause you little problem. Most managers can gauge how technically competent each subordinate is. With what you have learned thus far, you should be able to make some good guesses as to emotional competence. If you have doubts, it is hoped you can draw on the skills of a behavioral sciences counselor. Finally, you should make some good guesses as to how much potential a person has to learn how to cooperate with his peers under your guidance in your integrative role. Can he become an effective, group-building member who will help you develop a cohesive group?

Rank Your Subordinates Chances are that out of several people you should have a few who are outstanding and some who are good. These you can help. You also have some who are middling, and a few who are misfits. Plan your administering so that the outstanding and good ones can make their greatest contributions. Moreover, let them know you think they are good. Study your middling men. See if a way can be found to help them become more effective. Once you find that your help does not bring results, just assist them where you can. Some middling men need policing or coercion. Otherwise they will produce nothing. You will play "father" to others, providing them with emotional and intellectual support. Some will have to be steered or they will run off in all directions. Some will require continuous assurance that they are doing fine, so they can keep their anxiety under control. Some will have to be encouraged to slow down, so they do not end up as work addicts. Both an atmosphere of approval and consistent behavior by you in terms of the perceptions of each subordinate may be the anchor stone for his anxiety.

When you come to the misfits, however, the chances are that you, like most managers, find it difficult to take adverse action. There are a variety of underlying, strange, uncomfortable feelings. You may indulge in paternalistic soft-heartedness to protect them. You may have an underlying feeling of guilt for the way you have used them. Still, if a man is not doing what you think he should and you have tried to help him, do not waste your time. There is no good solution for the misfit. Find another spot if you can, but do not pass him off on someone else, although this is a popular game in corporation politics. Offer the man a job he can do in a satisfactory manner, even if it means demotion with a cut in salary. Although this seems hard, it is probably better for him in the long run. If he must be "dehired," encourage him to leave.

Games Subordinates Play   In your transactional analysis be alert to games subordinates play. Here are a few. Some of your normal subordinates may play "Blemish," reportedly the source of a large part of everyday dissension.[9] A subordinate who plays this game does not feel comfortable with you as his boss until he finds your blemish. His aim is reassurance and avoidance of an open relationship which might reveal his own blemish. Clues to his need to play "Blemish" may be found in the nature of his watchfulness, prying, and curiosity. Other clues may be his biases against people who wear clothes that are out of date, do not have enough money, are not sophisticated enough, or are not of the right color, class, or religion.

In "Kick Me," the player when he has provoked someone to kick him pleads that the sign he is wearing says, "Do not kick me." Then he asks, "Why does this always happen to me?" (In more extreme forms this is often found in paranoids.) This game is common with the job loser whose inverse pride makes him think that his misfortunes are better than those of anyone else.

"Look How Hard I've Tried" is the neurotic game of a hard-working man with a gastric ulcer. There are three degrees. The first degree is the man who tells his boss that he has an ulcer and that he will continue to work just as hard. His ulterior purpose is admiration which he gets from his boss, his wife, and friends. The second degree is when he keeps his condition a secret until he collapses at work. Now, boss and wife are not only supposed to admire him but also feel guilty for all the things they have done to him. The

---

[9] Berne, *op. cit.*, pp. 112–113. The other games in this section are drawn from pp. 84 and 106–107.

third degree is the progression of the secret ulcer to disability or death.

Job-Man Budget

Help your subordinates build their own jobs to the extent they can —self management by objectives. You help them think through what they want to accomplish and help them achieve it. Use the job-man budget.[10] You help them build their own jobs and thereby reduce their underutilization. In addition, you have the means to counteract the widespread disagreements that have been found to exist between boss and subordinate. Use the job-man budget as much as possible with your middling men and your misfits.

Systematic organization, job improvement, and self-improvement are not going to happen unless they are planned for as an integral part of a subordinate's work. Job-man budgeting provides for annual planning, budgeting, and feedback for each subordinate who is capable of doing this. He should take the initiative in working out *his* own work and career goals and how he is going to achieve them, in *his* appraising his own effectiveness in achieving them, in *his* evaluating his own accomplishments and developments. Through this approach, the subordinate participates actively in his being appraised, not in the usual terms of being told about his strengths and weaknesses but in terms of achieving his goals.

Let these job-man budgets be working drafts with only enough recorded to serve as a "memorandum of understanding" between your subordinate and you. He lists what the plans are, what they will cost, and how and when they will be accomplished. Expect the plans to be changed or modified in response to an ever-changing dynamic operation.

The job-man budget starts with a preliminary discussion between the subordinate and you as to how the year ahead looks, changes in the long-range plans or objectives of your organization, your overall view, and how these matters might affect the subordinate. If there was a job-man budget the year before, that is assessed and plans are discussed in relation to that memorandum. With these guides, the man goes to work on his program for the coming year. He may con-

---

[10] Abstracted from my book *Managing the Managers, op. cit.,* pp. 185–190.

sult with you several times as he works out his program, so that you two can come to a jointly developed set of plans.

Job Budget   The job phase of planning encompasses three major planning areas: work, projects, and improvements. *Work planning* covers the regular recurring activities. A review of his continuing work load provides a subordinate with a regular opportunity for a thorough evaluation of his work. *Project planning* covers the special, nonrecurring activities found in many management positions. Priorities and target completion dates should be set. Putting special projects in a separate category brings into focus the question of whether or not old projects should be continued, delegated, or eliminated. *Improvement planning* is the third major area of the job phase of planning. Out of his work activities, numbering somewhere around ten or twenty, and his special projects, usually one or two, a man might select five operations where significant improvements might be made.

Man Budget   The three major planning areas for the man budget all focus on personal growth: [11] job enlargement, personal development, and management development. *Job enlargement* is one of the best means for growth in work. Planned on an annual basis, job enlargement offers you the opportunity to help an individual with potential master new, higher-level, or broader tasks. *Personal development planning* includes those personal activities which the executive plans to carry out in the next year for his own growth. In terms of your being interested in what a subordinate is going to do to further his own personal development, accept the fact that if you make it an important facet of your concern about him, then it becomes important to him. With your help, he faces the issue of whether or not he is going to grow rather than vegetate and regress. Anything goes that adds to his personal development, such as community activities, nonbusiness courses, and constructive hobbies (see Your Personal Re-creation, Chapter 15). *Management development planning* includes any plans a subordinate has for taking courses paid for or

[11] Harry Levinson, "Is There an Obsolescent Executive in Your Company—or in Your Chair?" *Think*, vol. 34, no. 1, published by IBM, January-February, 1968, pp. 26–31. Levinson maintains that an organization must keep continuous pressure on its people to continue their self-development to avoid obsolescence.

put on by his organization, from participating in formal course work at a university on a part-time basis to attending a management conference. It is recommended that a man make his own plans, within company policies, for the kind of course he feels he can best profit from, with your counsel.

14
Help Your Peers

Open communications, mutual trust, and natural support may be helped or hampered, or even eliminated, by the actions of the leader, but he cannot bring about a high degree of any of them by the exercise of any of the forms of power available to him. They are characteristics of the system, affected by many other variables . . . and their degree is determined primarily by attitudes and interaction of *all* the individuals in the group, including the leader.

—DOUGLAS MC GREGOR, *The Professional Manager* [1]

IN WORKING WITH PEERS, man gets lost in a round of battles that are never won, only fought well. Such is the verdict of research. Yet, it is in your relations with your peers that you can do much to reduce the rat race. You need to secure (1) more knowledge about organizational roles, (2) better understanding of the nature of peer rivalry, (3) awareness of your own peer relations, (4) awareness of how you can help peers who will help you, and (5) information on how to help your boss in the integration of his subordinates.

[1] McGraw-Hill Book Company, New York, 1967, pp. 168–169.

Organization Roles

From the oversimplified boss-subordinate chain of command and line-staff concept of a few years ago, research has discovered a complex of peer roles that exist outside the chain of command. Exhibit 13 lists the organization roles.

Exhibit 13   ORGANIZATIONAL ROLES

Authority over People	Covered in Chapter
1. Administration	13
2. Integration	14
Authority over Actions	
3. Approval	14
4. Inspection	14
No Authority	
5. Subordinate	12
6. Staff	11
7. Service	14
8. Work flow	14
9. Group	14

Thus far we have analyzed three of these roles. In summary, the administration role is that of boss over each subordinate (Chapter 13). The subordinate role is that of working under a boss (Chapter 12). The staff role is essentially a peer role, helping another person who is responsible for the result (Chapter 11). Here the other peer roles as well as the integrative role of a boss are analyzed.

The approval role enables a person to give his approval before an action can be started. Because it has been established outside the *authority over people* roles, it indicates a distrust of the chain of command.[2] Worse, however, is the fact that the approval role adds another point of stress and evidence of distrust to the person who must secure the approval.

The inspection role is an auditing function. Whenever anyone who is not a supervisor reviews the work of others, he is occupying

[2] Leonard Sayles, *Managerial Behavior*, McGraw-Hill Book Company, New York, 1964, p. 103. This book is a major contribution to research on peer rivalry. Many of the roles in this chapter are based on Sayles's research and findings.

an inspector role. Inspecting may range from an occasional request by a superior to have you review a memorandum or proposal prepared by one of your peers to a full-time auditing or inspecting function. Private and public law are important to every organization. Police powers are necessary. But the police function tends to be grossly expanded because it nicely masquerades the pursuit of power. The inspector role enables its occupant not only to evaluate what is being accomplished but also to exercise authority ranging from pressure to veto. The proliferation of inspector roles particularly at the management level is additional testimony to the inability of management through the obsolete but traditional reward-and-punishment practices to feel that subordinates or their supervisors are doing a good job.

The service role encompasses a wide variety of service functions —maintenance activities, typing pool, cafeteria, health room, recreation program, house organ, tool room, and employment office. These result from the decision to centralize an activity and call it a service rather than permit each manager to spend time on it himself. The idea back of these services is that with a specialist or a special department devoting full time, a better job will be done at less expense. Many of these services go on without too much complaint. However, the more directly operating managers are dependent on these services for effective performance, the greater will be the conflicts between them and the service managers. The service manager has been found in the main to reward his friends and punish his enemies. For his enemies he is slower, more careless. Still, he usually caters to his most powerful adversaries in the belief that they can influence high management levels.

The work-flow role differs from the service role in that work under a supervisor is passed on to another unit under another supervisor for additional processing. Work flow covers the handling of work in stages. It includes the processing of papers, assembly of products, or the review of a problem by various departments. Managers involved in the work-flow process typically put pressure on each other to rearrange schedules, to improve the quality of the work they receive. Stalling, restricting information, playing politics, or manipulating are used to get into an earlier position in the work flow. From day-to-day processing, the work-flow concept can be expanded to include the interdependent work flow of the total company with the traditional expressions of hostility. Production insists that sales falls down on the job. Sales insists that production does not produce quality at a competitive price. Accounting insists that the others are not to be trusted and proceeds to prove its self-fulfilling prophecy.

The group role is where a man works with peers under one immediate boss. Collective or joint responsibility for results is becoming so common that we can no longer hold to the traditional organization theory where everyone has his own little box on an organization chart to indicate responsibilities for which he is solely accountable. Increasingly, with the growth of specialization and the complexity of operations, men are spending more of their time interacting with their peers in joint decision making and joint action. There are more and more staff meetings and collective deliberation. Task forces, where individuals with different bosses work together on a project to come out with a collective proposal, plan, procedure, product, or service, are continuing to accelerate at an increasing rate in many organizations.

Your Awareness as a Peer

In all the peer roles, the occupants have been found to practice one-upmanship. They try to move to a role where they have more control, power, and status. A man in a later stage of work flow tries to get into an earlier stage. Staff and service men strive for inspection. Inspection men strive for approval roles.[3]

Peer-Peer Transactions Open rivalry or individual competition is stage one of peer-peer transactions (Exhibit 10, Chapter 11). A Chinese expression, "Beware of honey on the knife," best typifies diplomacy, the second stage of peer transactions. This is subtle, rather than open rivalry. The expression also points up the ambivalent extremes of the need to win and the need to be accepted by peers. The emotional strain comes from subtle or diplomatic efforts in trying to get ahead of one's peers in both the win-lose complex of everyday competition and a success-failure complex of beating them up the ladder in the organizational hierarchy. There are also neu-

---

[3] Sayles, *op. cit.*, p. 114.

rotic needs to compete, as you have seen. As one who has succeeded, your own pecking-order instinct and your drive to achieve have served you well. To subordinate this to work for more effective peer-group effort is not an easy task.

Diplomacy contains a strong note of hypocrisy. You still try to get your way, but you give way gracefully if you find you cannot win. Popular synonyms for diplomacy are tact, respect, good manners. These are barriers between people. They are society's means for ensuring a superficial consideration of others as people. Good manners assure at least outwardly the control of aggression. Unfortunately, however, good manners require that you mask your feelings. At the diplomacy stage you can believe that you are working together and trying to help each other, when you are both in fact using "honey on the knife." In the ideal stage, mutuality, there is a spirit of mutual helpfulness where peers work together with the guidance of the boss or bosses.

Your Peer Transactions   In terms of what you can do to help your peers, look first at your own attitudes and actions. How effective are you in working with peers? For example, how much of your own personal feelings of insecurity have you projected into the need to dominate your peers? Or, how much of your own need for status and power have you projected into a belief that you need some leverage over the actions of your peers? It is here that you find the major difference between the power and maturation concepts of success.

In terms of how you help your peers, face the fact that they have feelings too. Accept the reality of these feelings and work with them. Even though they may not be particularly skilled in working at the peer level, many of your associates want to improve the functioning of their operations. Where this is not the case, you may find that an individual has real problems with himself.

Even in the best of groups, personal identification with a group of peers takes time. You are not likely to be accepted until you have become known to your peers and can be trusted by them. Your values and needs must be compatible in some measure with the values and needs of the group. At least you must accept the more important values of the group. When you have earned acceptance, you find that underneath the usual ribbing and razzing there is a supportive group atmosphere. You can take criticism and also give it. There is a personal feeling of security that comes with group identification so that you feel you can be frank and candid but at the same time concerned about the feelings of others. You know that you can count on the group to give you help when you need it. You come to feel that most of the members of your work group are friendly and want to help you. They give you recognition for a job well done.

Games Peers Play   Unconscious games by a peer (or boss or subordinate) start from the win-lose complex of "Now I've Got You, You Son of a Bitch." [4] The unconscious theme is to become highly indignant over some difference of opinion, a trivial matter or slight, rather than work through the situation on an adult basis. Since early childhood this person has overreacted to slight injustices or advantages taken of him. Your approach in dealing with him? Get your ego out of the way; see him for what he is. Be sure that you are right. Accept the fact that your dealings with him are always risky.

In "Why Don't You—Yes But," a peer presents a problem. You, as well as others, if it is a group situation, present solutions with "Why don't you . . . ?" To each suggested solution the player objects, "Yes, but. . . ." A good player can continue indefinitely until the others give up. The ulterior purpose is to reassure an inadequate child ego state. To stop this game, once you see it start, do not suggest solutions.

The "Schlemiel" game is for the player, in one way or another, to mess things up. Then there are profuse apologies. The player's child ego state enjoys itself in fouling things up. And the player wins whichever way you react. If you show anger, the player feels justified in reacting with anger. If you restrain yourself, then the player can continue to play "Schlemiel." Your cue to stop the game? Say to the player that he can do whatever he wants, but do not say "I'm sorry." If you do this, you may risk making an enemy.

[4] Eric Berne, M.D., *Games People Play*, Grove Press, Inc., New York, 1964, p. 85. The succeeding games are adapted from pp. 114 and 116–117.

How Can I Help?

If you are going to help your peers, do so when you can be reasonably sure that you will be helped in return.

Helpful Transactions Cultivate friendly, helpful associations with your peers where you can. Avoid the negative ones where possible. Do not call the grouchy man; call the pleasant one. Steer clear of those who are incompatible, unsympathetic, or too competitive. However, do not avoid feelings where there is a chance to work them through. Your work life should in the main be a friendly group life. You form associations which range from casual to good friends. You gravitate toward the people you like, your fellow associates who will help you and with whom you feel comfortable.

In your transactions with a peer, follow some of the steps we suggested earlier in an adult-adult transaction. First, assume a professional stance, helpful and empathic. Second, be aware of the organizational roles involved and try to help your peer become aware of his. Third, determine the purpose of the transaction. Fourth, evaluate your peer as to his compatibility, technical competence, emotional competence, and cooperative potential. If there is something lacking in any of these areas, do not expect too much and do not blame yourself. Fifth, look for a complementary transaction so as to avoid unconscious games.

In any joint deliberation where you may find yourself in organization life, you can at least not take a competitive stance even though there may be no opportunity to help secure greater joint effort. Just the ability to understand the process, develop group skills, and know what can and cannot work will give you a degree of sophistication that should reduce the business rat race for you.

Work for a Cohesive Group Whether peer, boss, or subordinate, whether chairman or member of a committee or task force, you can help for more effective group functioning. First, you can provide leadership-by-example in active consensus seeking. Second, you can work to develop the skills required for an effective group process, shared leadership.

Set a personal example as to how one should participate. Focus on the subject and be concerned not only with the various ideas advanced but with the emotional content. Speak quietly and easily, respond spontaneously and humorously on occasion, with good feeling and good fellowship. Think about your impact on the other members at the session. Do not move in with your ideas too quickly. Study reactions to your own behavior to see how you are being accepted. Accept members as they are and endeavor to understand them. You will find that some of them in turn become conscious of the impact of their behavior on others. If you can acknowledge other points of view as having pertinence and change your own point of view, you find that some of the others will respond in similar fashion.

Start with one fundamental: If the conditions are right, you can help yourself by helping your boss integrate his staff, the ideal goal. You can also help him move his group in improving communications toward leveling and in participation toward consensus, other ideal goals. You cannot establish, however, many helpful relations with your peers unless your boss is willing to move in this direction. He needs your help, too, for he cannot do it alone.

Group Stereotypes   First, however, become aware of the inaccuracies of the popular stereotypes about group effort. If you are a typical management man, you probably subscribe to these kinds of statements: "An individual should never submerge himself in the group." "If I join a group, I lose my individuality." These statements are fallacious. Man achieves his individuality only in groups, as *part* of a group. Man matures to the extent that he acknowledges his dependence on groups. He sees himself as part of the whole. If he sees himself as the whole with others as the parts, then he has severe emotional problems. In every sense man is the product of his group experiences.

Then there is the popular stereotype that group action is inefficient. It is phrased in various ways: "Only a committee could have conceived of a moose." "No group ever came up with a good idea." Typically, experiences with groups, such as committees and staff meetings, tend to make us leary of group action because they seem so inefficient. They often involve various individuals each trying to have his own way. Out of notions such as these has come the first stage of boss-subordinate staff transactions, coordination. In essence, coordination means that a manager controls the operations and the people by dealing with each subordinate individually. He personally coordinates all group effort. Each man is a pawn to be used for certain tasks. The most frequent analogy is that of a director of an orchestra. Each musician has specific music to play in a certain way. Only the director can hear all the parts and coordinate. Surely management people have much more to offer.

The second, or claimed stage, is teamwork: people working as a team. Critically think through the teamwork stereotype. Although "teamwork" is a popular term, it is much too simple a concept. Almost all teams are engaged in physical activity rather than intellectual. Relations between team members are well structured and well practiced to the point where they almost become automatic. Moreover, men selected for the team are chosen on the basis of not only their physical prowess but their high competitive drive. Each member of the team plays a highly specialized role. A coach moves men in and out at will. Teamwork also has the connotations of beating another group. Finally, in group management there is an emotional involvement at a much deeper, more significant, more permanent level. Men are not trying for a "winning team" but are engaged in joint pursuit of personal and organizational accomplishments.

Integration of a Staff

The ultimate in helping each other and achieving almost all the ideal stages in the various transactions comes in the integration of a staff into a cohesive work group by a boss. This involves trying to establish the conditions for an ideal work group. In addition members of the group learn how to carry out a variety of group-building transactions and group-task transactions.

Ideal Work Group   From the research on the group process, twelve basic conditions for integrating a group can be distilled. In reviewing these basic characteristics, rate your own peer group in terms of poor, fair, good, and excellent. You might also do this with your own subordinate group if you have one.

1. *Acceptance by the boss.* Basic to integration is the interest and capacity of the boss of the group to work with his subordinates. If he is opposed to the goal of consensus in participation, he automatically blocks the formation of an effective work group.

2. *Acceptance of the boss.* The subordinates must accept the manager as a good supervisor, dependent on the group and not a threat to it, sharing information and decision making with the group.

3. *Time.* No group will form overnight. It must have been in existence long enough so that individuals have had a chance to become acquainted, learn to get along, and have relaxed working relationships.

4. *Openness.* The supervisor and members of the group communicate frankly and fully all information which is germane to the group's activity. The group has been able to move from guarded and cautious to open and authentic communications, including leveling.

5. *Competence.* Differences in talent should not be too great. If individuals range from the extremes of very high to very low intelligence, creativity, technical competence, and training, drive to achieve, and cooperative skills, they may find it difficult to accept each other. Envy, rather than recognition for superior competence, is an enemy of group cohesiveness.

6. *Compatibility.* If the people do not actively like each other, at least they must not be more than indifferent to each other as individuals. Members of the group should be attracted to the group and feel accepted by it.

7. *Commitment.* A group can work *for* or *against* the organization. It is easier to organize group feeling against something than for it. A group can be cohesive and have as its goals mutual protection and mutual expression of hostilities toward the boss, with no commitment and low productivity and creativity. Its cooperativeness is not work related so much as emotionally related. However, if the group identifies itself with the boss, then its goals may well be work related under his guidance.

8. *Trust.* Mutual trust is difficult to achieve, coming more as the result of actions than words. It takes a long time to build and can be destroyed easily. Openness is a basic condition to both the development of trust and its continuance.

9. *Mutual support.* There is concern for each other without necessarily being close friends. Typically, members are gregarious enough to want to associate with each other, to be dependent on each other. They must feel that they are individually contributing and be able to see their own contributions.

10. *Helpful relations.* Comments, suggestions, information, ideas, and criticisms are all offered and received in a supportive atmosphere. The primary interest is in what "we can accomplish" not in "my way" or "his way." Members of the group are willing to help individuals with their problems.

11. *Leveling.* Not only is there an openness about ideas but there is genuinely open expression of feelings and leveling or feedback. Negative reactions or differences are not suppressed, underplayed, or masked. Rather, there is an attempt to work through differences because members can be themselves without fearing negative consequences. It is a climate of mutual trust and support with a genuine respect for differences. There are heated arguments. Tempers are lost. But these kinds of emotions are faced up to as something to be worked through for the long-term advantage of an effective group rather than ignored, belittled, or blocked. An individual who exhibits adverse feelings and actions such as anger, hostility, talking too much, and being unduly stubborn or insensitive is helped to work his problem through with consideration and patience by others.

12. *Shared leadership.* The supervisor of the group does not personally handle all the group leadership functions. Shared leadership means simply that the group members become skilled and interested in performance of a variety of leadership activities, that they share the responsibility for moving the group forward and helping others work and think together. They do not sit back and let the boss of the group (or a committee chairman) handle everything. Where there is interest in group integration and reaching consensus, the shared leadership functions have been classified into two broad categories—group-task and group-building transactions.[5]

Group-task Transactions   The following transactions or functions are concerned with the "product" or task of the group, *what* the group is going to accomplish. Most of them are self-explanatory.

Initiating activity covers such things as suggesting a new idea or

---

[5] These functions are drawn from a longer composite list compiled from a variety of sources and summarized by Warren G. Bennis and Herbert A. Shepard, "Group Observation," in W. G. Bennis, Kenneth D. Benne, and Robert Chin (eds.), *The Planning of Change*, Holt, Rinehart and Winston, Inc., New York, 1961, pp. 743–756.

another way of looking at the group problem or even suggesting a solution.

Seeking information may range from asking for clarification to asking for additional information.

Seeking opinion is trying to get clarification of the values that are involved in a suggestion or the opinions of others.

Information giving is offering fact, experience, or generalizations.

Opinion giving is volunteering beliefs or opinions relating to a suggestion that has been made.

Elaborating is either spelling out suggestions in terms of examples or trying to get others to expand on ideas or suggestions.

Coordinating is trying to bring the activities of various members of the group together or to pull ideas or suggestions together.

Summarizing is expressing what has happened thus far and seeing if the group views it this way.

Sifting feasibility is checking through with the group to see if there is a feeling that the idea or solution being considered by the group is thought to be feasible.

Evaluating is questioning the practicality of the quality of a procedure or suggestion.

Group-building Transactions   Group-building functions are concerned with the "process" of the group, *how* well they are working together —efforts to integrate the group.

Encouraging is done in a variety of ways: praising, agreeing with, listening attentively, being considerate.

Gatekeeping is attempting to expedite and keep communication channels open by encouraging the participation of others or by attempting to get others to permit the participation of the quieter members of the group.

Standard setting is expressing the quality of the group process, suggesting standards to the group, or helping the group to form its own standards.

Expressing group feeling is an attempt to verbalize the emotional level of the group.

Testing for consensus is a periodic attempt to see if there is a consensus.

Mediating is the attempt to work through differences between members of the group either at the emotional or the intellectual level so that they can be resolved and the group can move forward.

Relieving tenseness is accomplished by cracking a joke, changing the subject, suggesting a short break, or other such devices when the group appears to be at an emotional impasse.

Plan-Budget-Feedback System Underlying the group-task and group-building transactions, a plan-budget-feedback system is the determinant of what a group is to accomplish over a specified period. An extension of the job-man budget for an individual employee, its purpose is to enable people to plan intelligently both program and dollars, then be guided by the plan and the dollars. This approach to budgeting means that almost everyone will need to develop a new understanding of budgeting. Employees can work together intelligently to establish goals, assuring the maximum of individual freedom and conscious collective effort to make the management staff as effective and economical as possible.

The positive aspects of budgeting should be emphasized. Padding, competition, distrust, manipulation, and budget whacking can only develop an atmosphere of distrust. The purpose of budgeting, then, is planning the best program in light of dollars available and then establishing feedback to the individuals involved so they can know how well they are doing. Budgeting is not used as a weapon to put pressure on people. It is an integral part of the normal, ongoing management process.

Budgeting is a circular operation with much interchange. It should simultaneously be built up from the grass roots with every member of management responsible for taking the initiative for planning his own work programs, the costs involved, and then working within those costs—via the job-man budget.

One member of the staff should do the following:

1. Help put the budget together, including consolidating the plans and translating them into a comprehensive projection of financial conditions and results.

2. Record and report back comparisons of plans and results.

3. Assist management people to analyze, interpret, and react, including, where necessary, adjustments in the budget—a variable as opposed to a fixed budget.

4. Provide the management people with feedback reports geared to their needs in simple format, with charts or graphs wherever possible so that each person can plan and control his operations with the minimum of "paper work."

part 5

Help Yourself in the Pursuit of Happiness

*There are those who believe that the basic reason for
life is to seek "reduction of tension." Recent
researchers, beginning to be critical of this point of
view, point out that people who seek only tension
reduction may be neurotic or psychotic. These
people are preoccupied with their own irritations
and are continually trying to seek relief.*
—CHRIS ARGYRIS, *Personality and Organization* [1]

YOU HAVE THE RIGHT to life and liberty, but only to the pursuit of happiness. In spite of pretending to themselves and others that they are happy, almost everybody is not only not happy most of the time but actually unhappy, according to several of the professionals. Yet, it is only through the striving for happiness both at work and off your job that you survive in and beyond the business rat race. Pursuit of happiness is working for your total well-being not only in your work life but, as I suggest in this part of the book, in your personal life and your family life. Surely Jefferson and Franklin were too wise and knowledgeable to construe happiness as other than the pursuit of wisdom and democracy in the maturation concept of success.

[1] Harper & Row, Publishers, Incorporated, New York, 1957, p. 28.

Your nonwork life can be one of futility, powerlessness, emptiness, boredom, escape, reduction of tenseness, or superactive pleasure seeking, or it can be neglected for your business life. There are many other satisfactions which you need to get out of your life besides your job. Moreover, you are not only more productive and creative at work but also more cooperative when you live a full life.

For many of us today, life falls roughly into thirds: first, preparing for life; second, working for life; and last, "enjoying" retirement. It would be best if you did not retire, provided you have not succumbed in one way or another to the business rat race. Yet, with compulsory retirement, a vestige of the unemployment problem of the thirties, most of us have no choice. How important work is, if you have not prepared for a full life in retirement, is revealed by the recommendations of several mental health experts. They suggest that you find another kind of work. Yet, is this the answer when you have to do something which will underutilize you even more than what you did before retirement? No. The answer lies in the maturation concept of success. Then you can pursue your well-being into retirement. That, as you have seen, is the same answer for surviving the business rat race.

In this part of the book I suggest what the behavioral sciences, including the medical sciences, stress for the maturation concept of success in your personal life and your family life. Just as in your business life, so too in your personal and family lives you have three means—your mind, your body, and other people—through three kinds of activities—relaxation, work, and re-creation—the three by three by three formula.

15

Get More Out of Your Personal Life

You're old when:
1. You feel old.
2. You feel you've learned all you need to learn.
3. You feel tomorrow holds no promise.
4. You find no amusement in the youth frolics, and their lively banter irks you.
5. You would rather talk then listen.
6. You feel "the old days are best."
7. You find yourself saying, "I'm too old for that."
8. You won't help neighbors, friends or community.
9. You have no plan for tomorrow.
10. You would rather win an argument than be right.

—CHARLES E. THOMPSON, M.D., *What an Executive Should Know about His Health* [1]

HOWEVER YOU MAY APPROACH your personal life, you come to this question. How are you utilizing and building yourself for your own long-term feeling of well-being? All work and no play makes Jack not only a dull boy but very likely a neurotic. Just work and play,

[1] The Dartnell Corporation, Chicago, 1961, p. 198.

with no genuine relaxation and re-creation, can also make Jack an all-too-active go-go neurotic. Or, just work and reduction of tenseness can make Jack a dull, self-centered neurotic.

Start by separating your personal life from your work life and your family life. Seek relaxation, work, and re-creation through your mind, your body, and other people. Exhibit 14 contains some suggestions for relaxation, work, and re-creation in your personal life.

Exhibit 14   RELAXATION, WORK, AND RE-CREATION
IN YOUR PERSONAL LIFE

| | In These Activities: | | |
	Relaxation	Work	Re-creation
Through:			
Your Mind	Slow down Reduce tenseness Television, movies Light fiction Spectator sports Hobbies	Family duties (Chap. 16)	News reading Applied reading Pure reading See Chap. 17 for Major Life Crises; Rising Expectations; New American Realism
Your Body	Sleep and rest Physical therapy via re-creation	Home chores (Chap. 16)	Avoid soft living Vigorous exercise Run, walk
Other People	Non competitive games Fun with others	Community ser- vice	Learn from others Serious discussion

Modern Golden Mean

To achieve the art of personal living, you gradually develop an approach and follow it. You practice the *modern* Golden Mean as part of the maturation concept of success. While the prescription for personal living stresses a high level of activity, especially physical activity, it suggests more variety and more selectivity than the heedless habits of the typical businessman. It suggests a balanced or a rhythmic pattern of relaxation, extracurricular work activities, and re-creation of yourself.

As I said earlier, time becomes the governor, your budget. If you work beyond the normal work week, you subtract this time from either your personal or your family life. Therefore, it becomes imperative that you limit your work life to somewhere near the normal work week. There are enough suggestions outlined here so that you can find sufficient activity to fill the void. Follow the old maxim, a change is as good as a rest.

Personal Goals   If you want to succeed in the art of personal living, more of your time will be used to develop a greater feeling of intellectual, emotional, and physical well-being. Think through what you should do and then experiment. After you achieve your preliminary goals, you can then make a plan which is carefully organized and rigorously scheduled. It deals with specific points, covering the things you need to move away from as well as what you should move toward. In substituting new habits for old, move slowly and take short steps. Do not set unreasonable goals for yourself.

Work toward recapturing the verve and endurance, the vitality, curiosity, and enthusiasm you had as a young man. As suggested earlier, cultivate several sources of activity for the good life. With a multiplicity of these sources, if one source fails, you can use others. For example, if you are underutilized and underworked in your work life, you can secure your primary gratification from off-the-job sources. If you are underutilized and overworked where you cannot control your time, carefully select a few important extracurricular activities to enrich your life.

A planned program for personal living enables you to accept with much greater equanimity the stress, uncertainties, and ambiguities of the business rat race. You may well do better in the business world because you have a coherent sense of yourself and reality. You know what is right and what is wrong and your actions make sense in terms of stable values. Call it high frustration tolerance, self-control, emotional stability, or a mature mind. It comes only through your search for ways to become a more effective man, a less anxious man. Just as little things lead to anxiety, so too do little things, consciously and earnestly pursued, lead toward maturity.

Soft Living   Start with soft living. Many of us were brought up to believe that as we get older we should slow down, to our detriment in light of recent findings. Heart attack has become a leading killer. Its causes involve, not a germ, but such things as soft living, too little exercise and physical activity, tenseness, heredity, excessive cigarette smoking, excessive eating, being overweight, high levels of cholesterol, and high blood pressure.[2]

If you have any one of these conditions, risk of a premature heart attack is boosted two to six times over that of a person who has none. Your chances of having a heart attack before age sixty-five are one in fifty if you are in good health and are normal with respect to these risk factors. However, your chances are one in two or worse if you have a combination of two or more of the risk factors.

Relaxation

In your personal life, the first step is relaxation. Relax through your mind, your body, and other people. Suggestions made earlier for relaxing in your work life should be carried over into your personal life. The formula of relaxation is basically rest, play, and escape. It is not soft living, pampering, retreating, or avoiding strains, either physical or mental. Some physicians recommend that we drink frequently, but moderately. They feel that we need a "crutch" or a relaxer. Alcohol is judged by some physicians to be superior to tranquilizers.

Relax Your Mind   First, start with your mind. If you are going to reduce your tenseness and increase your emotional energy as well as enlarge your emotional capacity, there are many things your mind can do to help your emotions. The tremendous extra dividend is the direct help to your body and to your physical well-being. Check over the several nervousness signals listed in Chapter 9. Many of these can be attacked directly by developing new habits to replace those deadly habits. Boredom is one of the major barriers to relaxing. Some men feel a void within themselves when they have time on their hands. They are too tense to face leisure. "Sunday neu-

[2] Alton Blakeslee and Jeremiah Stamler, M.D., *Your Heart Has Nine Lives,* Prentice-Hall, Inc., Englewood Cliffs, N.J., 1963, p. 5. Victims of a rheumatic or defective heart are in a different class.

rosis" has been found to be a common complaint of the business-man who feels a void within himself because of the lack of content in his personal and family life. Boredom can be attacked directly by following the suggestions in this chapter to enlarge your personal life. Gulping breakfast, lunch, and dinner, an aspect of nervousness, can be counteracted by a conscious, deliberate program to slow down and cultivate a relaxed attitude.

Where do you fit in the normal curve of driving? The normal driver is a considerate and careful driver in his locale even though he may exceed the speed limit. Beyond normal is the driver who goes too slowly for the traffic. At the other end is the tense, overly aggressive driver who pushes too hard, too fast, to beat the others. Discipline yourself to follow the normal driving pattern. Establish a new driving habit, a conscious reduction of your undue tenseness.

Such things as fatigue, restlessness, or a feeling of being trapped require a deliberate effort to relax or find diversion. On your way home start thinking about home and the evening's activities. Home can be a wonderful place to come to if you and your wife consciously strive to make it that way. A major outlet for tenseness is to escape into amusements. Here a pleasant movie, a light book, such as one of the more popular novels, a crossword puzzle, or television are some of the best devices for escape. These kinds of amusements are especially helpful when things go wrong or you are faced with a painful problem. To make yourself suffer through it is not a good way to solve a problem, but a form of self-punishment. Move away for a while to get a new perspective and recover your balance.

There is danger in escape, for it is easy to become addicted. Accept the fact that you never get anything for nothing. A little of these amusements goes a long way. Not only does the time for escape consume time you need for more constructive things, but these amusements are well below your intellectual level. Because the masses have never learned how to live a full and meaningful life, they seek their fun-and-games morality as an opiate. They are cursed with boredom. You, however, as a successful man are a member of a small elite. Your cue for living in a meaningful way is to avoid that which attracts the mass of the new middle class, the blue-collar worker and the white-collar office worker. It is not a case of being snobbish, but a matter of being selective to achieve happiness.

Television, for example, not only provides for endless escape but creates daydreams of endless consumption and endless violence. Television fantasies, remnants of life for only a few people, have no resemblance to real life. You live vicariously but unconsciously the life of the heroes of violence. Evil rather than Good now triumphs. If you regularly watch television, you are accepting a "mother-narcotic" just as children do. Increasingly, television polls indicate that the more affluent and better educated are looking at it less. When they do, they look at movies, generally shunning the popular programs. More and more television is depending on the lower income groups. (Some advertisers who want to reach you are openly questioning the television trend.)

Spectator sports, particularly with the advent of television, offer another form of amusement. These in small doses are good escape. But their danger is that they might become a vicarious retreat into a simpler, sometimes a sadistic, competitive world. Some people clutter their minds with the details of what have always been basically juvenile sports and thereby keep out more vital information and knowledge.

If you do not regularly take a vacation, you have evidence of your tenseness. Get away from work completely now and then for a long enough period to refresh both your body and your mind. It is desirable to have one or more hobbies for relaxation. The test of a good hobby is that it not only interests you but is one into which you can throw yourself with pleasure and forget all about your work. Moreover, a hobby can be a mainstay for retirement.

Relax Your Body   Practice what you preach to your children. Relax your body by getting plenty of sleep. This is elementary, yet often ignored. It is another evidence of tenseness. Worse, a body that is tired offers a greater avenue for additional tenseness. Preparing for and having a good night's sleep is the key to successful relaxation. When we sleep, we all have periods of wakefulness, but even so we sleep or doze more than we realize, according to research.

Physical therapy, working and exercising your body, to be covered in re-creation, gives you many relaxation benefits. You work off tenseness that has built up within you. You relax not only physically but also mentally and emotionally. You also can work off your aggressive tendencies, your competitiveness, as well as your frustrations. As extra dividends, you not only have a feeling of physical

well-being, you have better physical and mental health, better diges-
tion, and sounder sleep. Hence, exercising your body provides not
only for a multiplicity of relaxations but for re-creation of yourself.

Relax with Others Games are good *if* you can reduce your need to
win and consider them strictly sociable. Be wary of competitive,
participative sports. Golf, tennis, volley ball, bowling, and other
competitive sports are assumed by many as a way of working off aggressions or relaxing. Unfortunately, this is not usually true. Psychiatric observations conclude that these activities are just another
form of competition and should be reduced. Even if you tell yourself that you are doing it to relax, chances are you are asking for
more competition because you want to beat someone. So, if you are
sports minded, make it a habit to limit your time at these kinds of
events. And when you play them, be as casual and easygoing as possible. On the other hand, if your work is boring and you work regular hours with little conflict, aggressive games may be your salvation.

To relax with others means that you must be aware of your own
ways of relating to others. How do you behave? For example, do
you talk too much? By watching yourself, you become aware of how
far beyond the normal bounds you go. You consciously slow down
your speech, lower your voice, and let others talk more.

Be moderate in your pursuit of fun with others. There is not only
excessive party going but excessive cocktailing. Some people cannot
be alone; they constantly seek to be with others. These people are
not able to converse intelligently. Using cocktails to secure sedation,
they escape from their loneliness by a regular round of cocktail parties. Too many parties brings the business rat race into your personal life when you mix business and pleasure.

Being with other people to relax means to find companionship,
relaxation, cocktails, and play with a few people. Try to find friends
with whom you can be genuinely open and intimate. Then form
close, trustful, and mutually supportive emotional attachments
where you talk about problems as well as pleasant things. Recall
the axiom, "A friend in need is a friend indeed." Make yourself
available to your friends. Reach out for them. Too often individuals feel that they are not wanted and increasingly expect their
friends to take the initiative in seeking them out. It is better, in

order to build strong friendships, for you to take the initiative and not sit back and wait. Go easy with criticism. Friends tend to be, because of close association, hypercritical of each other. This increases tenseness in the relationships. Therefore, give the other fellow a break and give in more than you might usually do to support the intimacy.

Your Personal Work

If you are a family man, much of your personal work will be your family work, as you shall see in the next chapter. There I cover your work with your body. Here I cover only those things which you do beyond your family. Your personal work is primarily that of using your mind to help others. This can be a community service activity such as PTA, civic club, or your church, or serving on a community committee, on a library board, or on more basic programs to help the have-nots.

Be sure that your motives are not those of public relations for your business or personal status seeking. In constructively giving of yourself to help others, more positive motives are necessary. These can range from a humane concern or identification with a good purpose to personal atonement.

Your Personal Re-creation

Build up to a vigorous program of re-creation. Relaxation reduces tenseness. Personal work gives you a sense of self-esteem and contribution through constructive activities. Re-creation is your rebuilding yourself, a program of personal improvement, so that

You make your mark on your organization.
You make your mark on your community.
You face retirement with many interesting things to do—not as the closing of your life.

Re-create Your Mind   There is an old saying that the clamor of the emotions is enormous, of the intellect very soft. The goal for your mind should be to broaden your vision and lead a more reflective, realistically oriented life.

Not too many years ago a man's formal learning, though limited, was enough to last him his lifetime in a stable, almost static environment. With the increasing pace of scientific, political, economic, and social developments today, a man must stretch his mind just to keep abreast. Unless he works at his own intellectual growth, he becomes obsolete—intellectually alienated. He cannot understand what is going on around him. He becomes unduly anxious or hides behind a false complacency. There is an ever-increasing need for broad-gauged men who are capable, productive, cooperative, creative, and growing. What is wanted is a broad-gauged thinker, one who can draw on his well-furnished mind to comprehend and meet creatively the problems of the larger job—one who does not resist change, but anticipates it, innovates, and capitalizes on it—to think as a manager should.

Yet no mind can be creative, generate ideas, and solve problems unless it draws regularly and generously on a wide variety of quality materials. Refurbishing the mind builds not only a store of ideas but also wisdom. Wisdom comes as a result of cultivating a long view (history), a large view (world problems), an open view (economics and politics), a rational view (behavioral sciences), a profound view (philosophy), and a humanistic view (literature and the arts).

Research indicates that many of the most successful businessmen do much more reading of serious books than do the less successful. You can take some measure of your interest in learning and culture in terms of a cross section of adult Americans.[3] One out of two have a good deal of interest in religion, sports, and music; one of three, in politics and government, international affairs, cooking, and home decoration. But only one out of five has a good deal of interest in history, science, presumably including the behavioral sciences, and literature. And only one out of ten in art. College graduates did better than high school graduates. But only a minority of the college graduates have a taste for cultural and intellectual activity. I recall earlier surveys of college graduates who had been out of school ten years. Only one out of ten had read any kind of a book in the last year.

[3] Elmo Roper, "How Culturally Active Are Americans?" *Saturday Review,* vol. 49, no. 20, May 14, 1966, p. 22. In this survey the respondents were asked to select subjects from a list in which they had "a good deal of interest."

If you gradually and systematically cultivate an interest in reading, you will understand better what is going on in the world and develop a habit and a hobby which will make your retirement more interesting and meaningful. The difficulty in reading is getting started. Once you do this, you find that reading itself is not hard, nor does it mean hours and hours of intense study. The mind of an adult is there waiting to be cultivated if there are not too many debilitating factors. It is generally agreed that adults can learn many things better than children, even though it may take them longer. Unfortunately, as you have seen, we want quick, easy answers, resisting the abstract and the difficult. We seek specific facts or simplistic "how to" answers, not ideas and the whys and wherefores. We react emotionally, too, rejecting what goes against our values.

To re-create your mind means to expand your reading time and to change your reading habits. Reduce your *news reading;* increase your *applied reading* and your *pure reading.* It is not a case of speed reading, but of carefully allocating your deliberately expanded reading time.

By *news reading,* many men think they are growing because they read newspapers and magazines. Look at the metropolitan businessmen who commute by train. Over 90 percent read a newspaper going to work in the morning and another coming home at night. They have never realized that what they are reading is well below their mental level—that newspaper wisdom is for the mass population, not for the small percentage of successful men. Nor do they realize that the warmed-over news of the morning and evening papers gives undue emphasis to the malevolent, the malicious, and the violent. It is debatable whether or not it is really news anymore. Some view it as a sad sort of entertainment for those who need to read about violence and malevolence or to avoid loneliness and boredom. With these as well as most of the trade, business, and management journals, skim for essentials.

You have already discovered many of the difficulties in *applied reading,* in the discussion of the management mess in Chapter 5. Ways for you to learn were outlined in Chapter 7 so as to develop your professional stance.

For *pure reading,* concentrate on nonbusiness, serious books and magazines which have only limited circulation. These are at your intellectual level as a successful businessman. They are designed to inform and instruct the one out of five who is genuinely interested in going beyond the oversimplified, superficial materials for mass circulation. Most of the limited circulation magazines and adult books can be comprehended by the intellectually oriented high school graduate. I know of men who did not finish high school who are able to read and learn and think at the level I suggest here. Serious books,[4] especially, offer a fruitful source for the pursuit of personal insight, knowledge, and an understanding of people. The classics and good plays come close to portraying real life and provide inspiration and pleasure. Also keep up with what you might want to read by looking at current books and book reviews. Too, you will find that your friends who are readers will suggest books.

Your vacation or leisure time may be a time not only for relaxation but also for re-creation. For example, a noted heart specialist has moved from general history for its own sake to the history of archeology and medicine. On vacations he visits ancient cities both in the old and new worlds to collect old medical books. These fit in with his medical educational endeavors.[5]

Re-create Your Body   Just as the clamor of the emotions drowns out the soft voice of the intellect, so too may the complaints of the body nullify the soft clamor of your general feeling of physical well-being. You listen and overreact to what is going on inside your body.

Which comes first, diet or energy? It has been found that well-fed persons are characteristically enthusiastic and energetic. Overeaters have less tolerance for activity and stress. And undereaters, who eat the wrong foods or too little food, tend to suffer from tenseness, moodiness, boredom, and inability to make decisions. They are also prone to digestive trouble, anemia, gallbladder trouble, vitamin deficiency, and constipation. If you are overweight, you probably know that there is practically no difference among the reducing diets. All are equally effective or futile. The significant difference is in the dieters. Only about 1 percent of the people who go on diets are emotionally able to stay slim over a long period of time.

[4] There is a paperback guide listing over 15,000 titles in many fields, called *Good Reading*, prepared by the Committee on College Reading, J. Sherwood Weber (ed.), Mentor Books, New American Library, Inc., 501 Madison Ave., New York, 1935, revised 1956.

[5] Paul Dudley White, M.D., "My Own Prescription for Life," *Saturday Review*, vol. 50, no. 50, Dec. 16, 1967, p. 19.

The all-too-evident message about exercise to re-create your body is this. Take a few minutes each day and make it a habit you do not break to keep yourself alive and vital. Huff and puff by running and walking to build a strong heart, tone up your glandular system, put your mind and emotions at ease. And it is free! You can do it alone at your convenience or join a neighborhood jogging group. If you jog on a hard surface, I suggest from my own experience that you use a thick, soft-soled running shoe. It is so important that it bears repeating. By exercising the body, you not only release emotional aggressions but you relax and re-create your total being. Some medical men claim that exercise is the master conditioner for the healthy and the major therapy for those that are ill.[6] Heart patients and people with mental breakdowns are encouraged to huff and puff for recovery.

It is never too late to begin if you do two obvious things: check with your physician and start slowly to build yourself up. Get out and run and walk—or at least walk, the universal exercise. You can work under a point system which indicates how well you are doing and how much exercise you are getting.[7] To achieve a needed minimum of 30 points a week, run and walk five days a week, one mile in under six and a half minutes, two miles in twenty to twenty-four minutes. You can substitute points by swimming, bicycling, walking, or playing handball, squash, basketball, football, or golf without carts. But these all take more time. To get 30 points a week, you would have to play eighteen holes ten times a week.

Re-create Yourself through Others   Re-creating yourself through others means both participating in learning or discussion groups and opening your mind to others individually and collectively. Your objective? Learn from others. When you engage in intellectual growth, you find that there are others who also do it. They like to think about larger issues and the major problems with which all of us are faced. With a better understanding of them, they are more philosophical about them. Seek joint participation in reading and

---

[6] Blakeslee and Stamler, *op. cit.*, p. 129.

[7] Kenneth H. Cooper, M.D., *Aerobics*, M. Evans and Company, Philadelphia, 1968. Based on U.S. Air Force research and experimentation. Cooper has worked out points for a wide variety of activities. Calisthenics, viewed as body cosmetics, and isometrics receive no points.

discussion through adult education groups or groups which you might form. You undoubtedly can find some people in your community. There are various reading and discussion groups, sometimes with an outsider to act as a resource person and discussion leader. Sometimes the group itself rotates the leadership among its own members.

Another major step in re-creating yourself through others is to reach out for individuals who are unlike you and have opposing views. For example, pick a college student, someone older, and someone younger. Visit with them to learn from them. Talk with them and listen to them.

Most important, if you fear self-expression, you can help yourself through others. Some men have been able to work on the problem directly by consciously but very gradually striving to become a little more open with others. They pick a friend who gives evidence of being not only a good listener but also understanding and helpful. They find the opportunity to talk more about themselves when the two of them are together for a fairly long period, since then other subjects are exhausted. Another means is through serious group discussions. Here you gradually move from talking about things outside yourself to things inside. Not to work at the problem, even if it means psychiatric help, is a major barrier to your surviving in and beyond the business rat race. Ideally, the best person to be open with is your wife.

16

Capitalize on the Sexual Imperative

> Human males form sexual associations with females
> not out of a tiresome, dutiful, pious, half-unwilling
> obedience to the demands of the culture but in ful-
> fillment of the biological nature of the beast.
> —WESTON LA BARRE, *The Human Animal* [1]

POTENTIALLY, THE MOST IMPORTANT "OTHER" in your life is your
wife. To help her help you requires that both of you accept the
realities of the sexual imperative about both of you, the feminine
mystique, your true role in your family, and how to achieve companionship. Even though my treatment must necessarily be brief, I
can cite enough of the major common findings to give you a good
basis for coming to a better understanding of your family life, the
third major facet of your life. The rewards of the maturation concept of success in your family are great.

In your case, does your work come before your wife and your
family? If you are like most businessmen, you will say no. You may
work long hours, perhaps including a lot of travel, but you still
deny it. Even a neurotic competitor is likely to say no. Yet for him
his wife is often only a prize he won in competition with other men.

[1] The University of Chicago Press, Chicago, 1954, p. 210.

206

He competes with her because he has never learned any other type of relationship. He also unconsciously but subtly competes with his children for attention from his wife.[2] If you are going to face reality in your family life, you should be aware that for man, work comes before woman [3]—except for the moments of sex. Your own success in business if you neglect your wife is a threat to your marriage, as many newspaper columns testify. Yet, the maturation concept of success enables you to be a success at work and at home as well as in your personal life.

You may rationalize your overinvolvement in your work life with excuses or alibis, but to an outsider they are patently false. Here are a few symptoms [4] of the problem:

"My wife is interested only in the children, not in me." In the little time you are at home you still think primarily about your work.

"My wife talks, but never listens." If you bide your time, you probably will find that your wife is interested in your work.

"All I am is a handyman around my house." Should not a businessman share in the household chores if he wants to be part of the family? His wife does them. And for him, if he can see them in the true light, they are good physical and emotional therapy.

"I am too busy." Both your wife and children soon get this message with the rest of it implied, "I am more interested in my work than in my wife and family." You are escaping from your family into work—neglect.

"My wife is obsolete. I have outgrown her." This is nothing more than sadistic treatment of a human female for which there can be no rationalization.

The Confused Human Animal

Our tremendous interest in sex, evidenced by four-letter words and pornography, is not matched by research. Although we really do

[2] C. Knight Aldrich, M.D., "The Neurotic Competitor in the World of Business," *Executive Behavior, Selected Papers,* no. 5, Graduate School of Business, University of Chicago, Chicago, 2d printing, April, 1966, p. 11. Reported on in Chapter 9.

[3] Theodore Reik, M.D., *Of Love and Lust,* Farrar, Straus & Cudahy, Inc., New York, 1957.

[4] For a description of more symptoms, see Mortimer R. Feinberg, "Corporate Bigamy," a reprint from *Business Management,* 1965.

not know much about sex, especially among normal people, we talk a great deal about it.[5] We know less about the female than the male. Both the human male and female animals have the strongest sex drives, the most developed sexual equipment, the most sexual activity, and the greatest sexual experience of any animal species.

Sexiest Sex In contrast to other primates and other animals, the normal female of our species is interested in sex and receptive most of the time and over a longer period, even into her eighties. Neither love nor proper psychological preparation of the female are important variables for satisfaction of the sexual act. And her orgasm, as explosive as that of the human male, apparently is not anywhere near as strong in other animals. Even the permanently enlarged female breasts, unique among animals, are not for maternal use as much as they are another device for sexual signaling.[6]

That we have not done too well with sex demonstrates our own incapability of dealing with this open primary instinct. True, we have covered our bodies, but then the female accentuates her sex signals, starting with lipstick. True, we have sexual restrictions, but then our high level of sexuality causes us to trigger it off in non-acceptable ways. Just as the need to work is built by our culture on the open instinct for survival, and on the open instinct of the pecking order, so too is wife and family built on an open sexual instinct. However, we are all mixed up about sex. It has now become so twisted in our culture that a significant number of women are frigid, nymphomaniacs, or lesbians. And a significant number of men are impotent, women chasers, or homosexuals.[7] Moreover, a sexual basis is often found in kleptomania, fire setting, reckless car driving, various types of physical violence, and extensive gambling.[8] In our single-standard culture, we are still told that sex is a sin if practiced before or beyond the bounds of matrimony. It seems that even if we tried, we could not have done worse with such a basic instinct.

[5] William Simon and John H. Gagnon, "The Pedagogy of Sex," *Saturday Review*, vol. 50, no. 46, Nov. 18, 1967, p. 91.

[6] Desmond Morris, *The Naked Ape*, McGraw-Hill Book Company, New York, 1967, p. 70. Some experts disagree with the last point.

[7] It is estimated that 4 percent of the adult males are homosexuals.

[8] Karl Menninger, M.D., with Martin Mayman and Paul Pruyser, *The Vital Balance*, The Viking Press, Inc., New York, 1963, p. 191.

Repression in the Christian World   Religion is the bugaboo. Several studies conclude that those groups in our society least subject to the demands of religion are more at ease with sex, men in general, non-church goers, Negroes, liberals, and the highly educated. The popular notion that America is undergoing a sexual revolution appears to be a myth. The great change is in our open attitude toward sexual behavior.

The Christian church has a long history of opposition to earthly pleasures, particularly sex. The medieval sexual ideal of the Catholic Church provides the basis for our present feelings about sex. It is also the base of our sexual regulations in the United States. Even within marriage the sexual act should not be performed for pleasure. This ideal continues to the present day, especially in the Catholic Church.[9]

The written history of England, as well as the stories resulting from it, do not reflect the actual conditions. Christian authorities and historians have either rewritten the stories or prudishly ignored the facts. For example, King Arthur and his Knights of the Round Table lived at a time when neither the morals of the knights nor those of the ladies were very strict. When Catholic missionaries first came to England during medieval times, they found that marriage was a temporary, often polygamous arrangement frequently preceded by children. It was a different system of sexual morality. A woman was free to take a lover, either before or after marriage. A man was free to seduce a woman of lower rank and might hope to attract a woman of higher rank. That the missionaries had a great deal of difficulty in succeeding is well documented by historical events. For example, Henry the VIII's break with the Catholic Church and his several marriages can be more easily understood if it is realized that not only was Henry the VIII apparently syphilitic but also in his time marriages were temporary affairs.

On the European continent there were also severe Protestant attitudes toward sexual matters embodied in both Lutheranism and Calvinism. In all of their prohibitions they sought to reduce both spontaneity and pleasure. Man was expected to work diligently and find no pleasure on this earth—in work, sex, family life, or personal life. In the sixteenth century, Luther laid the foundation of the Pu-

[9] G. Rattray Taylor, *Sex in History*, Vanguard Press, Inc., New York, 1954, p. 51. Much of the information here is drawn from this book.

ritan work ethic. Luther, in his revolt against the established church, gave voice to hard work when he established a new religious individualism. He was opposed to improving one's lot or enjoying life. It was well after Henry the VIII's break with the Catholic Church that the Puritans became the primary reformers. They had the status of a minority opposition which was unable to impose its restrictive regime on others. Hence, many of them went to Amsterdam and finally to America, thus endowing this country with the Puritan ethic.

In contrast, premarital sexual relations are allowed in 70 percent of 158 non-Western societies covered in one study.[10] Moreover, women initiate sexual advances as often as do men.[11] The family is a biological event. Marriage is cultural. Looking at marriage from an anthropological standpoint, the family came first and the wide variety of marital arrangements are cultural sanctions.

Male Misconceptions   In order to give you a better understanding of some of the forces and values of the male human animal, we need to clear up some misconceptions. Here are some facts.

You have no paternal instinct as such. Man is conditioned to accept fatherhood. It has been generally found that when a young wife announces that she is going to have a baby, her pleasure is not shared by her husband. He is likely to be dismayed, disgusted, afraid, or jealous.[12] Typically, the father badly needs mothering himself and resents the fact that his wife is too absorbed with the coming child to give it to him. Most husbands are found to be jealous of their wives. Some show their envy by insisting that their wives continue to help with all the usual chores. Some are repelled by the embarrassing evidence of their sexual behavior, the generous curves of the pregnant female. Moreover, half of the fathers develop one or another of the symptoms of pregnancy—fatigue, muscle aches, headache, nausea and vomiting, stomach trouble, and a weight gain.

You are not really the head of the family. Although women are

[10] George P. Murdock, *Social Structure*, The Macmillan Company, New York, 1949, p. 265.

[11] Clellan S. Ford and Frank A. Beach, *Patterns of Sexual Behavior*, Harper & Row, Publishers, Incorporated, New York, 1951, p. 105.

[12] Beatrice Liebenberg, "Expectant Fathers," a paper presented to the Orthopsychiatric Association, Washington, D.C., March, 1967. Based on interviews with sixty-four young husbands about to become parents for the first time.

nowhere near having equal rights with their husbands, a father is only a minor influence in raising children. About the most a father can do, and it is important, is to play the authoritative masculine father role. The basic influence is mother.

Permanent monogamy is not instinctive with you. Contrary to a popular notion that children bring the mother and father closer together, there is research evidence indicating that husband and wife tend to be happier with each other before the children arrive and again after they leave the home.

You do not go through a "change of life." Although man typically slows down in sexual activity from the late twenties on, there is no such thing as male menopause. However, according to professional observation, there is a surprisingly high rate of impotence among businessmen forty years of age and over. Chronic emotional or mental fatigue or even continued unhappiness at work may cause a loss of sexual interest. Physical and emotional infirmities, as well as tendencies to overindulge in food and drink, are other causes of sexual regression. In some cases women stop demonstrating sexual concern for their husbands and the husband, feeling slighted, may withdraw.

You cannot have sex without some companionship. If you attempt this, odds are you will lose not only sex but your children. Wives pull away from this one-sided deal and imply to the children that you are not interested in them.

A double standard is wishful thinking and dangerous. Some psychiatrists believe that a man who plays around is as difficult to help as an alcoholic. Promiscuity is an errant form of immature behavior. There are several causes. There are those men who keep going from one woman to another either through a series of marriages or outside of wedlock unconsciously trying to find their mother again. Then there are men who are really competitive and see women as objects to be conquered, then discarded, such as the egotist, Don Juan, cited earlier. Some men indulge in promiscuousness because they had unfortunate relationships with their mothers, the first woman in their lives, and have never been able to work out a normal relationship with a woman. There also are those men who have grave doubts about their masculinity because of their own personal feelings of inadequacy. This feeling may well come around middle age when a man turns to a younger woman because of his fear of failure at home. Then there are those who have become impotent at home and are promiscuous to reassert to themselves their masculinity. Finally, there are men who cannot handle the monogamous state. They fear continuing, sustained relationships with one woman. For them several affairs provide them with an unusual concept of personal "security."

Mystique of the Human Female

Biologically the human female has one function: to bear and raise children to perpetuate the species. Man because of his greater physical power and freedom (he is not tied to children) has determined the fate of woman and established for her a subservient position. In early times a woman was selected for her beauty, defined in terms of toil, not toilette. For man it was a sexual-economic advantage, not a sexual-social advantage. A man would buy his bride in order to reduce the loss her father suffered in giving up a daughter. With the industrial age, the economic value of a woman decreased and her sexual value increased.

Now both men and women take man's prejudice as a law of nature. Not too many years ago women were accused of having those traits once attributed to the Negro—less intelligent than men, more emotional, weaker, less sense of judgment, fit only for menial tasks.[13] Once man has been able to see through his prejudices, he finds that women have a natural superiority. Constitutionally, not physically, the female is the stronger sex. In psychological and social qualities, woman is superior to man. Women in their greater loving-kindness and humanity become the nurturers of life and the civilizing influence. Man, as we have seen, more often tends to be the destroyer of life. Several behavioral scientists suggest that men should accept the fact that the sexes should complement each other and that women must be granted complete equality by men. You should start it in your own home.

Man or Child   For woman it is not the man but the child. With her instinctive need for the child, woman in most of the world today marries to obtain economic support for herself and her children. Hence, woman is not able to accept man for what he is. In order to have the child, she must have the man. Moreover, after the baby

[13] Ashley Montagu, *The Natural Superiority of Women*, Lancer Books, The Macmillan Company, New York, 1952, p. 11.

comes, her "feminine intelligence" about the child bewilders many fathers. She senses when the baby is hungry, thirsty, soiled, and when it is ill, tired, or in a bad temper.[14]

Although a woman loves a man because he alone can give her the baby, a woman in our culture usually learns that sex is dirty, immoral, or risky. Hence, her attitudes toward the sexual act are at best ambivalent. Still, to get and keep her man, woman is conditioned to become a female sex symbol. She dresses to excite man sexually. She joins the cult of synthetic youth and erotic beauty. However, once woman has a man and children, the apparatus cannot be shut off. She continues to look the role of the erotic female symbol. She may not openly stare at a man, but her quick, sweeping glance tells her whether or not men are openly staring at her. A woman who goes beyond normal bounds is using cosmetics in a neurotic way. Psychiatrically, she is viewed as trying to find her own sense of identity through attempting to look like the unreal but alluring pictures of professional models. Men generally encourage their wives to be as attractive as possible, thereby encouraging the cult of synthetic youth and erotic beauty. Years ago it was pointed out that men used their wives as evidences of "conspicuous consumption." [15] In ancient China women of the upper classes had their feet broken when they were babies in order to "prove" that they were economically useless. Today we might term it "conspicuous sexual consumption."

The prospect of growing old causes woman real concern. While age is a problem to men, it becomes a worrisome state for women. Conditioned as they are to try to stay forever young, the importance of their sexual attractiveness causes them anxiety for the time when it must diminish as they grow older. Menopause is especially threatening. In one survey over half the women stated that the prospect of losing their husbands would be the worst thing about middle age.[16] The next worst category was getting older, where one-fifth of the women felt that this was the worst thing about middle age. Yet only 1 percent of the women were concerned about changes in sex-

---

[14] LaBarre, *op. cit.*, p. 167.

[15] Thorstein Veblen, *The Theory of the Leisure Class*, Modern Library, Random House, Inc., New York, 1899.

[16] Bernice L. Neugarten, "A New Look at Menopause," *Psychology Today* magazine, vol. 1, no. 7, December, 1967, pp. 43–45, 67–70. Copyright Communications Research Machines, Inc. Reprinted by permission.

ual feelings and behavior. As for the prospect of menopause, many were concerned about not knowing what to expect and possible discomfort. Again, the second greatest concern was the fact that it was a sign of growing old. When asked about the best thing about menopause, 74 percent of the women reported not having to worry about getting pregnant and not having to bother with menstruation. Only 3 percent reported that the best thing would be greater enjoyment of sex life. And only another 11 percent thought that the best thing would be better relationships with their husbands.

Woman's Work   Granted that a woman may get herself out of focus sexually. Still, a woman as a homemaker is not shortchanging her husband. In her noneconomic, nonsexual function of housewife, she works for no direct economic reward and does not see herself as an economic asset. Economists continue to try to produce figures on the worth of woman's work. A woman's approach to her housework has several implications for man. If she is normal, she cannot be idle; she must be busy. She sets her own goals and standards—with active encouragement from advertisers. She chooses her own time for doing things and sets her own pace, giving in to the many and frequent requirements of the children. She does the humdrum, the routine, the backbreaking, and the dirty jobs. She typically works in a situation which provides for less adult association than man experiences. Her day, although not as physically demanding as years ago, still requires many hours of work. Yet she has the total "product" under her command.

Too Narrow a Base   As with men, the consensus among professional observers of women is that in our culture they try to build their lives on too narrow a base of underutilization. Being a sex symbol for man in order to get the child also results in a dependent attitude. But in her priorities her husband takes a back seat to the child. In one survey, over 80 percent of the women mentioned children as most important for the role of mother. Most of them, 87 percent, saw their husbands as providers; 65 percent listed father; and only 46 percent listed husband. Only 62 percent mentioned the role of wife and only 33 percent gave it first place.[17]

[17] Helen Lopata, "The Secondary Features of a Primary Relationship," *Human Organization*, vol. 24, no. 2, Summer, 1965, pp. 116–123. A survey of over 600 young housewives and older women.

Woman has an almost tragic yearning for youth. She fails to evaluate her qualities outside the erotic sphere, qualities best characterized as poise, autonomy, independence, judgment, and wisdom.[18] Once women were concerned with their legal, political, and economic rights. Today they are concerned with personal, private, and sexual rights. A woman has a lack of interest in high-level positions and settles for jobs rather than careers.[19] A woman's human qualities, as opposed to the strictly female qualities, should be developed. Women are human beings *before* they are women, and they should develop themselves as human beings. Women are urged to get the housework done as quickly as possible, see marriage for what it really is, not the overglorification imposed by the feminine mystique. Then, just as man must do, a woman should strive for her maturation concept of success.

Female Achievers So, too, in her way, does woman face the same problem as man—becoming as much of a person as she can become. Man may lose himself in the business rat race. Woman may lose herself in her family or her personal life and push her husband away. When a woman cannot face growing older with some equanimity, she not only loses her charms of youth but demonstrates that she has emotional problems. As a wife, a woman has her particular levels of the achiever:

Mature achiever. With the qualities of a mature person, a wife is a companion to her husband. She maintains a good balance of her three lives—her family life (children and home), her personal life, and her marital life. In the latter she is particularly open, helpful, and effective in her relationships with her husband, both personal and sexual, an achieving companion.

Average normal achiever. The "life-cycle" wife has a husband-oriented period until the first child is born. With the coming of the children, her primary interest is in motherhood. After the children have left she tends to go back to the husband-oriented stage with an overriding interest in children and grandchildren.

Low normal achiever. A "homemaker" tends to be more involved with the home and its furnishing than with anything else. She is

[18] Neugarten, *op. cit.,* p. 70.
[19] Jessie Bernard, "The Status of Women in Modern Patterns of Culture," *The Annals of the American Academy of Political and Social Science,* January, 1968.

usually unrealistic and overly concerned about the appearance of her home and having everything spic and span all the time. She tends to see both her children and her husband as secondary to her home or even as infringers.

Undue normal achiever. The "mother" wife considers the basic family unit herself and her children. The husband is not a member of this group, but a bystander. Both while the children are home and after they have gone, her primary concern is the children—and then the grandchildren—almost to the exclusion of any real concern about her husband. In some surveys at least a third of the wives are found in this category.

Neurotic underachiever. Overly dependent or a clinging vine best typifies this underachiever—a childlike need to be taken care of. Some wives become overly dependent after the children have left home, as a result of boredom and emptiness.

Neurotic overachiever. The authoritarian wife has almost all the manifestations of the authoritarian overachiever described in Chapter 13. She is a dictator both for the children and for the husband.

Marital Win-Lose Complex

What is widely advertised as living happily ever after is actually a win or lose contest between two fiercely individualistic human beings, each bent on getting his own way. Fighting about what? The most common conflicts are found to be sex, money, children, man's work and career, personal activities of husband or wife, and how to drive the car.

Unhappy Marriages   People are inclined to marry those who satisfy their psychological needs. Opposites do attract. They tend to be unlike and complementary in their needs.[20] Even then only about half of the marriages are successful. In half of the world marriages are not based on romantic love. They are business propositions. Still, there is no greater percentage of marital discontent than in our

[20] Robert F. Winch, *Mate Selection: A Study of Complementary Needs,* Harper & Row, Publishers, Incorporated, New York, 1958, p. 354.

"love-match" marriages. About half of the couples in both cases are definitely without joy in each other.[21]

Achieving Companionship

If you and your wife find no joy in your relationship and see no hope of achieving compatibility, the thing to do is to seek professional counsel. If that does not work, end the relationship. A complete break is best. If your religion does not condone divorce, separate. Just as in the work relationship, it is better to end the association if there is no hope for compatibility. Living together in hostility and conflict can cause emotional damage. But, if you and your wife want to and can, strive to achieve the third of three marital stages:

Stage one: minimum-interaction marriage. This is the marriage that continues out of religious or social necessity or economic convenience. Various surveys show that this type of marriage is common among ambitious businessmen [22] who are caught up in the business rat race. Or, the wife may be the undue normal achiever who considers the basic family unit the children and herself with the husband as a bystander.

Stage two: child-oriented marriage. In this case both mother and father do everything for the children. In being overly concerned about the children, parents lose touch with each other. Hence, when the children leave home, there is a void between husband and wife.

Stage three: companionship marriage. This is the ideal, a goal. Few couples achieve it. Here there is not only the sexual sharing companionship but also friendly sharing companionship. The satisfaction of being together is so strong that they plan to be together as much as possible. As close friends, they quarrel as much as or perhaps more than other couples. They are very critical of each other. But they remain the best of friends who want above everything else to be together and to help each other. Both young and old accept sex as a biologically, emotionally, and socially normal

---

[21] David Mace and Vera Mace, *Marriage: East and West,* Doubleday and Company, Inc., Garden City, N.Y., 1960. In our country this includes the 25 percent of the marriages that end in divorce.

[22] This is also common among blue-collar workers.

need. Sex is clean and fun rather than something shameful, dirty, and evil. Rather than the traditional pattern of male dominance in the sexual act and the submissive woman, the two share their sexual life.

Increase Compatibility Compatibility can be increased if a conscientious effort is made to reduce the areas of conflict. Perhaps the best way to approach it is for you to face up to those areas where it is exceedingly important for your wife to have her way. Recall what your most heated arguments have been about. You may well find that you can give in on things about which she is particularly touchy, because they are not too important to you. She may also be willing to ease off on certain areas which are important to you, after evidence of your consideration for her.

Think of your relationship with your wife as consisting of five areas. The first and most important is that of mutuality. Include here your joint interests, the things you do with and for each other for the utmost in relaxation, work, and re-creation. This is the area of love in all its senses ranging from sex to intimacy to spontaneity and helpfulness.

The next two areas should be called the areas of danger. One should be marked *his* and the other *hers*. Include here those things which cause small spats. If you and your wife are able to level with each other about these, you might find that you could move some of them to the area of mutuality.

Finally, you come to two other areas which should be marked *fatal hers* and *fatal his*. These are the long-term issues where there never has been agreement. And there appears to be little chance of getting together. Take money, for example. Odds are that you view your wife as either too extravagant or too conservative. Much of your perception rests on values which you acquired in childhood. By the same token, your wife might view you as too extravagant or too conservative with money. The values of both of you are so basic that much emotion is involved: impetuousness for the extravagant and anxiety for the conservative. The best way to attempt to resolve the money question is to try to conform to the wishes of the person who is having unpleasant anxiety because of his or her conservative nature.

Games Couples Play Another way to improve your companionship is to think through the games you play, the unconscious games that hurt. Recall the ego states of child, parent, and adult and the crossed transactions in Chapter 12. To avoid games, try to develop with your wife an increased awareness of the potential for complementary transactions. As one example, face up to the game of Uproar to avoid sexual intimacy, if this is one of your games. Behind the uproar game, you may find your wife playing a Frigid Woman who thinks that all men are beasts. On the other hand, you may have selected this kind of a wife because you are afraid of sexual intimacy and overtaxing your disturbed potency.[23]

A common misconception is to think that a wife should be a good counselor, that she is able to listen and mirror back. Most wives are too emotionally involved and too maternal to counsel. Expect that much of the time your wife, if she is interested in you, will play the mother role, a maternal ego state. She treats you as a child and is "bringing you up" for your own good. Even when she fusses about your bad habits, respond as from your child ego state to keep the transaction complementary.

Relaxation, Work, and Re-creation Suggestions for family relaxation, work, and re-creation in Exhibit 15 are self-explanatory for the most part. When you get home, deliberately move into your father-husband role. Although you may feel reluctant to do so, play the role of the sympathetic listener. If your wife is tired and harassed, she may start from the child ego state. You move into the parent ego state to form a complementary transaction.

You are working toward the goal of companionship when you:

Consciously develop a program of joint relaxation, joint work, and joint re-creation. A woman should get as much vigorous physical exercise as a man.[24]

Help your wife raise the children, respecting the limits she sets for them, loving them in your masculine way so that they have a stable father figure. Do not shield them from your own unpleasant

[23] Eric Berne, M.D., *Games People Play*, Grove Press Inc., New York, 1964, pp. 98–99.

[24] Kenneth H. Cooper, M.D., *Aerobics*, M. Evans and Company, Philadelphia, 1968. Some experts say two-thirds.

Exhibit 15   RELAXATION, WORK, AND RE-CREATION
IN YOUR FAMILY LIFE

| | In These Activities: | | |
	Relaxation	Work	Re-creation
Through: Your Mind	Television Relaxing together Games with children	Family business affairs Father-husband role	Learn together Good plays Good music Good standards for children
Your Body	Sex Family sports, especially noncompetitive	Easy routine chores	Nonroutine do-it-yourself and routine hard jobs
Other People	The family	The family	The family

childhood experiences such as your anxieties, grief, and loneliness. Follow the qualities of a good boss, father, and teacher, given in Chapter 3. High intellectual academic standards are set for your children by practice, not by your preaching.

Help your wife around the house and become a do-it-yourselfer. The projects have several advantages besides saving money. They are noncompetitive, reduce your tenseness, and are re-creative. Also they give you a sense of tangible accomplishment—something to look at which is so different from your verbal-paper world of work. The number and kinds of do-it-yourself projects range from gardening to wallpapering, mowing the lawn to painting, plumbing to electricity. Many a man comes home from the office emotionally fatigued and frustrated. After leisurely cocktails and dinner, he climbs into his work clothes and goes to it. His fatigue drops away. He forgets his office problems as he becomes involved in a do-it-yourself project. Finally, he can see his handiwork.

For both you and your wife, your goal should be to get as much joy out of marriage as possible and to have as little conflict as possible. The goals should be that of companionship with sharing, helpfulness, and re-creation for both. Once your goals have been set, so much becomes self-evident. You both look for more ways to keep in frequent touch even when you are working. You find ways to express approval and avoid disapproval, thereby reducing the times for instinctively aggressing. Share each other's lives, both the failures and successes. Married companionship is the ultimate in helping another to help yourself. As your children grow up and grow away from you, you both can see evidence of what you two have done to help them develop as young maturing achievers—if you can accept the big generation gap and the fact that they do not achieve all your high goals for them.

part **6**

Help Yourself for the Long Pull

*To accept the importance of your own humanness
in the lives of others is to understand an important
meaning of your own life.*
—HARRY LEVINSON, *Emotional Health in the
World of Work* [1]

BEFORE GETTING INTO the final phase of the total program for the total man, let me summarize. In trying to do better, you follow the maturation concept of success to survive in and beyond the business rat race. The salvation, organization, or power concepts must ultimately be your undoing. In your work life, your personal life, and your family life, you plan and budget yourself so that you relax, work, and re-create yourself through your mind, your body, and other people, the "three by three by three" formula.

In your business life, you try for more from your work and you build your own career. You adopt the behavioral sciences consensus and develop a professional stance. To help yourself directly, you acquire knowledge to become aware of yourself and your achieving tendencies. Then you

[1] Harper & Row, Publishers, Incorporated, New York, 1964, p. 294.

223

relax and work as well as re-create yourself for more maturity. To reduce your own business rat race, you help your boss, subordinates, and peers where they can help you in turn.

To survive in and beyond the business rat race with a feeling of well-being, you relax, work, and re-create yourself in your personal life, through your mind, your body, and other people. For you, as for many businessmen, you undoubtedly find that the greatest temptation is relaxation through escape. Your common sense deceitfully tells you that after the business rat race you need to relax. Then you stop trying to do better and set the trap for your own undoing. To give in to your impulses for fun and games is the road to emotional ill health. It is no small order to practice the *modern* Golden Mean and turn from your work life to strive for your personal growth and physical fitness. You find there are no bargains. Greater maturity, the goal in the maturation concept of success, is uphill. It is uphill until you get near the summit. Then you find that you get a sense of achieving, well-being, and even pleasure from trying to do better.

In your family life, the important "other" is your wife, then your children. Here you relax, work, and re-create yourself through them as well as your mind and your body. To understand your wife, a woman, may well be one of the greatest challenges and accomplishments in your life. (She has a similar problem with you.)

In all three of your lives, you develop new habits for old, new and more knowledgeable values and emotions for your childhood conditioned ones. Dropping the old and picking up the new can never be complete. It is a case of working continuously with yourself so that you do not fall back into the old habits, emotions, and values. As you have seen, what you expect is frequently unreal and can affect your emotional health. In a very profound sense, ignorance is *not* bliss. Ignorance may even cause you more frustration and obsolescence, an inability to face realities of

Yourself and others
Business life and fellow businessmen
Personal and family life
Your community and the world

To help yourself over the long pull is the final aspect of this total program for the total man.

17

Break Through
to a Larger Awareness

Less and less are we able to locate our lives meaningfully in the pageant of history. More and more do
we find ourselves retreating to the sanctuary of an in-
sulated individualism, sealed off in our private concerns from the larger events which surround us.
—ROBERT L. HEILBRONER, *The Future as History* [1]

THE LAST ASPECT of the maturation concept of success is acquiring
an intellectual realism for a larger awareness. Re-create your mind
to influence your instincts, emotions, and values so that you can accept

The major crises of your life
The revolution of rising expectations
The new American realism

These are but three cases of major changes occurring today. The
only way to reduce your pessimism and anxiety is to invigorate your
intellectual life—not to become an egghead but simply "to be in on
the know." Then, you can take the long and large view. You can
examine things from both the historical and the process-of-change
standpoints.

[1] Grove Press, Inc., New York, 1960, p. 209.

For example, in the last 100 years man has had four of his greatest dreams shattered. Darwin shattered the dream that we were a separate, special kind of being and not part of the rest of the animal species. Freud shattered the dream of a conscious or free will. Einstein shattered the dream of the significance of this planet with his theory of relativity. Oppenheimer shattered the dream of national safety in directing the research on the atom bomb.

You and Your Tomorrows

The most that many businessmen do to prepare for the future is tangible—life insurance, investments, and participation in the company pension plan. It is rare when an individual prepares himself intelligently and intellectually for his own future. Hence, each adjustment in his life can be a major crisis. If he is not living a full and well-rounded life, he may be catapulted into a neurosis.

Major Crises of Life   Aside from unusual things such as being permanently disabled, being "dehired," or the death of a loved one, there are these typical major adjustments: (1) teens, (2) college, (3) career, (4) identity, (5) marriage, (6) management, (7) middle age, (8) children gone, (9) preretirement, (10) retirement, and (11) old age.

Teens. The first stage is the teens when the adolescent tries to get free, to rebel from parental restrictions, to become an adult in his own right. He has the usual high level of normal anxiety of the teenager. This is the time when he typically comes to the realization that there are wide gaps between the standards his parents set for him, what they practice themselves, and what he wants to practice. He finds himself in a credibility gap. (Those of you who are or have been parents of teenagers know what I mean. It is best illustrated by the famous routine: "Where did you go?" "Out." "What did you do?" "Nothing.") He succeeds in making this adjustment to the extent that he is able to free himself emotionally from his parents, particularly his mother. If he does not, he carries over into adulthood an overpowering load of unsolved problems of childhood.

College. Although a boy looks forward to getting away from home and being on his own, college is another anxious crisis. He is without any continuing supervision for the first time in his life. Colleges with their requirements for more study and higher performance standards can cause young men serious problems. This is particularly true today when college no longer is the place where a student can fall flat on his face, pick himself up, and start over.

Career. Here for the first time a man faces the realities of work life. They are different from anything he has experienced before. It can be a particularly frustrating experience, as we have seen, when he learns that he must be "practical." Moreover, it is here that he finally comes face to face with the fact that he must, for the most part, experiment, probably by changing jobs, in his search for the kind of work and career he likes.

Identity. The need to establish "who I am" or "what I should be" comes at a time when a young man is either in college or in his first job. He finds that he has no one to lean on anymore. With our open, ever-changing society, as opposed to a static class system, identity conflict is an acute struggle for many.[2]

Marriage. Recall that one-half of the marriages are without joy. Can there be any worse evidence of the difficulty in working out a satisfactory adjustment in man's love life? Marriage is usually complicated by the fact that it comes at a time when a man is trying to find himself in the business world.

Management. The fifth stage comes when a man starts supervising others (see Chapter 13).

Middle age. A most critical stage in a man's career comes somewhere between ages forty and fifty. He can no longer dream about the big success he would like to be. He can see the years running out and has heard all too often that death of a career begins at age forty. Moreover, as he has climbed the management ladder, his anxiety increases. Struggling to get ahead in his own lonely world, he sees fewer and fewer jobs as he approaches the apex of the organization pyramid. He must accept the fact that he is not going to go up much further. He must endure the rather drab things he is doing until retirement. Middle age is typically too a time when a man becomes uncertain about his values. He may become restless, plagued by a free-floating anxiety: Where am I going? What have I been doing that is worthwhile?

Children gone. When the children have left home either to go to college or to establish their own families, a man faces a real test of

[2] Harry Levinson, *Emotional Health in the World of Work,* Harper & Row, Publishers, Incorporated, New York, 1964, p. 148.

his marriage. Often it comes at the same time as his own middle-age crisis, making matters more difficult. He finds that he has only his wife left. She usually feels an emptiness, for she has finished her primary instinctive function of raising children. If the two of them have not worked for companionship, they find themselves "separated." Although they are not really mad at each other, they may stumble into a middle-age divorce.

Preretirement. For many a man the greatest difficulty is facing the fact that in a few years he is going to retire. Work, with all its frustration and exasperations, is the main thread of life. To think that the organization does not really want you when you reach age sixty-five is a realization that is difficult to face.

Retirement. This is the big test as to how well you have mastered the maturation concept of success. If you have, you can face a healthy, happy, and active retirement.

Old age. Old age is the culmination of the plusses and the minuses of life. For some it is a second childhood with a crotchety self-centeredness. If the body has not been taken care of, it means senility and often disability. For others, it means a pleasant, active, outward-oriented life.

Live a Life of Change   If you take a long view, your work is a comparatively short, part-time occupation in terms of current life expectancy. You learn about and accept your tomorrows. Face up to retirement and old age. Prepare for them as early as possible. As I pointed out before, your chance of changing grows progressively less decade by decade. Worse, building a healthy body cannot be started if you have acquired a disability. Live in transition. Fight against slowing down, intellectually, emotionally, and physically. You accept the indifferences and mysteriousness of unknown forces, both human and nonhuman, against which you live out your conscious existence.

The Revolution of Rising Expectations

As a member of the establishment of the successful, you may find it difficult to accept what is now known as the "revolution of rising expectations." The have-nots, the young and those who have not made it, want much more. Increasing competition among the news media may overdramatize the macabre and the violent for your eyes and ears. Hence, you are undoubtedly more concerned about the facts which increasingly seem to get pushed into the background. You may well feel that you have slipped from victor to victim.

But start with your own rising expectations. As a citizen you want better police protection. As a father you are concerned about the use of questionable chemicals in foods for your children and yourself. As a man you do not want your life shortened or "crippled" by pollution of the air or water. As a family man you want the best medical care for yourself and yours. You are afraid that you cannot handle financially any long illness for yourself, your wife, or your children. You can easily add to this list, in terms of your own situation.

By approaching your rising expectations from your own vantage point, you may be able to learn about those in the forefront of the revolution. Again, you need knowledge to weigh the issues. Remember that the question of man's destructive instinct has not been resolved. Ask yourself if any minority group ever got anything without a power struggle. You find that the revolution is not as bad as some of the more violent ones in history. Recall the War between the States, or the great strife and bloodshed when the unions were trying to get themselves established. Recent recurring strikes by labor and farmers often result in bloodshed. Can you find any decade in the history of our country when there was not some major kind of violence?

Critically think through your values about people of other classes, nationalities, and colors. Prejudice, hostility, and hatred all can be evidence of bias. Moreover, they also work against your need to have faith in people generally, for your emotional health. Be careful that you do not deceive yourself. Open prejudice is less evident than it used to be. Racism is still prevalent though more subtle. To condemn, openly or subtly, is to block any chance to learn and to understand.

To move beyond your biases, find your answers to questions such as these:

1. What makes some businessmen operate outside the law?
2. Why should a "buyer beware," i.e., *caveat emptor?*

3. Why do the poor stay poor, whether they are black or white?
4. What makes some people resort to violence in the new revolution?

From American Pessimism to American Realism

Our great American dream of power is shattered. True, our drive, our natural resources, and our technical abilities have brought many of us substantial affluence and conveniences beyond the comprehension of most of the world. The affluence gap between us and the rest of the world continues to increase at a substantial rate. Yet our American optimism has turned to pessimism. Rather than look upon these events as a personal defeat, consider them the process of worldwide evolution. Through knowledge, awareness, and understanding, your pessimism moves to realism.[3]

Think through your attitudes toward other countries. Through your intellectual efforts, you come to develop a long and enlarged view about what has happened and what is now happening in the world. Try to accept the fact that the peoples of each nation are trying, in their own way, to work out their destiny. They have internal power struggles. Our democratic way of life is a long way off for most of those who are struggling to move forward. Moreover, their envy of our affluence is another facet of the have-nots against the haves.

Toward Maturation and Success

In these last few pages you have had a glimpse as to why it is vitally important for you to strive for the maturation concept of success—for your own sense of well-being, for your surviving in and beyond the business rat race. The behavioral sciences consensus urges you to learn about the realities of your life and the world. First, become emancipated from blind belief, ancestral order, tradition, nationalism, and established authority. Second, think your way out of your parental, ethnic, social, economic, religious, and educational background to awareness of yourself. Third, throw off the weight of business, political, and cultural tradition. Fourth, reevaluate your

[3] Heilbroner, *op. cit.*, p. 208.

business life, your personal life, and your family life in terms of your own success and survival as a person. Fifth, relax, work, and re-create yourself through your mind, your body, and other people in your business, personal, and family lives.

Then no longer do you, like a rat in an experimental maze, rush or wander through a blind network of passages toward unknown ends. You gain an overview of the world. You see your life as a whole, as it really is, through the maturation concept of success. You strive to become a physically fit, self-actualizing, autonomous, helpful, enterprising achiever in your business, personal, and family lives.

Bibliography

Adorno, T. W., E. Frenkel-Brunswick, D. J. Levinson, and R. W. Sanford: *The Authoritarian Personality,* Harper & Row, Publishers, Incorporated, New York, 1950.

Aldrich, C. Knight, M.D.: "The Neurotic Competitor in the World of Business," *Executive Behavior, Selected Papers,* no. 5, Graduate School of Business, University of Chicago, Chicago, 2d printing, April, 1966, p. 9.

Argyris, Chris: *Executive Leadership and Appraisal of a Manager in Action,* Harper & Row, Publishers, Incorporated, New York, 1953.

————: "How Tomorrow's Executives Will Make Decisions," *Think,* vol. 33, no. 6, published by IBM, November–December, 1967, pp. 18–24.

————: *Interpersonal Competence and Organizational Effectiveness,* Dow Jones-Irwin, Inc., Homewood, Ill., 1962.

————: *Personality and Organization,* Harper & Row, Publishers, Incorporated, New York, 1957.

Bakal, Carl: *The Right to Bear Arms,* McGraw-Hill Book Company, New York, 1966.

Barger, J. P.: "The Managing Process," in H. B. Maynard (ed.), *Handbook of Business Administration,* McGraw-Hill Book Company, New York, 1967, sec. 1, pp. 1–14.

Baritz, Loren: *The Servants of Power,* Science Editions paperback, Wesleyan University Press, Middletown, Conn., 1965.

Barkin, Solomon: "Diversity in Time Study Practices," *Industrial and Labor Relations Review,* vol. 7, no. 4, July, 1954, pp. 537–549.

Barnard, Chester I.: *The Functions of the Executive,* Harvard University Press, Cambridge, Mass., 1938.

Batten, J. D.: *Developing a Tough-minded Climate—for Results,* American Management Association, New York, 1965.

————: *Tough-minded Management,* American Management Association, New York, 1963.

Baumhart, Raymond C.: "How Ethical Are Businessmen?" *Harvard Business Review,* vol. 39, no. 4, July–August, 1961, pp. 6–7.

Bennis, Warren G., and Herbert A. Shepard: "Group Observation," in W. G.

Bennis, Kenneth D. Benne, and Robert Chin (eds.), *The Planning of Change*, Holt, Rinehart and Winston, Inc., New York, 1961, pp. 743–756.

Bernard, Jessie: "The Status of Women in Modern Patterns of Culture," *The Annals of the American Academy of Political and Social Science*, January, 1968.

Berne, Eric, M.D.: *Games People Play*, Grove Press, Inc., New York, 1964.

———: *A Layman's Guide to Psychiatry & Psychoanalysis*, Simon & Schuster, Inc., New York, 1947.

Bixler, Ray H.: "Ostracize Them," *Saturday Review*, vol. 49, no. 27, July 2, 1966, pp. 47–48.

Blakeslee, Alton, and Jeremiah Stamler, M.D.: *Your Heart Has Nine Lives*, Prentice-Hall, Inc., Englewood Cliffs, N.J., 1963.

Bradley, Nelson, M.D.: "The Work Addict," *Sales Management*, July 7, 1961.

Brussel, James A., M.D.: *A Layman's Guide to Psychiatry*, Barnes & Noble, Inc., New York, 1967.

Cantor, Nathaniel: *The Learning Process for Managers*, Harper & Row, Publishers, Incorporated, New York, 1958.

Cawelti, John G.: *Apostles of the Self-made Man*, The University of Chicago Press, Chicago, 1965.

Chase, Stuart: *The Proper Study of Mankind*, Harper & Row, Publishers, Incorporated, New York, 1963.

Clark, James V.: *Education for the Use of Behavioral Science*, Institute of Industrial Relations, University of California, Los Angeles, 1962.

Collins, Orvis F., David G. Moore, and Darab B. Unwalla: *The Enterprising Man*, Graduate School of Business Administration, Michigan State University, East Lansing, 1964.

Cooper, Kenneth H., M.D.: *Aerobics*, M. Evans and Company, Philadelphia, 1968.

Dale, Ernest: *The Great Organizers*, McGraw-Hill Book Company, New York, 1960.

Dalton, Melville: "Informal Factors in Career Achievement," *American Journal of Sociology*, vol. 56, March, 1951, p. 414.

Dill, William R., Thomas L. Hilton, and Walter R. Reitman: "How Aspiring Managers Promote Their Own Careers," reprint from *California Management Review*, vol. 2., no. 4, Summer, 1960.

Drucker, Peter F.: *The Effective Executive*, Harper & Row, Publishers, Incorporated, New York, 1966.

———: *The Practice of Management*, Harper & Row, Publishers, Incorporated, New York, 1954.

Dubin, Robert, and S. Lee Spray: "Executive Behavior and Interaction," *Industrial Relations*, Institute of Industrial Relations, University of California, Los Angeles, February, 1964.

Feinberg, Mortimer R.: "Corporate Bigamy," reprint from *Business Management*, 1965.

Ferguson, Lawrence L.: "Social Scientists in the Plant," *Harvard Business Review*, vol. 42, no. 3, May–June, 1964, p. 134.

Fleishman, E. A., and D. R. Peters: "Interpersonal Values, Leadership Attitudes and Managerial 'Success,' " *Personal Psychology*, Summer, 1962, pp. 127–143.

Ford, Clellan S., and Frank A. Beach: *Patterns of Sexual Behavior*, Harper & Row, Publishers, Incorporated, New York, 1951.

Fromm, Erich, M.D.: *Man for Himself*, Holt, Rinehart and Winston, Inc., New York, 1947.

———: *The Sane Society*, Harper & Row, Publishers, Incorporated, New York, 1955.

Galbraith, John Kenneth: *The Affluent Society*, Mentor Books, New American Library, Inc., New York, 1958.

———: *The New Industrial State*, Houghton Mifflin Company, Boston, 1967.

Gouldner, A. W.: "Cosmopolitans and Locals: Toward an Analysis of Latent Social Roles, I," *Administrative Science Quarterly*, vol. 2, December, 1957, pp. 281–306.

Guth, William D., and Renato Tagiuri: "Personal Values and Corporate Strategy," *Harvard Business Review*, vol. 43, no. 5, September–October, 1965, pp. 123–132.

Hall, Calvin, and Gardner Lindzey: *Theories of Personality*, John Wiley & Sons, Inc., New York, 1957.

Hamilton, Edith: *The Greek Way*, W. W. Norton & Company, New York, 1930, 1943. Copyright renewed in 1958 by Edith Hamilton.

Hanvey, Robert G.: "Social Myth vs. Social Science," *Saturday Review*, vol. 50, no. 46, Nov. 18, 1967, pp. 80–95.

Hawkes, Jacquetta: "Automation and Imagination," *Harpers Magazine*, vol. 231, no. 1385, October, 1965, pp. 92–98.

Heath, Roy: *The Reasonable Adventurer*, The University of Pittsburgh Press, Pittsburgh, 1964.

Heilbroner, Robert L.: *The Future as History*, Grove Press, Inc., New York, 1960.

———: *The Worldly Philosophers*, Simon & Schuster, Inc., New York, 1967.

Herzberg, Frederick, Bernard Mausner, and Barbara Snyderman: *The Motivation to Work*, John Wiley & Sons, Inc., New York, 1959.

Horney, Karen, M.D.: *Self-analysis*, W. W. Norton & Company, Inc., New York, 1942.

"How Do You Pick an Executive Winner?" *Business Week*, no. 1905, Mar. 5, 1966, pp. 108–110.

Jennings, Eugene Emerson: *The Executive in Crisis*, Graduate School of Business Administration, Michigan State University, East Lansing, 1965.

Kahn, R. L.: "The Prediction of Productivity," *Journal of Social Issues*, vol. 12, no. 2, Fall, 1956, pp. 41–49.

LaBarre, Weston: *The Human Animal*, The University of Chicago Press, Chicago, 1954.

Levinson, Harry: *Emotional Health in the World of Work*, Harper & Row, Publishers, Incorporated, New York, 1964.

———: "Is There an Obsolescent Executive in Your Company—or in Your Chair?" *Think*, vol. 34, no. 1, published by IBM, January–February, 1968, pp. 26–31.

————, Charlton R. Price, Kenneth J. Munden, Harold J. Mandl, and Charles M. Solley: *Men, Management, and Mental Health,* Harvard University Press, Cambridge, Mass., 1962.

Liebenberg, Beatrice: "Expectant Fathers," a paper to the Orthopsychiatric Association, Washington, D.C., March, 1967.

The Life Extension Foundation: *Report of a Survey on Executive Tension in Business,* Life Extension Institute, New York, about 1960.

Likert, Rensis: *The Human Organization,* McGraw-Hill Book Company, New York, 1967.

————: *New Patterns of Management,* McGraw-Hill Book Company, New York, 1961.

Lopata, Helen: "The Secondary Features of a Primary Relationship," *Human Organization,* vol. 24, no. 2, Summer, 1965.

Lorenz, Konrad: *On Aggression,* Harcourt, Brace & World, Inc., New York, 1966.

Lundberg, Craig C.: "Evolving Conceptions of the Administrator," *MSU Business Topics,* vol. 16, no. 1, Michigan State University, Winter, 1968, pp. 68–72.

McClelland, David C.: *The Achieving Society,* Litton Educational Publishing, Inc., New York, N.Y., 1961. By permission of Van Nostrand Reinhold Co.

————: "That Urge to Achieve," *Think,* vol. 32, no. 6, published by IBM, November–December, 1966, pp. 19–23.

Mace, David, and Vera Mace: *Marriage: East and West,* Doubleday & Company, Inc., Garden City, N.Y., 1960.

McGregor, Douglas: *The Human Side of Enterprise,* McGraw-Hill Book Company, New York, 1960.

————: *The Professional Manager,* McGraw-Hill Book Company, New York, 1967.

Maier, Norman R. F., L. Richard Hoffman, John J. Hooven, and William H. Read: *Superior-Subordinate Communications,* American Management Association, New York, 1961.

Martinez, Thomas M.: "Why Employment Agency Counselors Lower Their Clients' Self-esteem," *Trans-Action,* vol. 5, no. 4, March, 1968, pp. 20–25.

Maslow, A. H.: *Motivation and Personality,* Harper & Row, Publishers, Incorporated, New York, 1954.

————: "Self Actualizing Attributes," in Clark E. Moustakes (ed.), *The Self,* Harper & Row, Publishers, Incorporated, New York, 1956, chap. 14.

May, Rollo: *Man's Search for Himself,* W. W. Norton & Company, Inc., New York, 1953.

Menninger, Karl, M.D., with Martin Mayman and Paul Pruyser: *The Vital Balance,* The Viking Press, Inc., New York, 1963.

Meyer, Donald B.: "The Confidence Man," *New Republic,* vol. 133, July 11, 1955, pp. 8–10.

————: "Successful De-bunker of Success," *New Republic,* vol. 133, Aug. 22, 1955, pp. 8–10.

Mills, C. Wright: *The Power Elite,* Oxford University Press, New York, 1959.

————: *White Collar: The American Middle Classes,* Oxford University Press, New York, 1951.

Montagu, M. F. Ashley: *The Direction of Human Development,* Harper & Row, Publishers, Incorporated, New York, 1955.

———: *The Natural Superiority of Women,* Lancer Books, Inc., published by arrangement with The Macmillan Company, New York, 1952.

Moore, Wilbert E.: *The Conduct of the Corporation,* Random House, Inc., New York, 1962.

Morris, Desmond: *The Naked Ape,* McGraw-Hill Book Company, New York, 1967.

Murdock, George P.: *Social Structure,* The Macmillan Company, New York, 1949.

Neugarten, Bernice: "A New Look at Menopause," *Psychology Today,* vol.1, no. 7, December, 1967, pp. 43–45, 67–70.

Packard, Vance: *The Pyramid Climbers,* Crest Reprint, Fawcett World Library, published by arrangement with McGraw-Hill Book Company, Inc., New York, 1962.

———: *The Status Seekers,* David McKay Company, Inc., New York, 1959.

Palmer, Stuart: *Understanding Other People,* Premier Books, Fawcett World Library, published by arrangement with Thomas Y. Crowell Company, New York, 1964.

Pell, Sydney, and C. Anthony D'Alonzo: "Acute Myocardial Infarction in a Large Industrial Population," *Journal of the American Medical Association,* vol. 185, no. 11, Sept. 14, 1963, pp. 831–838.

Presthus, Robert: *The Organizational Society,* Vintage Books, Random House, Inc., New York, 1962.

Purcell, T.: *The Worker Speaks His Mind on Company and Union,* Harvard University Press, Cambridge, Mass., 1953.

Reik, Theodore, M.D.: *Of Love and Lust,* Farrar, Straus & Cudahy, Inc., New York, 1957.

Riesman, David, Nathan Glazer, and Reuel Denny: *The Lonely Crowd,* Doubleday & Company, Inc., Garden City, N.Y., 1953.

Robertiello, Richard C.: *A Handbook of Mental Illness and Treatment,* Argonaut Books, Inc., Larchmont, N.Y., 1961.

Roethlisberger, F. J., and W. J. Dickson: *Management and the Worker,* Harvard University Press, Cambridge, Mass., 1947.

———, and Carl R. Rogers: "Barriers and Gateways to Communication," *Harvard Business Review,* July–August, 1952, pp. 18ff.

Rogers, Carl R.: *On Becoming a Person,* Houghton Mifflin Company, Boston, 1961.

Roper, Elmo: "How Culturally Active Are Americans?" *Saturday Review,* vol. 49, no. 20, May 14, 1966, pp. 22–23.

Sampson, Robert C.: "Management and the Behavioral Sciences," in H. B. Maynard (ed.), *Handbook of Business Administration,* McGraw-Hill Book Company, 1967, sec. 11, pp. 3–16.

———: *Managing the Managers,* McGraw-Hill Book Company, New York, 1965.

———: "Personality Problems," *For Executives Only, An Anthology of the Best Management Thought,* The Dartnell Corporation, Chicago, Ill. 60640, 1967, Chapter 24, pp. 380–392.

————: *The Staff Role in Management*, Harper & Row, Publishers, Incorporated, New York, 1955.

Sayles, Leonard: *Managerial Behavior*, McGraw-Hill Book Company, New York, 1964.

Schein, Edgar H.: "How to Break in the College Graduate," reprint from *Harvard Business Review*, vol. 42, no. 6, November–December, 1964.

————, and Douglas T. Hall: "The Student Image of the Teacher," *The Journal of Applied Behavioral Science*, vol. 3, no. 3, July–August–September, 1967, pp. 323ff.

Sheehan, Robert: "New Report Card on the Business Schools," *Fortune*, vol. 70, no. 6, December, 1964, p. 148.

Simon, William, and John H. Gagnon: "The Pedagogy of Sex," *Saturday Review*, vol. 50, no. 46, Nov. 18, 1967, pp. 74–76, 91–92.

Sloan, Alfred P., Jr.: *My Years with General Motors*, Doubleday & Company, Inc., Garden City, N.Y., 1964.

Stevenson, George S., M.D.: *How to Deal with Your Tensions*, National Association for Mental Health, New York, 1958.

Stevenson, Ian, M.D.: "Scientists with Half-closed Minds," *Harper's* Magazine, November, 1958, pp. 66–71.

Tannenbaum, Robert: *New Approaches to Stresses on the Job*, Institute of Industrial Relations, University of California, Berkeley, reprint no. 137. 1064.

Taylor, F. W.: *Scientific Management*, Harper & Row, Publishers, Incorporated, New York, 1947.

Taylor, G. Rattray: *Sex in History*, Vanguard Press, Inc., New York, 1954.

Thompson, Charles Edward, M.D.: *What an Executive Should Know about His Health*, The Dartnell Corporation, Chicago, 1961.

Tompkins, Sylvan: "The Psychology of Being Right—and Left," *Trans-Action*, vol. 3, no. 1, November–December, 1966, pp. 23–27.

Townsend, Robert: *Up the Organization*, Alfred Knopf, New York, 1970.

"The Truth Hurts: Some Companies See More Harm than Good in Sensitivity Training," *Wall Street Journal*, vol. 49, no. 191, July 14, 1969, p. 1.

Uris, Auren: *The Executive Job Market*, McGraw-Hill Book Company, New York, 1965.

Urwick, Lyndall F.: "Have We Lost Our Way in the Jungle of Management Theory?" *Personnel*, May–June, 1965, pp. 8–18.

Veblen, Thorstein: *The Theory of the Leisure Class*, Modern Library, Random House, Inc., New York, 1899.

Verner, Coolie, and Gary Dickinson: "An Analysis and Review of Research" (lecture), *Adult Education Magazine*, vol. 17, no. 2, Winter, 1967, pp. 85–95.

Ward, Lewis B.: "Do You Want a Weak Subordinate?" *Harvard Business Review*, vol. 39, September–October, 1961, pp. 6–8.

————: "The Ethnics of Executive Selection," reprint from *Harvard Business Review*, vol. 43, no. 2, March–April, 1963.

Warner, W. Lloyd, and James C. Abegglen: *Big Business Leaders in America*, Harper & Row, Publishers, Incorporated, New York, 1955.

Wasserman, Paul, and Fred S. Silander: *Decision-Making: An Annotated Bibliography*, Cornell University Press, Ithaca, N. Y., 1958.

Weber, J. Sherwood (ed.): *Good Reading,* rev. ed., prepared by Committee on College Reading, Mentor Books, New American Library, Inc., New York, 1956.

Weiss, Edward, M.D., and O. Spurgeon English, M.D.: *Psychosomatic Medicine,* W. B. Saunders Company, Philadelphia, 1943.

Welles, Chris: "Test by Stress," *Life* Magazine, vol. 63, no. 7, Aug. 18, 1967, pp. 69–74.

Wellington, C. Burleigh, and Jean Wellington: *The Underachiever: Challenges and Guidelines,* Rand McNally Curriculum Series, Rand McNally & Company, Chicago, no date.

White, Paul Dudley, M.D.: "My Own Prescription for Life," *Saturday Review,* vol. 50, no. 50, Dec. 16, 1967, pp. 17–20.

White, Robert W.: *Lives in Progress,* The Dryden Press, Inc., New York, 1952.

Whyte, William Foote: *Money and Motivation,* Harper & Row, Publishers, Incorporated, New York, 1955.

Whyte, William H., Jr.: *The Organization Man,* Simon & Schuster, Inc., New York, 1956.

Winch, Robert F.: *Mate Selection: A Study of Complementary Needs,* Harper & Row, Publishers, Incorporated, New York, 1958.

Wrapp, H. Edward: "Good Managers Don't Make Policy Decisions," *Selected Papers,* no. 26, Graduate School of Business, University of Chicago, Chicago, Apr. 27, 1967.

Zaleznik, Abraham: *Human Dilemmas of Leadership,* Harper & Row, Publishers, Incorporated, New York, 1966.

Name Index

Subject Index

243